Cultural Text Studies 1:
An Introduction

Edited by:
Camelia Elias & Bent Sørensen

Aalborg University Press • 2006

Cultural Text Studies 1:
An Introduction

Edited by:
Camelia Elias & Bent Sørensen

© The Authors and Aalborg University Press, 2005

Cover: Camelia Elias
Lay-out: Camelia Elias
Printed by Narayana, 2006
ISBN 87-7307-753-4
ISSN 1901-1911

Distribution:
Aalborg University Press
Niels Jernes Vej 6B
9220 Aalborg Ø
Denmark
Phone: (+45) 9635 7140, Fax (+45) 9635 0076
E-mail: aauf@forlag.aau.dk
Homepage: http://www.forlag.aau.dk

All rights reserved. No part of this book may be reprinted or reproduced or utilized in any form or by any electronic, mechanical, or other means, now known or hereafter invented, including photocopying and recording, or in any information storage or retrieval system, without permission in writing from the publishers, except for reviews and short excerpts in scholarly publications.

Table of Contents

Bent Sørensen
Introduction   5

Jørgen Riber Christensen
Remediating Shakespeare: The Boydell Shakespeare Gallery   17

Jens Kirk
Books and Selves: John Stuart Mill's Autobiography   37

Jørgen Riber Christensen
Dickens and Kipling: Two Good Victorians   57

Jesper Trier Gissel
Poetic Means for Social Ends:
Reading Positions in Modernist Interwar Poetry   77

Lene Yding Pedersen
Imagining Ireland: The Cultural Space of the Irish Free State   93

Bent Sørensen
"Small, but exalted": Otherness in Nella Larsen's Novels   117

Jens Kirk
The Production of the Martians   135

Ben Dorfman
The ABCs, or GHQs, of Global Text Reading   157

Steen Christiansen
Hollywood as Cultural Text 171

Tore Rye Andersen
Down with the Rebels!
David Foster Wallace and Postironical Literature 187

Camelia Elias
A Mile in Her Shoes:
Culture Metamorphoses in Rebecca Miller's Personal Velocity 209

Steen Christiansen
Transtextuality, Paranoia, and Apophenia in Pattern Recognition 229

Contributors 243

Introduction

Bent Sørensen

Cultural Text Studies (CTS) is a research project initiated by the Department of Languages, Culture and Aesthetics at Aalborg University. The present introductory volume launches a series of themed monographs which will be edited by researchers at the Dept., occasionally aided by friends and associates from other programmes. The purpose of the series is to be a forum for the publication of results of research in the broadly defined area of cultural text. This particular volume engages with a wide range of Anglophone texts and cultural phenomena which are read in each their particular historical framework (the synchronic dimension to the research), and which, when presented in a suite of essays, provide a chronologically structured primer in cultural text studies (the diachronic dimension to the work).

This interdisciplinary field of research springs from an emergent interest in both studying texts culturally *and* in studying culture as text. Thus it is "*cultural text* studies" in the sense that the object of study consists of all readable cultural phenomena which are regarded as texts in a much more broadly defined sense than in the traditional field of literary studies. Yet it is also "cultural *text studies*", in the sense that, while the approach is "cultural" as opposed to, say, formalist, the work often entails an intense engagement with texts and close readings thereof[1], usually combining reading strategies inspired by literature or film studies, in tandem with application of continental cultural theory, such as the German hermeneutic tradition,

---

1 I am indebted to Lene Yding Pedersen for first formulating this dialectic relationship clearly in her contribution to the 2003 conference on *Complexity* I co-organized with several of the contributors to the present volume. The proceedings from this event will appear as the CTS 3 monograph later this year.

French deconstruction, or sociological approaches to aesthetic products such as Pierre Bourdieu's contribution.

This methodology by nature yields hybrid readings, and the teaching of cultural text studies in this form is unique to the English programme at Aalborg University, in the sense that while other English departments in Denmark offer cultural studies courses, they do not offer sufficient theory to support these courses, nor do they engage with such a wide array of text types. The whole idea behind the CTS project therefore springs from teaching activities in the programme, such as our long running lecture series in textual history, entitled "Fashioning Self and Identity", which came about as an idea fostered by our long time programme mentor, associate professor Torben Ditlevsen. The idea to collect the lectures in textual history into a volume and to supplement the sequence with extra essays to consolidate our research focus areas also came from him. After several years of preparation we are proud to finally present our collective efforts.

The essays in this volume are thus all authored by present and past members of the English programme's teaching staff in the fields of culture, literature, and media studies. The pieces range widely in terms of the period, genre and medium of the texts investigated. Focus areas include Victorian literature and art; high modernism, especially approached from the point of view of a centre/margin discourse; and finally postmodernist aesthetics and its embedded move from literary into cultural studies, as witnessed by essays on world music, shoes, Hollywood, the post-ironic, the de-territorialized, and the post-human condition as cultural texts.

~~~

The collection commences with Riber Christensen's analysis of the cultural and aesthetic function of The Boydell Shakespeare Gallery, at the very beginning of the 19th century. The essay shows how the paintings and prints exhibited and sold by the Gallery remediated the works of Shakespeare, and provided the growing middle class audience of art and culture with access to de-auralized versions or reproductions of high art. The works of Shakespeare therefore were transposed from a dynamic, performance oriented art form such as the theatre, into static tableaux which could be consumed in the newly defined private space of the bourgeois home. The prerequisites for this transformation of art from auratic to non-auratic are theorized via the well-known work of Walter Benjamin, whereas the distinction between private and public spheres draws on the work of Habermas and Bourdieu. The close reading portions of Riber Christensen's essay illuminate the technological developments in engraving techniques that paved the way for cheap mass reproduction and distribution of the images. We are also treated to an analysis of the various genres of painting represented in the Gallery, and the point is offered that the remediation process leads to a destabilization of the traditional hierarchy of genres with history painting at the top. The Boydell images can thus be seen to pave the way towards a new paradigm in art and culture consumption, which, while it has its roots in the post-Glorious Revolution era and the 18th century struggle between an emergent but immature bourgeoisie and a moribund aristocracy, also leads forward into the Victorian era where the hegemony of the bourgeoisie becomes ever more firmly established, including that class's full sway of both private and public spaces within Britain and ultimately the whole British Empire. This analysis of a curious phenomenon of the Georgian age, thus serves as the perfect staging for the two essays to come on the making and breaking of three eminent Victorians.

In the first of these essays Jens Kirk analyzes the relationship between the construction of self and identity and the writing of autobiographies and other books. He takes as his specific object of interest the life and works of John Stuart Mill, an uncommonly well-educated person by the standards of any historical period. Kirk's essay draws on the twin disciplines of book history and the history of reading to situate Mill's efforts of self-fashioning within a social-constructivist paradigm. His reading is inspired by the insights generated by New Historicist approaches to textual studies, as exemplified by the work of Stephen Greenblatt, and the essay shows how the issues of authority/power and authorship are irrevocably intertwined. Kirk further uses Roman Jakobsen's notion of the conative function of language (and by extension books) to discuss the impact of texts and books on readers. Mill's particular construction of self is read closely in the case of his relationship with his father and with his wife, Harriet Taylor Mill, whose contribution to Mill's book *On Liberty* receives particular attention in Mill's *Autobiography*. Kirk argues that Mill attempted to create a unified self, and to communicate this self image, through the revisions of his life and life's work performed by the writing of and in the *Autobiography*, and that the acknowledgement of his by then deceased wife's contribution functions as a prerequisite for internal unification within Mill's understanding of his identity as author.

Riber Christensen returns with a comparative essay discussing two of the most widely read Victorian authors, Dickens and Kipling. His essay commences with the postulate that the Victorian period in fact should be read as an era of thoroughgoing modernization and innovation, which he documents with a number of graphs and maps showing internal and external, imperial expansion and technological growth. The textual engagement with the two authors picks lesser known texts by the two authors, so that the famous novelist Dickens is represented via a short story, and so that Kipling's best known longer prose works and poems take the back seat to far more obscure short fictions. Dickens is shown to have deep-seated anxieties vis-à-vis technological progress, partly due to personal traumas incurred because of his unfortunate involvement in the train accident known as the "Staplehurst Railway Accident". This event not only jeopardized his life but also his reputation, as he was traveling with his mistress, and a leakage between his private and public personae could have occurred with potentially career damaging consequences. The short narrative "The Signal-Man" is analyzed by Riber Christensen with the use of Todorov's theory of hesitation in the reading of texts within the fantastic paradigm. Dickens uses the hesitation between a fantastic and a pseudo-ghost story reading protocol to establish a critique of the consequences for man's spirit and faith of too rapid and pervasive technological development. In contrast, Kipling is shown – via an analysis of some of his fictions thematizing whites passing for natives in India (particularly the short story "Lispeth") – to not be as uniformly jingoist in his ideology of empire and racial hierarchies as has popularly been assumed by faulty, decontextualized and dehistoricized analyses of poems such as "The White Man's Burden". Rather Kipling must be regarded as in favour of colonialism in the public sphere, but thoroughly against it in the private sphere of love and marital relations. Both authors are thus shown to be good Victorians, yet ultimately they have become undone by their own ideologies for a more contemporary reading public by their attempts to parcel out a waterproof distinction between the two spheres.

~~~

The focus of the collection then shifts to the modernist period, and the next three essays read canonical as well as marginal modernist authors in various contexts that all highlight these authors' questionable belongings to nations, groups and – ultimately – periods.

INTRODUCTION 9

Jesper Trier frames his essay on T.S. Eliot and Yeats with a discussion of the problematics of period definition, but still offers to synthesize a common poetics for these two very different poets, via an analysis of the use of reader manifestations and inscribed reader positions in some of the best known poems by the two authors. The essay offers a description of the construct of modernism and modernist aesthetics as a cultural text, with a number of poets organizing themselves loosely around the figure of Ezra Pound and his declared aesthetic programme. Through Poggioli and others' ideas of avant-garde versus more integrated artistic expressions and 'schools' Trier conceptualizes both Eliot and Yeats's positions as critical of the alienation associated with life in the modern world, especially post-WWI. Their differences are, however, also emphasized, as Eliot is shown to rapidly develop into a more conservative figure lamenting the fragmentation of life and thinking in his famous essay "Tradition and the Individual Talent", where he suggests the objective and catalytic role as ideal for the poet. Eliot's own poetic practice is discussed through an analysis of the poem "Sweeney Among the Nightingales", where the reader is inscribed as a drab non-participant figure clad in brown. In contrast Yeats is shown, through an analysis of some of the paratext surrounding *A Vision*, to be an advocate for the poet to exert active influence and work for a change to the better. This desire is seen as more of a moral or religious/philosophical endeavour than an aesthetic one, and this insight is evolved in an analysis of one of Yeats's most apocalyptic texts, the poem "The Second Coming". Ultimately the shared project between Eliot and Yeats is shown to consist in a desire or moral obligation ascribed to the poet to educate his readers in how to navigate modern life with its lack of moral and social guidelines.

Lene Yding Pedersen also reads Yeats, but she engages with him as one of several writers engaged in a project of (re)imagining Ireland in the years leasing up to and immediately after the establishment of the Irish Free State in 1922. Her theoretical framework draws on Benedict Anderson's notion of imagined communities, which entails reading the construction of nations and national identity as a mainly textual project. Belonging and non-belonging is in Anderson and Yding's optics a matter of construction of unified selves and groups bound together by shared narratives of origin, development and common *telos*. Yeats's participation in this project as regards the so-called Celtic Renaissance is analyzed through a number of essays and other non-fiction writings by Yeats as well as through a reading of his poem "The Fisherman". While Yding admits that an Andersonian reading of this or any poem is necessarily highly reductive, she still documents that the relations between history and myth and past and present become particularly poignant when viewed through a social-constructive lens. Yding proceeds to treat the particular case of the role of the Gaelic language in the Irish revival, and here she focuses on some of the oppositional voices ironizing over the elevation of the Gaelic tongue to a key to the Irish Ur-identity. Joyce is mentioned in passing, but the particular, representative voice analyzed in depth is that of Flann O'Brien's novel, *The Poor Mouth*, which contains hilarious passages satirizing among other things the academic *faible* for all things Gaelic, including the squeals of a particular piglet which sound especially authentic to the scholars of Gaelic. Yding concludes with a perspective on the other not so Irish Irish writers, Shaw and Beckett who both spoke out against the (self)censorship practiced by the Irish Free State on key issues related to sexuality, public morals and the Catholic Church. Yding concludes that even these oppositional voices were engaged in an imagining of Ireland as a cultural (free) space in the interwar years and post-WWII period.

Free spaces are also among the main topics of Bent Sørensen's essay on the Harlem renaissance and one of its lesser known writers, Nella Larsen, whose connection to Denmark is currently being re-mapped and re-interpreted. His essay participates in this unearthing of Larsen as a forgotten literary figure whose life is very illustrative when read as a social and cultural text, exemplifying exclusion form and a quest for sanctuary and belonging in groups, classes and ethnicities. Sørensen's theoretical point of departure is in his attempt to develop a trans-generic tool for the reading of cultural texts, which combines semiotics as a general philosophy of sign and meaning with a historicist credo, leading to the claim that all texts can be read as expressive of a few central difference discourses (of say, gender, race, age, class, nation/region and belief), but these texts cannot be fully understood unless read in a cultural specificity. New Historicism here also serves as a significant source of inspiration, but departing from the generic New Historicist circulation perspective Sørensen also insists upon the necessity of further specificity which calls for close reading techniques to supplement the reception and circulation analysis. Here Bourdieu's notions of the field of cultural production and the Habermasian distinction between private and public life and text play a role as influences on his methodology. To open the case of Nella Larsen as a culturally significant text, Sørensen situates her in three concentric circles of contextualizations: The modernist period in the USA and its specific manifestation in African-American and diasporic literature and art of the 1920s, i.e. The Harlem Renaissance; the

INTRODUCTION 11

pressures of negotiating double minority differences within that group, e.g. female and black identities, with its attendant numerous victim positions, both as regards the author's life and the life of her literary characters; and finally the individual biography of Larsen and its reflections in her works. Larsen is particularly interesting in the latter respect because many layers of obscurity still persist and competing biographical narratives produced by herself and, belatedly, by academics do little to shed light on the lacunae in our understanding of her life and works. Sørensen's strategy is here to apply the difference discourse theory to all three circles of engagement with Nella Larsen and her texts, her peer group, and the socio-economic reality she had to operate within. This analysis shows her as a victim of discrimination, silencing and character assassination from a variety of agencies, including some of her closest peers. Her own works are read as containing sophisticated oppositional discourses signaling these silencing attempts and offering us as contemporary academics a cultural text that can be read as quite sophisticated in its feminist and interracial critiques.

~~~

The final and largest cluster of essays in the volume treats postmodern and even more recent texts. That this is the largest area in terms of contributions also reflects the predominant teaching and research focus of the English department which squarely engages with postmodern poetics, aesthetics and textual practices across media and genres, and the potential labeling of that which is to come, or has come, after postmodernism. The six essays in this latter half of the volume stake out several of the posts in this field of study, starting with English poetry of the 1970s and 80s, 1980s global texts and world music, and Hollywood (historically, as well as in the contemporary period) viewed as a cultural text, before moving into the 1990s and the early 21st century in the choice of object texts, focusing on trends that surpass post-modern concerns and venture into analyses of the new literary sincerity (or the post-ironic), of shoes as cultural texts (or post-constructivist identity issues), and finally of transtextuality in post-cyberpunk literature (or post-human identities).

The first of these essays is Jens Kirk's analysis of the socio-literary production of the so-called 'Martian School' in English poetry in the 1970s and 80s. Using Pierre Bourdieu's theory of the field of cultural production, Kirk meticulously traces the construction by certain critics of a group of poets as both a unified school and a trend representing literary value in the shape of a neo-Eliotian sensibility. This consecration of, especially, the poets Craig Raine and Christopher Reid is shown to have its specific origin in a one-page article appearing in the *New Statesman* in 1978, wherein critic James Fenton performs a dual operation of appraisal of the above-mentioned poets and desecration of several critics of a previous generation, thereby in effect also auto-consecrating himself as a taste-maker and gate-keeper in the field of cultural production. While it appears that Fenton's actions are motivated by a desire for renewal of the canon of consecrated poetry in England, Kirk further shows that the actual values praised by Fenton and later critics that participate in the production of the Martians are considerably more conventional and all hinge on the reading of emotionality into the works of Raine in particular. Thus the new consecration of Martian poets cannot be said to be subversive in itself, but rather constitutes a struggle for the power to consecrate. Kirk ends by reminding us that we all as cultural analysts are implicated in this struggle and cannot ultimately take a stand outside the field of cultural production.

Ben Dorfman, in his essay on global text reading, takes an intellectual historian's approach to what he wishes to consecrate as a new genre or label for a field of analysis. Commencing with a reminder that we live in an age of globalization, he proposes that we examine what that implies for our engagement with texts that themselves are global in the sense that they embody the dual move of time-space compression and deterritorialization. Dorfman sees globalization itself as a process that first connects and then integrates units into global wholes. He proposes that certain texts can be seen to be ruled by this logic, and proposes the term 'global texts' for this trans-generic body of works. While globalization in itself is not a new phenomenon, as Dorfman's excursus on the Roman Empire illustrates, he nevertheless argues that compression and de-territorialization as proposed by Deleuze and Guattari are more common phenomena in postmodernity than ever before. As an example of a trans-national, indeed global, cultural product, which is both conceived, produced, disseminated and consumed globally, Dorfman selects Paul Simon's album *Graceland*, which features a fusion of several musical influences or roots, a collaboration between musicians across spatial distances, and global consumer appeal. Dorfman illustrates how this text evinces a time-space compression and 'transports' its listeners effortlessly from American blues/country roots to contemporary *mbaqanga* style South African music, and metaphorically allows us to simultaneously be in Tennessee and Soweto, while we are in Simon's land of grace. This imagined suspension of distance in time/space echoes Yding's analysis of the imagined cultural spaces in Ireland and Sørensen's observations on constructed concentric circles of sanctuary in the case of Nella Larsen. Dorfman concludes his essay with a three-step reading programme for global, cultural text studies, which strongly echoes the engagement with text that New Historicism and social constructivism teach us: global texts must be read in awareness of global history, i.e. they produce meaning fully only when situated historically and globally; texts co-produce the history they partake in, and finally, we become involved in globalization ourselves when performing readings and analyses of such texts. The latter point, of course, echoes Kirk's conclusions in the Martians' article.

The first of Steen Christiansen's essays proposes that the whole of Hollywood's production, dissemination and reception system can be read as a cultural text, or a set of specific global texts, to use Dorfman's terminology. His point of departure is in a critique of film studies agendas that focus narrowly on auteur films (seen as film's version of high art) or on genre studies which either are naively quantitative in scope or else purely formalist and therefore prone to bizarre miscategorizations. Instead Christiansen proposes to read film in general and the Hollywood system in particular from a reception oriented perspective. He claims that films have in them reader positions (to revitalize Trier's point about modernist poetry), and that these reader positions are historically specific and often ideologically expressive of certain expectations on behalf of the filmmakers. The historical situatedness is dealt with in the portion of the essay that discusses the technological innovations within filmmaking from the introduction of sound onwards, where the point is that Hollywood has used innovation and globalization techniques in combination to ensure a continuing role as the dominant force in film, while remaining a national film industry. Hollywood film thus remains steadily American in its view of the world it impacts on and attempts to teach. While Christiansen does not disregard psychoanalytic film theory as important for a reception oriented approach he prefers reader-response ideas that allow the audience more agency in filling out the blanks in the interpretative process of film viewing. Brief analysis of films such as *Deep Blue Sea*, *Boyz N the Hood*, and *Se7en* show that the reader positions are partly engendered within the film, but that reader competence and playfulness as a dialogic (i.e. two-way producer-reader constructed) process cannot be ignored especially in the work of interpreting postmodern meta-films. Christiansen concludes by proposing that we adopt John Fiske's idea of an extension of Roland Barthes's distinction between 'readerly' and 'writerly' texts to also encompass the position of 'producerly' texts. This position affords us a middle ground between hermeneutics and empty formalist categorization where we can speak of a cultural text reading of Hollywood itself and its products.

Tore R. Andersen, in his essay on post-ironic positions within or beyond postmodern literature, focuses in particular on David Foster Wallace's constructions of sincerity in his 1996 novel, *Infinite Jest*. Andersen, however, identifies a whole generation of American novelists who both are the inheritors of and rebels against what has become postmodern conformity and hegemony within the American literary establishment. The first generation of ironic postmodernists, spearheaded by John Barth, Thomas Pynchon and Don de Lillo have reached levels of consecration that are quite astounding considering the contents of their paranoid quasi-nihilistic works often written in a hard-to-engage-with, alienating style. The new 'wannabe' patricidal generation of Wallace, Jonathan Franzen, Rick Moody and others offer a return to teleological narratives and a new sincere belief in the function of story-telling. This is seen by Andersen as a generational move towards the post-ironic, both within the literary texts themselves and in the construction of author personae, which differs considerably from the strategies chosen by the older ironists. While the post-ironists are not always successful in avoiding the trap of repeating old ironies inherent in the writing styles and favourite subject matters of their predecessors, the essay argues that *Infinite Jest* is a fully successful post-ironic text, while still remaining a vibrant social satire of contemporary USA. This novel is seen as an example of 'radical realism' as much in the tradition of Raymond Carver as that of political, dissident postmodernists such as those identified by Paul Maltby in his seminal work of that title from 1991. Andersen in sum offers an update of Maltby's distinction between introverted and extroverted postmodernists, an endeavour complicated by the return of some of the ironical patriarchs (such as de Lillo and Pynchon) to the joys of storytelling. This tentative poetics of the post-ironical includes a renewed focus on the personal and on the family as the quintessential identity unit. It is therefore ironic in itself (!) that this tendency towards the post-ironic can potentially be seen as a return to an avant-garde aesthetics, as Andersen proposes in his concluding perspectives which also comment on Danish filmmaker Lars von Trier as a post-ironist.

The penultimate essay in the volume at hand offers a reading of the various cultural metamorphoses surrounding the career and works of Rebecca Miller. Camelia Elias reads Miller's career as a navigation of the field of cultural production, as theorized in Bourdieu's volume of that title.

Miller is a multi-talented woman whose varied heritage from gifted and consecrated parents (Arthur Miller and Inge Morath) has stood her in good stead in her career-shifts between acting, art, writing and filmmaking. Elias's point is also that Miller in some of her latest works, both entitled *Personal Velocity* (one is a collection of short stories and the other an episodic film), overtly thematizes the position a number of gifted young women find themselves in when attempting to negotiate new careers and new identity positions for themselves. While the stories and film episodes are not autobiographical in a conventional sense, Elias argues that they all thematize the desire for being interesting – a desire Miller herself has ample biographical reasons for being fuelled by. Elias's most controversial point is that the symbol of choice in Miller's work, as in the work of many other authors and purveyors of cultural artifacts throughout the history of cultural text production (from at least Chaucer onwards), is shoes. Elias shows how shoes pervade not only Miller's own texts but also references in the reception of her career. Culturally speaking, shoes are therefore among the most well-worn artifacts, also when academics subject them to analysis when walking through the field of cultural production.

The volume closes with Steen Christiansen's second contribution, which tackles a very recent text by William Gibson, who pioneered the sub-genre of cyberpunk within the field of science fiction. Gibson's *Pattern Recognition* questions what defines us as human, particularly in a fragmented, paranoid, amnesiac or apophenic culture. Christiansen's approach to these issues is again reader and reception oriented, this time utilizing the charting of transtextual phenomena carried out by French theorist Gerard Genette in a number of volumes of textual history and criticism from the 1980s and 90s. Transtextuality is a common term for all that creates links between texts and their readers and between texts and other texts. Christiansen shows how Genette's detailed catalogue of phenomena of intertextuality, hypertextuality, and architextuality (and to a lesser degree meta- and paratextuality) can help us read even a text such as Gibson's which endeavours to play games with its readers that go beyond the standard catalogue of postmodern poetics. Christiansen shows first that apparently innocent intertextual games such as quoting and misquoting canonical works can have radically different aesthetic functions according to reader competence and reading protocol applied to such phenomena. *Pattern Recognition* turns out to relate transtextually to other texts as diverse as Melville's *Moby-Dick*, Gibson's own *Neuromancer* and Pynchon's *The Crying of Lot 49*. Different readers will of course recognize these patterns of transtextuality to different degrees. Christiansen utilizes Umberto Eco's notion of the open and the closed text to conceptualize these reading protocols, and concludes radically that Gibson's version of problematizing the postmodern notion of paranoia over the connectedness of everything is by questioning and leaving open the very notion of any purpose or intentionality behind these trans-textual connections. Interpretation may therefore ultimately be redundant, and Gibson may therefore fall in the trap the post-ironists seek to avoid: that of dying of his own textual exhaustion.

~~~

This collection thus ends on an open question applied to an open text. This spirit of openness to approaches is of course no coincidence. The credo of cultural text studies is that any object text can be situated in an interesting context and be given an interesting reading. The wide range of theoretical approaches from New Historicism and literary sociology, over reception aesthetics to close readings shows the interdisciplinary and eclectic method cultural text studies must embrace to make texts relevant in a contemporary research and teaching environment. Sometimes Shakespeare must be stippled and stroked, Ireland imagined as Gaelic piglets, Martians produced out of thin air, silk shoes donned in muddy fields, and patterns recognized where none exist, all in order to make fresh research done and the communication of its findings to reluctant students possible. Should we succeed, as I am confident we will, that would be no small accomplishment.

Remediating Shakespeare:
The Boydell Shakespeare Gallery

Jørgen Riber Christensen

The birth of a new cultural publicness in the 18th century in Britain meant a changed relationship between audience and text, between text and its form of distribution and also of the media and form of the text itself. The place of consumption of the text itself developed from a public place, e.g. the theatre, with collective reception through a public place with individual reception, e.g. the gallery to a private place with individual reception, i.e. the home. This narrowing of the world of the text has its paradoxical counterpart in a widening relationship between the author or textual producer and his or her audience. By and large the artistic producer moved from a well-defined connection to a patron to an obscure and impersonal relationship to an anonymous mass market.

This general movement is reflected in the Boydell Shakespeare Gallery, which opened in London in 1789 and exhibited a large number of specially commissioned oil paintings with scenes from Shakespeare's plays, until it closed in 1805. Engraved prints were made from the paintings, and they were sold to the general public at reasonable prices in very large quantities. This migration of Shakespeare's plays from the theatres over oil painting to prints can be regarded as remediation. This remediation not only changed the reception of Shakespeare's texts and their form. Also the media changed. The remediation or reproduction of oil painting with its soft tones, colors and gradients was improved by a new delicate engraving technique, the stipple process, which was promoted in England and used by one of the Shakespeare Gallery engravers, Francesco Bartolozzi (1727–1815) at the close of the eighteenth century.

The Boydell Shakespeare Gallery and its publication of Shakespeare prints, but also its subsequent financial failure in 1805, reflect a new paradigm of the production and consumption of culture. This change of paradigms is basically one from aristocratic feudal publicness with a system of patrons to a market system with the new mercantile middle classes as consumers of culture. Already before Boydell poets such as Dryden (1631–1700) and Pope (1688–1744) were gradually starting to look for less dependence on the patronage of the aristocracy. They used a system of subscribed editions, where buyers of their books subscribed to paying in advance. The first seven pages of James Thomson's (1700–1748) *The Seasons* from 1730 consist of a list of both noble and bourgeois subscribers (Thomson 1979). For instance The Right Hon. George Dodington Esq. had ordered no less than twenty books, it appears. Public subscription is a bridge between aristocratic patronage and the free culture market of the general public.

The new commercial system of artistic distribution and consumption meant the rise of new forms of mass publication and new technologies. It also meant new themes, genres and subjects of art. In the Boydell Shakespeare Gallery there was a preference for a certain content of the Shakespearian scenes reproduced that bore witness to a new kind of sensibility, and which had its own melodramatic style.

The Boydell Shakespeare Gallery and its History

A gallery with an exhibition of paintings with scenes from the plays of Shakespeare opened in London in June 1789 at 52 Pall Mall. The large building had a façade in copper; over the entrance there was a relief of Shakespeare with the Dramatic Muse to his right and the Genius of Painting to his left. The first year 34 paintings were displayed; this number grew each year so that when the gallery closed in 1805 there were 167 paintings by 33 different artists.

The initiator and owner of the gallery was "Alderman" John Boydell (1719–1804). He became the Mayor of London in 1790. The idea for the gallery arose at a dinner in November 1786. Boydell and his nephew Josiah were printers and publishers of engraved prints. John Boydell had grown rich as a publisher of books and prints that were sold in Britain and in France. Boydell and his nephew hit upon the idea of publishing a fine illustrated edition of Shakespeare like the ones the French had published with their most celebrated authors. This idea grew into not only publishing such an edition, but also opening a Shakespeare gallery where the most famous artists of the time would be commissioned into painting scenes and characters from Shakespeare's plays. First the paintings were to be exhibited at the gallery with an entrance fee, and then prints were to be engraved based on the paintings. The painters employed were among others: Sir Joshua Reynolds, George Romney, James Barry, Thomas Stothard, James Northcote, Benjamin West, Johann Heinrich Füssli (Henry Fuseli) and Angelika Kauffmann. Two sets of engravings were produced: a large one for a picture-only edition, and a smaller one for an illustrated text edition. The editions, which were based on public subscriptions, appeared between 1791 and 1805, when a large or folio edition was published with 100 prints. However, there were no profits, as the war with France in 1793 put a stop to export for the lucrative European market. In comparison it may be mentioned that in 1786 exports of Boydell's English prints to France valued 200,000 pounds annually. The expenditure of the Shakespeare paintings and print production was too large, over £100,000, as Boydell was magnanimous with his contracts with painters and engravers. He may seem more to be a patron of the arts or a Maecenas than an acute businessman in this respect. Sale of individual prints and proofs was at a price of one guinea each.

When the firm had lost almost its whole capital the Boydells managed to get permission from the House of Commons to dispose of the gallery through a national lottery. The Boydell firm issued 22,000 three-guinea tickets. The holder of a ticket received a Shakespeare print from the enormous stores of the gallery. At John Boydell's death in December 1804 all the tickets had been sold. The winner of the lottery, who turned out to be a Mr. Tassie, won the entire gallery and its contents. The still enterprising nephew, Josiah Boydell, offered Mr. Tassie £10,000 for the gallery; but Tassie refused and auctioned the 167 oil paintings at Christy's where they only fetched around £6,000. The Boydell Shakespeare Gallery ceased to exist in 1805, and around 40 of the paintings still exist today.

Marketing Shakespeare

The Shakespeare Gallery is an example of what happened to the societal reception of culture and art in the historical movement from a largely feudal and aristocratic societal formation towards a bourgeois one. Painters were beginning to be loosened from patronage and had to function in a mass market. Here the Boydell Shakespeare Gallery is a curious example of a transitory stage, where paintings were exhibited publicly, but the public had to pay a fee in order to enter this part of the cultural sphere. An art gallery with an entrance fee may be considered part market and part exhibition; but a more obvious consequence of art being produced for a mass market is to turn the production of art into mass production, and here Boydell's trade as a printer is very apt. John Boydell combined the Shakespeare dramas and original and unique oil paintings in a gallery with mass-produced prints of the oil paintings. This complex transaction and remediation may be viewed as an early step in the process that liberated art and the artist from the ties of patronage, but this freedom meant an insecure position in an anonymous mass market, which was still immature at Boydell's time. The subsequent bankruptcy of Boydell's firm is a consequence of a market that was not quite ready for this kind of artistic production, just as Boydell's innovative project may seem understandably unfocussed.

A consequence of the development of a mass market for pictorial art was the development of engraving and printing techniques. In the case of the Boydell Shakespeare Gallery especially two techniques were used. Francesco Bartolozzi developed the stipple or 'dotted' process which could give gradients, soft tones and shades and which was relatively fast to execute for the trained engraver. The gradients and soft look of stipple engravings were a translation of the colors and chiaroscuro of oil paintings into the grayscale shades of engravings. Furthermore, copper plates engraved with the stipple technique could stand for thousands of prints before the plates were worn out. It was not until around 1820 that steel plates were used for engraving. More impressions can be made from steel plates than from copper plates, but copper produces finer results. When working with the stipple technique the engraver hammers fine dots into the copper plate, so that dots or flecks create the shapes in the image instead of lines doing it. By varying the size and proximity of the dots of the stipple technique it was possible for the engraver to accomplish the most delicate gradations of tone. As recorded in Joseph Farrinton's diary he and another of the Boydell-engravers, Robert Smirke, had discussed the relative merits of the two engraving techniques, stipple and line. Smirke had remarked that that "the excellence of stroke [or line] engraving consisted of the difficulty of execution and... dotted [or stipple] engraving produced a better imitation of color and effect" (Joseph Farrington's diary (1793–1831). Typescript deposited in the print room of the British Museum. Quoted by Frederick Burwick, in Pape and Burwick, 1996: 19).

Usually, however, a mixture of stipple engraving and line engraving was used in the Shakespeare prints, just as they had some initial etching. Where the ink in stipple engraving is deposited in the small holes or specks in the copperplate, in line engraving the ink is deposited in long lines or furrows incised into the copperplate. In contrast to stipple engraving line engraving is precise and has sharp outlines of the shapes of the design. Where line engraving has an identity of its own, stipple engraving approaches other techniques such as etching or as mentioned above oil painting, though stipple engraving usually is monochrome. If the precise and well-defined outlines are to be softened or if large areas are to be filled in line engraving they are filled with a minute pattern of dot- and especially lozenge-shapes.

Line engraving uses a technique that has the narrative and aesthetic qualities of precision, sharpness and economy of its expressions. Sharp outlines may be the effect that is desirable. As such line engraving is a first-class technique of its own, and stipple engraving may lose these qualities in its attempt to emulate the characteristics of oil painting. So there is no intrinsic reason that stipple engraving should supplant line engraving, unless it is oil painting that is remediated and that it is the remediation itself that is decisive in the choice of engraving technique.

When the whole image has been cut into the metal plate, the plate is inked and then wiped clean on its surface. The ink fills the channel or holes cut by the engraver and the plate is then passed through a printing press having a damp sheet of paper pressed into the cut lines, so that the ink is absorbed from the furrows or holes in the plate into paper. Printing processes where the ink is not deposited on the surface of the plates but in incisions in the plates is called intaglio printing.

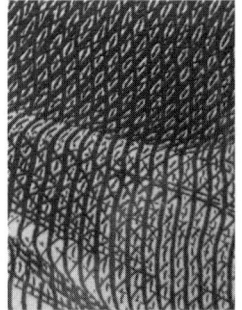
Line engraving with
contours of dot-and-lozenge

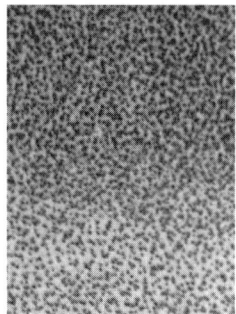
Stipple engraving with
soft tones and atmosphere

In his essay "The Work of Art in the Age of Mechanical Reproduction" from 1934 Walter Benjamin (1892–1940) wrote about how mechanical reproduction technologies had made it possible to distribute works of art in large numbers. Before such technologies as printing and photography works of art such as oil paintings had been made manually, and they were unique and original. Some works of art such as frescoes were even tied physically to a specific location, and their production was tied to a specific time and age. This had the consequence that art was the domain of relatively few people, i.e. the upper classes, but it also meant that the act of reception of a work of art could produce what Benjamin calls aura. Aura is the ability of a unique work of art to contain its history in itself including its time and place, so that the beholder may experience the history of the authentic and unique work of art during the process of reception. This history may be seen in the many tiny traces of patina and age, and perhaps one may experience its provenance. Aura is a form of transhistoricity, and it has an emotional effect on the beholder.

> Die Echtheit einer Sache ist der Inbegriff alles von Ursprung her an ihr Tradierbaren, von ihrer materiellen Dauer bis zu ihrer geschichtlichen Zeugenschaft. Da die letztere auf der ersteren fundiert ist, so gerät in der Reproduktion, wo die erstere sich dem Menschen entzogen hat, auch die letztere: die geschichtliche Zeugenschaft der Sache ins Wanken. Freilich nur diese; was aber dergestalt ins Wanken gerät, das ist die Autorität der Sache.
>
> Man kann, was hier ausfällt, im Begriff der Aura zusammenfassen und sagen: was im Zeitalter der technischen Reproduzierbarkeit des Kunstwerks verkümmert, das ist seine Aura. Der Vorgang ist symptomatisch; seine Bedeutung weist über den Bereich der Kunst hinaus. Die Reproduktionstechnik, so ließe sich allgemein formulieren, löst das Reproduzierte aus dem Bereich der Tradition ab. Indem sie die Reproduktion vervielfältigt, setzt sie an die Stelle seines einmaligen Vorkommens sein massenweises.[1] (Benjamin, 1974: 477)

---

[1] The authenticity of a thing is the essence of all that is transmissible from its beginning, ranging from its substantive duration to its testimony to the history which it has experienced. Since the historical testimony rests on the authenticity, the former, too, is jeopardized by reproduction when substantive duration ceases to matter. And what is really jeopardized when the historical testimony is affected is the authority of the object. One might subsume the eliminated element in the term "aura" and go on to say: that which withers in the age of mechanical reproduction is the aura of the work of art. This is a symptomatic process whose significance points beyond the realm of art. One might generalize by saying: the technique of reproduction detaches the reproduced object from the domain of tradition. By making many reproductions it substitutes a plurality of copies for a unique existence (English translation by Harry Zohn).

Negatively seen mechanically reproduced works of art negate history and tradition, but positively seen mechanical reproduction is a reformulation of the reception of works of art in a popular and democratic direction as it to some extent is the history of the elitist upper-class culture and its history that are leveled by the reproduction techniques, which literally reduce the number of codes of its sources and cultural products during the process of reproduction so that originality and authenticity are translated with accessibility for many. But as Benjamin points out, this translation is not direct and complete. Mechanical reproduction always reduces the number of codes so that the work of art is simplified.

There are two versions of a scene from King Lear. One is an original oil painting hanging in a museum in London (James Barry, (1741–1806): *King Lear Weeping over the Dead Body of Cordelia*, 1786–8, oil on canvas, 269,2 x 367 cm, Tate Gallery, London), where an alarm will go off if a visitor gets too close to the painting. The painting may be seen in a digital reproduction at *Tate Online* (see references list). The other version is a print made after the painting and printed in thousands of copies (James Barry, *King Lear Weeping over the Dead Body of Cordelia*, 1792, copperplate engraved by Francis Legat, 49,5 x 62,5 cm).

James Barry, *King Lear Weeping over the Dead Body of Cordelia*, 1792, copperplate engraved by Francis Legat, 49,5 x 62,5 cm.

This print could be bought cheaply (at one guinea) and put on the wall at home with four pins. However, not only authenticity and aura are lost. The most obvious loss of codes is colors, but also details are lost, and the size of the image has been reduced considerably. Strangely enough no contemporary critics complained about the loss of color-coding, but then again the translation of the image into grayscale may not actually be a loss, but rather a coding that is concentrated and economic.

The predominance of stipple engraving in the Boydell Gallery is an indication that an attempt was made to partially overcome some of the consequences of mechanical reproduction, as the stipple engravings sought to imitate the oil painting originals or sources. At the same time the Boydell Shakespeare Gallery sought to keep the better of two worlds. It exhibited original oil paintings, which drew on the rich Shakespearian history and tradition, and it made these oil paintings available to the public both in their original form at the gallery and in the cheap and popular form of prints. The fact that the Boydell Shakespeare Gallery catered for both the auratic and non-auratic taste may be explained by the gallery's own historical position when a societal paradigm was shifting in Europe from an aristocratic world towards a society dominated by the middle classes.

Genres

In 1768 The Royal Academy of Arts was founded, and its first president was Sir Joshua Reynolds, who was one of the artists of the Boydell Shakespeare Gallery. Academism within art history may be seen as an aspect of the strict neo-classicist normative view of culture. A hierarchy of genres goes back to Aristotle, but through the 17th-century French Royal Academy of Painting and Sculpture with its Chancellor Le Brun and The Royal Academy of Arts in London sought to establish a set of rules, which also defined genre and placed them in a hierarchy. History painting was at the top. Reynolds writes about this genre in his Discourses on Art (1769–91), of which he gave one each year to the students of the Academy:

> [A] painter of history shows the man by showing his actions. A painter must compensate the natural deficiencies of his art. He has but one sentence to utter, but one moment to exhibit. He cannot, like the poet or historian, expatiate, and impress the mind with great veneration for the character of the hero or saint he represents, though he lets us know at the same time that the saint was deformed, or the hero lame. The painter has no other means of giving an idea of the dignity of the mind, but by that external appearance which grandeur of thought does generally, though not always, impress on the countenance, and by that correspondence of figure to sentiment and

situation which all men wish, but cannot command. The painter, who may in this one particular attain with ease what others desire in vain, ought to give all that he possibly can, since there are so many circumstances of true greatness that he cannot give at all. He cannot make his hero talk like a great man; he must make him look like one. For which reason he ought to be well studied in the analysis of those circumstances which constitute dignity of appearance in real life. (Reynolds, 1769: http)

Portraits came below history painting. Reynolds states this reason: "A history painter paints man in general; a portrait painter, a particular man, and consequently a defective model" (http). Landscapes, animal painting and still life were even lower in the hierarchy. Boydell himself saw his enterprise as a way of developing the genre history painting in the grand style. In the preface to a catalogue of the paintings in the Shakespeare Gallery John Boydell had written in 1789: " – To advance the art towards maturity, and establish an *English School of Historical Painting* was the great object of the present design" (Boydell, 1979: 5).

An examination of the prints from the gallery raises the questions whether a genre classification is so straightforward as Boydell's objective would suggest. Four genres and hybrids between them seem to appear: history painting, landscape painting, portrait painting and theatre painting.

History Painting

History painting is a genre that has a representative character as it depicts past memorable or historical moments in order to influence the present. For instance history painting may promote national identity or it may buttress a ruling class. In this way history painting always interprets a historical event with a purpose. Certain stylistic traits are common to most history paintings. The characters wear historical clothes, sometimes even antique Roman ones. The historical hero is also the center of the composition. This means that the composition in itself is relatively simple, so that the hero is placed at the top of a triangle, at the centre of a circle, or in the middle of symmetrical shapes. Action lines in the image must point towards the hero or heroine. Other shapes must not overlap the hero. The background is used to interpret the historical action in the sense that it creates an atmosphere. History paintings are very large, of panoramic scale, which may be regarded as part of their representative function. History painting has a wider definition than just historiography. Its subjects may also be mythological, religious or literary, in so far as these subjects have an ideological function.

Battle scenes are typical subjects of history paintings. The antique *The Alexander Mosaic or The Battle of Alexander at Issus* from ca. 333 BC is the archetypal example. In the Boydell Shakespeare Gallery there are several battle scenes. John Francis Rigaud's *First Part of King Henry the Fourth*: Act. V, scene IV. *Plain near Shrewsbury. Prince Henry, Hotspur, and Falstaff*, engraved by Thomas Ryder, 1796 is one. The measurements of the engraving are 51x38 cm. The painting is lost. While the battle rages in the background the showdown between Prince Hal and Hotspur fills the foreground. Falstaff who cowardly is lying on the ground hidden under his shield connects the foreground with the background through the man lying really dead on the ground with an arrow in his chest.

The standing Prince Hal is the top of a triangle the left side of which is formed by his right arm with the sword, and its right side is formed by the gaze or action line from Hotspurs' eyes to Prince Hal's head. Prince Hal is also accentuated by his position in the left golden section of the image. This image belongs to the genre of history painting. It presents heroic deeds (and their opposite as a contrast). Though the direct source of the image is literary, indirectly the source is historical, as Shakespeare used Holinshed's *The Chronicles of England, Scotland and Ireland*, 1578 as his source. The death of Hotspur at the Battle of Shrewsbury took place in 1403. However, the connection between historiographic and literary sources is even closer, as the Shakespeare texts themselves are an important part of British historical heritage.

Landscape Painting

This genre is primarily tied to the 19th century, especially the early part, and it valued nature in the spirit of Romanticism. It is crucial to an understanding of this genre whether human characters are placed in the natural setting or not. With regard to the Shakespeare images a reading of nature in them will be a question of to what extent nature is just a background or backdrop to the foreground's (Shakespearean) action, or whether nature in its own right plays an active and independent role. What natural elements are there, and how large a proportion of the pictorial space do they occupy, would be initial questions to ask.

In the British social and historical context there is a part of landscape tradition tied to the landed gentry where ownership of land and land as a means of production influence the rendition of natural scenes, as it may for instance be seen in Thomas Gainsborough's *Mr & Mrs Andrews* (1748–9). Just as there was an uneasy relationship between the historiographer and the painter of history, so there was between the map-drawing topographer and the landscape painter. In the Boydell period this latter relationship was further complicated by the predominance of history painting as the ideal and highest art form. Even the landscape painter sought to embellish his art by borrowing stylistic traits from history painting, and also to elevate the function of landscape painting to that of history painting. The landscape painter Edward Dayes compared in 1801 in his essay "On the Principles of Composition as Connected with Landscape Painting" the two genres, when he writes about landscape painting: "The principles that govern this branch of composition, extend to every other connected with the art of painting, whether the subject be history, or otherwise" (Edward Dayes, *The Works of the Late Edward Dayes*, London, E.W. Brayley, 1805: 191 as quoted by Kriz, 1997: 23). Landscape painting must have the same didactic effect on the spectators as history painting. Just as the past incidents of history painting must elevate the spectator, so nature must be perfected for the sake of the same effect, so the landscape painters must "endeavor to create a nature of our own, if possible, more dignified and noble than the one that strikes our senses: we should feel an enthusiasm in our pursuits not to be satisfied with a perfection short of divine" (Dayes, 1805: 202).

The views expressed by Edward Dyes in 1801 may lie behind the wide-ranging depiction of nature and landscape in the Boydell Shakespeare Gallery, where generally there is no conflict between the action of the foreground and the landscapes of the background or middleground, which

Johann Heinrich Fuseli (Füssli), *The Tempest*, Act I, scene II, engraved by Jean Pierre Simon, 1797.

extend the meaning of the foreground action. In James Barry, *King Lear Weeping over the Dead Body of Cordelia* (see p. 23) the background is both landscape and historical as it contains Stonehenge. Barry has been free with his geography in order to connect the tragic ending of the play with ancient British history. He has moved Stonehenge from the plains of Salisbury to hills near Dover, where the stage directions set Edgar's camp.

Barry has also been free with his meteorology as he makes Lear's hair blow rhetorically so that it points toward Stonehenge and Cordelia's body at the same time as he lets the feathers on the soldier's helmet blow in the opposite direction in order to achieve the same pointing effect. Where the landscape and its landmarks only take up a small proportion of the total area of the image in *King Lear Weeping over the Dead Body of Cordelia*, the landscape may fill almost the whole frame in other images in the gallery as in William Hodges, *The Merchant of Venice*, Act V, scene I, William Hodges, *As You Like It*, Act II, scene I, Joseph Wright, *Winter's Tale*, Act III, scene III, Robert Smirke and Joseph Farrington, *First Part of King Henry the Fourth*, Act II, scene II, and Joseph Hoppner, *Cymbeline*, Act III, scene IV.

In Joseph Hoppner, *Cymbeline*, Act III, scene IV the natural background is used as a compositional device to frame Imogen and Pisanio so that they are tied together, and so that the dynamics of Imogen's emotions and the stunned bewilderment of Pisano's are reflected in the shapes surrounding them. In Fuseli's *The Tempest*, Act I, scene II, this framing function of the natural background plays even more closely together with the foreground human action. The lit circle, which is made up from the opening of the cave, contains the monodrama of the triad of Prospero, Caliban and Ariel, so that the empty space between them both sets them apart and ties them together in a silent dialogue.

Portrait Painting and Theatre Painting

Two points are important with regard to portraits. One is that the sitter must be rendered so that he or she is identifiable. There must be some degree of likeness. The other is that the sitter may be psychologically characterized and interpreted by the artist. As such this kind of portraits is a relative to the novel, which is basically a bourgeois form. The sitter may also be portrayed not as an individual but as a social function. In this case the portrait will be representative, as when a king is portrayed. This representative function of portraits is basically an aristocratic form. It may seem that many British portraits of the period before 1800 are actually both representative and psychologically oriented. This may be a reflection of Britain having an aristocracy and ruling class that were partially influenced by a bourgeois mode of life.

George Romney, *The Tempest*, Act I, scene I and II, *The Inchanted Island: before the cell of Prospero*, engraved by Benjamin Smith, 1797

In the case of the Shakespeare Gallery, which reflected not real life, but dramatic texts and the theatre, any portrayal would be of leading actors, and as such the portrait genre is hybridized with the genre of theatre painting. However, the hybridization reaches further, as portraits of the leading actors are of the actors in the role of a historical or literary personage, so that the actor's interpretation of this personage is doubled by the painter's and subsequently the engraver's interpretation.

When the more private and intimate portrait genre is inscribed in the representative and public genre of history painting one of the first consequences is canvas size and scope. The small close-up of a face is altered into a large-scale design, e.g. a panorama, where the sitter usually is part of an action. George Romney's enormous painting *The Tempest*, Act I, scene I and II, *The inchanted Island: before the cell of Prospero*, engraved by Benjamin Smith, 1797 includes a portrait of a celebrity from the time. Lady Emma Hamilton (1765–1815), mistress of the British naval hero Horatio Nelson and friend of Queen Marie Caroline, posed as Miranda (upper right corner). In this way the upper classes of the day could be inscribed into the national Shakespearian heritage. Only a few fragments survive of the original painting.

When looking at the Shakespeare Gallery one often wonders whether the scene depicted is the artist's conception of a part of a play, or whether the artist has used his or her sketches from a theatre performance with a

Josiah Boydell, *Henry VI, part 1*, Act II, scene VI, *Richard Plantagenet at the rose bush*, engraved by John Ogborne, 1795

tableau from the stage as the motive. In many of the images the depth is shallow, and the middle and background seem to be vertical. In this case, we are dealing with theatre painting, in particular when the characters have a striking likeness with known actors. Josiah Boydell's *Richard Plantagenet at the rose bush* bears all the signs of a staged theatre tableau with its symmetrical frieze of characters with the actor's frozen and theatrical poses in front of a vertical backdrop.

Ut Pictura Poesis

The relationship between visual art and poetry (literature) has been discussed through history. The basis of this discussion is Horace's (65–8 BC) *Ars Poetica*, which states "Ut pictura poesis" – As in painting, so in poetry. Especially during the Renaissance and during the Neo-Classicist period Horace's rules were revived, discussed and elaborated. One of the crucial points in this discussion is that the visual artist's medium is space, no matter whether he or she produces three-dimensional sculpture or two-dimensional painting, whereas the writer's medium is time. So the artist must create an illusion of time, and the writer must create an illusion of space.

The question of the iconography of visual art is often one of intertextuality, as narrative visual art often depicts a story already told within other media, especially literature. Here we are in other words dealing with adaptation or remediation, as it is the case with the Boydell Shakespeare Gallery where both written and performed plays are recoded into visual art. To achieve this recoding visual art has developed some methods to overcome the temporal limitation. Or in other words: how does a painting tell a story like a play, as there is no temporal sequence in an image? Basically two methods have been used. The image may choose to combine within its frame or setting various parts of the action of the story that it narrates, so that they are to be seen in a specific and temporal sequence. Much more often, however, the image records just one appropriate moment, e.g. a climax, in its adaptation of a literary text, or of any story for that matter. The Boydell Shakespeare Gallery also in this respect chose hybridity. As drama is both visual and verbal, the remediation of it is complex. The visual codes of the play in question can be transferred by and large, whereas the verbal codes must be adapted so that they can be substituted by visual ones. The tableau (defined as action frozen in time) is a relatively simple way of transferring the visual codes of a play into an image. When it comes to the adaptation of the verbal codes, the Boydell Shakespeare Gallery in its form of prints mediated between the arts in a double way. As printing as such is a technology that is primarily connected to the printing of books or other verbal texts, the remediation of the Shakespeare paintings into prints was accompanied by an inclusion of text or caption. Beneath each of the images there are always several captions. They take the form of both anchorage and relay. For instance Fuseli's Hamlet-image with the ghost is anchored by its title, which is also the title of the play:

> SHAKESPEARE, *Hamlet, Prince of Denmark.*
> ACT I, SCENE IV.

The anchorage is continued with the stage directions from the play itself: *The Platform before the Palace of Elsineur. – Hamlet, Horatio, Marcellus and the Ghost.* And just as Shakespeare is mentioned as the author of the play, so both the painter and the engraver are credited: *"Painted by H. Fuseli R.A."* and *"Engraved by R. Thew, Hist. Engraver to H.R.H. to the P. of Wales."* The relay takes the form of the lines actually spoken by the characters depicted in the image:

> HAM. *Still am I call'd. – unhand me gentlemen;*
> [Breaking from them.]
> *By heaven, I'll make a Ghost of him that lets me: –*
> *I say, away: – Go on, I'll follow thee.*

In this way Boydell's prints actually combine literature (printed captions etc.) with the visual arts, so that some of the effects of spoken and acted drama are retained.

The Boydell Shakespeare Gallery also mediates between the two ut-pictura-poesis poles in another way. The gallery as a whole combines the two methods that may be used when a text is visualized. Each play is represented by several images so that the action is shown in a kind of temporal sequence, and each of the images shows a climax or crucial moment from its part of the play.

Style and the Audience – A New Paradigm on its Way

The Boydell Shakespeare Gallery is a complex and hybrid conglomerate full of mediations and also contradictions. Its very form of remediation is complex as the source of the remediated sources is double. The Shakespeare plays are found in their verbal-textual form in the published scripts as well as in the stage performances, which in some cases were the direct source for some of the artists. The doubleness of the source is also there in the remediated texts themselves, which first took the form of auratic oil paintings in a public, yet commercial gallery, and subsequently the paintings were remediated again into non-auratic, mechanically reproduced prints meant for private consumption. The stipple engraving technique was the reproduction technology best suited for this purpose. Even the commercialization of the prints took a transitory form, as they were initially offered for sale in a subscription form.

The ut-pictura-poesis mechanism of the Shakespeare Gallery transcends and even solves some of the traditional problems of narrative images. The Shakespeare prints are multi-modal, as not only anchorage, but especially relay text is an integral part of the prints, and the fact that each play was remediated in a series of prints and not just one central is in itself a mediation between the temporal form of verbal texts and the spatial form of images.

The genre of the images in the Shakespeare Gallery is not pure history painting. This dominant genre has been diluted with landscape painting, portrait painting to some extent, and especially with theatre painting, so that in most of the images there is genre hybridity. There is stylistic confusion. This confusion is the consequence of the merging of various social and historical paradigms, chiefly an immature bourgeois one with an aristocratic, which in itself was the result of the historical convergence of the Glorious Revolution in 1689. The most precise stylistic genre description of the whole gallery is presumably that history painting dominates, but in each historical scene there is a foregrounding of sentiment and personal feelings, quite often between family members. The foregrounding of feelings may of course be described as just theatrical, but the very theatricality of the images is their raison d'être. The inclusion of theatre painting with the gestures of actors on the stage made it possible to overcode sentiment. This mixture of neo-classicist rules and bourgeois sentiment is a result of the Boydell Shakespeare Gallery's position in the creation of a new private and middle-class publicness, which argued for its own existence by turning feelings into rhetorical melodrama and pathos, so that gesticulation and facial expressions seem exaggerated today. When the characters in the images look at something or each other their gazes are so powerful that they turn into action lines or vectors that become part of the compositional structure. In this respect outstretched hands and arms are invariably pro-

Benjamin West: King Lear Act III, scene IV,
engraved by William Sharpe, 1793

longed into compositional action lines, too. Passionate feelings become a rebellious organizing trait in the images, and the decorum of neo-classicism is modified by these pre-Romantic tendencies. In Benjamin West's *King Lear*, Act III, scene IV, the frenzy of feelings create a compositional centrifugal force around the central Lear. The conglomerate nature of the Boydell Shakespeare Gallery points to how its period is one of transition between two societal systems or world pictures. The gallery and its fate document the changing form of consumption of culture as well as the changing role of art in society.

References

Benjamin, Walter (1974) *Gesammelte Schriften*. Frankfurt am Main: Suhrkamp. "Das Kunstwerk im Zeitalter seiner technischen Reproduzierbarkeit" (1935) Band I, 2, pp. 471–508

Boydell, Josiah (1979/1803) *The Boydell Shakespeare Prints*. New York: Arno Press

Bruntjen, Hermann Arnold (1974) *John Boydell (1719–1804): A Study of Art Patronage and Publishing in Georgian London*. PhD thesis: Stanford University

Hauser, Arnold (1972 /1951) *The Social History of Art*, 1–4. London: Routledge

Honour, Hugh (1979 /1968) *Neo-Classicism*. Harmondsworth: Penguin

Kriz, Kay Dian (1997) *The Idea of the English Landscape Painter*. New Haven: Yale University Press

Lee, Rensselaer W. (1940) "Ut pictura poesis: the humanistic theory of painting". *The Art Bulletin*, 22, pp. 197–269

Pape, Walter and Frederick Burwick (eds.) (1996) *The Boydell Shakespeare Gallery*, Pomp, Essen, Bottrop

Reynolds, Joshua (1769–91) *Discourses on Art*. [http://ibiblio.org/gutenberg/etext00/artds10.txt] – last consulted Jan. 2006

Tate Online [http://www.tate.org.uk/servlet/ViewWork?workid=739&tabview=work] – last consulted Jan. 2006

Thomson, James (1979 /1730) *The Seasons*. London: Scholar Press

Books and Selves:
John Stuart Mill's *Autobiography*

JENS KIRK

After the preface-like first paragraph of his *Autobiography*, John Stuart Mill outlines his beginnings as if he entered this world as a compromise between a boy and a book:

> I was born in London, on the 20th of May 1806, and was the eldest son of James Mill, the author of *The History of British India*". (Mill, 1981: 5)

The sentence creates this impression by functioning in a strikingly straightforward and roundabout manner at the same time. On the one hand, it speaks the literal truth by rendering the time and place of the autobiographer's birth correctly. On the other hand, there is something decidedly odd about the way in which his discourse represents the genesis of his life story. First, Mill claims that he "was born", yet his mother is conspicuously absent from the scenario of origin.[1] In this manner he succeeds in representing his father as if *he* were solely responsible for his birth. Secondly, not only does Mill figure his father as his only point of origin at the expense of his mother, he also evokes his father in a peculiar fashion, i.e. as "the author of *The History of British India*". The post-modification of James Mill is crucial since it functions by evoking a particular feature of his, i.e. his occupation, as if he were an author-father compound. Thus, by suppressing his mother and by portraying his father as author, Mill succeeds in creating a dehumanised image of his early self as if "the eldest son" were actually another of James Mill's books. Thirdly, although James Mill wrote several books and numerous articles, John Stuart Mill singles out

---

1   And from the rest of the *Autobiography*, as a matter of fact.

The History of British India as especially noteworthy. In fact, at a later point of the *Autobiography*, the reader learns that he has the highest regard of this work, rating "it if not the most, one of the most instructive histories ever written". The value of *The History of British India*, according to Mill, depends upon the fact that it is highly unconventional. In fact, it is "saturated [...] with the opinions and modes of judgement of a democratic radicalism then regarded as extreme; and treating with a severity at that time most unusual the English Constitution, the English Law, and all parties and classes who possessed any considerable influence in the country" (29). Thus, Mill casts his early self as if, originally, he were a major radical book conceived by his author-father.[2]

This essay deals with the relationships between books and selves in Mill's *Autobiography*. More particularly, I focus on two books which for very different reasons are singled out by the autobiographer as particularly important in relation to his self: Pierre Etienne Louis Dumont's *Traités de législation civile et pénale* (1802), and his own *On Liberty* (1859). In my conclusion I sum up my main points and sketch out positions on the subject in the twentieth century. But first I take a closer look at the role of the printed book in relation to the self.

Books and Self-fashioning

The relationship between printed books and selves is one of the subjects of book history, which includes "the study of practices which in various ways take hold of these objects or forms [e.g. books and printed matter in general] and produce usages and differentiated meanings" (Chartier, 2002: 48), and its sister discipline the history of reading, which deals with "the various ways of reading that have been characteristic of Western societies since classical antiquity" (Cavallo and Chartier, 1999: 2).

Among other things, this is studied by Greenblatt (1980) in the context of the early sixteenth century, which saw "a crucial moment of passage from one mode of interiority to another" (85). Speaking especially of the early Protestants, who challenged the power that Catholic institutions held over the individual, he claims that for the former the printed book took on a "crucial significance" (84) as a new site of power at the expense of the authority of the Catholic Church (76). According to Greenblatt, Protestant

---

2 Similar points are made by, e.g., Glassman (1982: 196) and Zerilli (1992: 198).

books such as William Tyndale's *The Obedience of a Christian Man* (1528) and the English New Testament (1525) replaced the Catholic modes of controlling interiority, especially "formal auricular confession and the power of the keys" (86), and became one of "the primary sources of self-fashioning".[3] This "passage from one mode of interiority to another" involved important changes for the printed book – changes that Jakobson's model of communication conceptualises effectively. Of the six "constitutive factors" (Jakobson, 1988: 35) of communication, the addressee is highlighted. Similarly, of the six corresponding functions of language, the conative is emphasised. Because man's salvation now depends upon printed books, they are oriented towards their addressees in new ways, for instance, books are now printed in the native tongue and include images and pictures, i.e. non-verbal signs, designed to facilitate the reader's understanding (Chartier, 1989: 7).

As an example of the printed book as an authoritative force and source of self-fashioning – an example that highlights the conative function of a particular book by outlining its effect on a particular reader, Greenblatt discusses the fate of James Bainham, a Protestant who was burned at the stake in 1531. After he had been accused of heresy, arrested, and tortured, Bainham abjured his faith. However, regretting his abjuration soon afterwards, he "came openly to Saint Austin's church, stood up 'with the New Testament in his hand in English and the Obedience of a Christian Man in his bosom,' and, weeping, declared to the congregants that he had denied God" (1980: 74).[4] According to Greenblatt:

> It is hard to tell if there is one book here or two, for 'the Obedience of a Christian Man' may refer to Bainham's inner state or to Tyndale's book of the same name, which Bainham owned and may have carried next to his heart. The ambiguity here is felicitous, for Tyndale's manual […] is precisely

---

[3] The power of the printed book is well documented. For instance, McKenzie (1982) summarises the following technological and economic aspects that all combine to create books as unprecedented forms of power: the use of movable type, the perfection of the codex form, the use of paper, the standardisation of letters, the use of the vernacular (208–9). Last but not least, the fact that books are printed in editions vastly expands the number of potential readers and secures that they actually read the same text (209–10). Recently scholars have tended to tone down the relative impact of print (e.g. Cavallo and Chartier, 1999: 24). Similarly, today scholars are interested in the similarities rather than the differences between Protestant and Catholic uses of the early printed book. However, for my purposes Greenblatt's notion that books and selves became related in new ways in the early sixteenth century remains useful.

[4] Greenblatt is quoting John Foxe (1516–87), *Acts and Monuments* (1563).

designed to be absorbed: one should not, in principle, be able to say where the book stops and identity begins. This absorption of the book, at once provides a way of being in the world and shapes the reader's inner life; Christian obedience is simultaneously a form of action and an internal state. (84)

Greenblatt's image of reading as absorption casts the printed book as a compelling force demanding to be assimilated by the reader – demanding that the reading subject performs the action of becoming like the book. Greenblatt regards Tyndale's book "as an extreme version of the less drastic but widespread influence exerted in the period by conduct manuals" (87) – a form of courtesy literature, which taught "courtiers and others good manners and morals" (Drabble and Stringer, 1990: 130).

According to Greenblatt, the active, absorbing power of printed books in relation to identity goes hand in hand with their special kind of presence – a presence which maximises their effect on their readers, moreover. Speaking generally of early protestant books and particularly of the printed English New Testament, which Greenblatt regards as "above all, *a form of power* […] invested with the ability to control, guide, discipline, console, exalt, and punish" (1980: 97), he recounts how:

> [W]hen in 1529 [Thomas] More went to Antwerp with his friend Cuthbert Tunstall, the bishop of London, the latter bought up and burned as many copies of Tyndale's New Testament and other heretical works as he could find, but this was pre-Guthenberg strategy. The money Tunstall spent for the books only helped Tyndale to hasten the production of the second edition of his translation, which appeared in 1534. (96)

In contrast to manuscripts, which "have a certain innate intimacy and presence" (85), Greenblatt's example shows that printed books can always be made present since they are reproduced mechanically. In fact, printed books have a special kind of power that involves a complex relation between their absence and presence within the cultural field, amounting to a reversal of cause and effect patterns: paradoxically, their destruction advances their production.

According to Greenblatt, then, the printed book functions as a unique form of power, authority, and presence in the context of early Protestantism. More particularly, the force of the book exerts itself in relation to the process Greenblatt calls self-fashioning. In its most general sense, self-fashioning refers to "the forming of a self" (2) either "understood quite literally as the imposition upon a person of physical form" or as "the achievement of a less tangible shape: a distinctive personality, a characteristic address to the world, a consistent mode of perceiving and behaving". Apart from the "submission to an absolute power or authority situated at least partially outside the self – God, a sacred book, an institution such as church, court, colonial or military administration" (9), self-fashioning depends upon "something perceived as alien, strange, or hostile. This threatening Other – heretic, savage, witch, adulteress, traitor, Antichrist – must be discovered or invented in order to be attacked and destroyed". Lastly, self-fashioning always involves the imitation of a "model", either religious or secular (2–3), for instance, Jesus. The conative function of books, their authoritative effect on readers, then, interacts with other forces such as aliens and models in the fashioning of selves. In the following, I focus on the relationship between books and power rather than on the notions of alien and model.

The Autobiography: Two Books – Two Selves

Earlier I pointed out that Mill, in the opening of his *Autobiography*, presents his original self as if it in part were another of his father's radical books. And, generally speaking, books are extremely prominent in the account of his early years. Thus, between the ages of three and sixteen (1809–1822) his "unusual and remarkable" (Mill, 1981: 5) education involved reading hundreds of books on a range of different issues: history, philosophy, government, economics, and similar subjects (Robson and Stillinger, 1981b: 551–81). In the following discussion, I focus on two of the innumerable books mentioned in the *Autobiography*: Pierre Etienne Louis Dumont's *Traités de législation civile et pénale* (1802) and Mill's *On Liberty* (1859). They have been singled out for special attention since Mill considers them uniquely important in relation to the fashioning of his self as a unified whole.[5] While the former at first appears to function as an authority and model in the fashioning of his first unified self, the autobiographer demonstrates that the conative function of the printed book is illusory. Not only does its effect always depend upon on various forms of support, eventually it fails completely in maintaining a sense of a unified self. After the failure of the *Traités*, books never function in that way again. Instead, absolute authority is transferred to human beings, particularly to Harriet Taylor Mill, who both before and after their marriage, functions as a powerful influence in rela-

---

5 According to Mill a unified self is an indivisible whole. Thus, his idea of the self partakes in the notion of "the 'sovereign individual'" which came into being "between the Renaissance humanism of the sixteenth century and the Enlightenment of the eighteenth century" (Hall, 1994: 119).

tion to Mill. The printed book, nevertheless, reasserts its importance. In the *Autobiography*, Mill repeatedly highlights the emotive or expressive function of the *Liberty* by constructing it as co-written with his wife, as a kind of monument to his and his wife's unified self – an entity that was shattered irretrievably by her death.

Pierre Etienne Louis Dumont's *Traités de législation civile et pénale*

According to Mill, the most important book by far in the fashioning of his first unified self was "the *Traité* [sic] *de Législation*" (Mill, 1981: 67), Dumont's redaction of "Jeremy Bentham's *An Introduction to the Principles of Morals and Legislation*" (1789) (67n), which he read in 1821 at the age of 15.[6] We are told that it marked "an epoch" in his life and constituted "one of the turning points" in his intellectual and moral development. He elaborates:

> When I laid down the last volume of the *Traité* I had become a different being. The "principle of utility," understood as Bentham understood it, and applied in the manner in which he applied it through these three volumes, fell exactly into its place as the keystone which held together the detached and fragmentary component parts of my knowledge and beliefs. It gave unity to my conception of things. I now had opinions; a creed, a doctrine, a philosophy; in one among the best senses of the word, a religion; the inculcation and diffusion of which could be made the principle outward purpose of a life. And I had a grand conception laid before me of changes to be affected in the condition of mankind through that doctrine. (69)

Here Mill demonstrates how Dumont's *Traités* functioned in relation to his teenage self as a sixteenth-century form of absolute power responsible for his "becom[ing] a different being". More particularly, he singles out Bentham's "principle of utility",[7] the theory and practice of which is outlined by the *Traités*, as the central doctrine in the creation of his new identity.

---

6 James McConnell also deals with the importance of this book in relation to the young Mill (1977: 775).

7 The principle of utility signifies a particular notion of man: "Nature has placed mankind under the governance of two sovereign masters, *Pleasure* and *Pain*. To them [...] we refer all our decisions, every resolve that we make in life. The man who affects to have withdrawn himself from their despotic sway does not know what he is talking about. To seek pleasure and to shun pain is his sole aim, even at the moment when he is denying himself the greatest enjoyment or courting penalties the most severe [...] To these two motives the *principle of utility* subjects everything" (Bentham quoted in Jones, 1975: 165).

Through the image of the keystone, he casts the function of the greatest happiness principle as that which finalised or rounded off his previously disjointed identity by holding it "together" and giving it "unity". The importance of Dumont's *Traités* is underlined by the use of the adverbial, "now", creating a border between past and present selves, between a useless fragmentary self and a useful unified one. The utility of the new self rests on three things. First of all, Mill now contained a systematic set of beliefs and values, "a creed, a doctrine, a philosophy; [...] a religion". Secondly, this set determined his orientation towards the future by giving him a mission, an "outward purpose", i.e., to instil and disseminate, to teach, the set of beliefs and values. And thirdly, this pedagogical purpose was linked to a master plan, "a grand conception" for the reform of mankind.

However, while the above passage certainly points to the central role of the book in the fashioning of a unified self, it also relativises the power of the book. Significantly, the *Traités* is not Bentham's original work, but a French version of it. Thus, not only does Mill's self-fashioning depend upon a French translation of a work originally written in English, it relies also on an act of redaction, which, according to the *Oxford English Dictionary*, involves revision, rearrangement, and adaptation. In fact, the autobiographer explicitly foregrounds the power of the redaction at the expense of the original by calling our attention to the fact that the presentation of certain issues is "much more clear, compact, and imposing in Dumont's *redaction*, than in the original work of Bentham" (67–68). This suggests that a book cannot stand alone, but need some sort of interpretative support that is capable of effectively clarifying its meaning. Similarly, Dumont's *Traités* cannot function on its own. Its meaning and value depends precisely on its relation to Bentham's original.[8]

The notion that books are in need of something that is capable of mediating their meaning and reinforcing their effect upon their readers is actually a predominant one in Mill's story of his early years, where his development is shown not only to hinge upon books, but, more importantly, also upon spoken language. For example, Mill outlines how his reading of books was always followed by oral reports delivered to his father, "giving

---

8   According to the editors of the *Autobiography*, John Stuart Mill, when "writing of Dumont's redaction [...] quotes words in English that suggest a reference not to the translation, but to Bentham's original work, which he must have read then or soon after" (577). This strengthens the notion that both the original and the redaction are interdependent. They appear to have remained that way. When Jones 1975 quotes Bentham he uses an English translation of Dumont's redaction (see note 7).

each day to him, in our walks, a minute account of what I had read, and answering his numerous and searching questions" (21). Similarly, Mill depicts how another aspect of the reading of books was policed by his father. Speaking of his reading of Plato and Demosthenes, he recalls that he was required not only "[t]o read them aloud to my father, answering questions when asked" (26) in the usual manner. His "elocution", i.e. his way of reading aloud, was also controlled by his father:

> He had thought much on the principles of the art of reading, especially the most neglected part of it, the inflections of the voice, or *modulation* as writers on elocution call it (in contrast with *articulation* on the one side, and *expression* on the other), and had reduced it to rules, grounded on the logical analysis of a sentence. These rules he strongly impressed upon me, and took me severely to task for every violation of them […] (26–27).

Thus, Mill's early self was fashioned internally and externally and a specific shape was imposed on his personality and speech. Books played a prominent role in these processes, exercising a sixteenth-century authority and power over identity. However, the *Autobiography* also shows that, ultimately, books failed and were in need of authoritative forms of support of meaning through translation into a foreign language, redaction, or elocution. The absolute power of books in relation to the reader's self, their conative function, is shown to be problematic.

Five years after reading the *Traités* for the first time, the problematic relationship between books and the twenty-year old Mill comes to a head. In the fifth chapter of the *Autobiography*, "A Crisis in My Mental History. One Stage Onwards", we learn:

> The time came when I awakened from this as from a dream. It was in the autumn of 1826. I was in a dull state of nerves, such as everybody is occasionally liable to: […] In this frame of mind it occurred to me to put the question directly to myself, "Suppose that all your objects in life were realized; that all the changes in institutions and opinions which you are looking forward to, could be completely effected at this very instant: would this be a great joy and happiness to you?" And an irrepressible self-consciousness distinctly answered, "No!" At this time my heart sank within me: the whole foundation on which my life was constructed fell down. All my happiness was to have been found in the continual pursuit of this end. The end had ceased to charm, and how could there ever again be any interest in the means? I seemed to have nothing left to live for (138–39).

The passage delineates the collapse of his unified self fashioned exclusively according to Dumont's *Traités* and Bentham's idea of utility. First the image of awakening demotes his Utilitarian self to the realm of dreams, fantasy, and delusion, leaving Mill in the world of reality. This sense of coming to consciousness, which is developed by the image of spell breaking later in the paragraph, is coloured by a feeling of despair. While the image of demolition reverses the unifying effect which he earlier enjoyed from the "principle of utility" (69), the disappearance of the "keystone" does not return him to his earlier "fragmentary" self. Instead, the images of falling and sinking suggest that the shattering threatens to destroy the self: The realization that "the end", i.e. the fulfilment of his master plan for mankind, has fallen away places himself at the end of his own life with "nothing left to live for." Now Mill's appeals to his books – those mainsprings of unity and purpose of character – are unsuccessful: "in vain I sought relief from my favourite books" (139).

Thus, so far the *Autobiography* has outlined the rise and fall of the kind of fashioning of a unified self that depends on a printed book as a form of absolute power and model, first and foremost, the *Traités*. In the remainder of the *Autobiography*, individual books are never depicted as producing the same unifying effect in relation to the self again.[9] Instead, books are brought into play with each other in an attempt to create a form of inclusive, expanding, multi-volume authority. The best example of what John Stuart Mill had in mind as a replacement of the powerful single book is perhaps found in his 1840 essay on Coleridge. Here he points out that the ideas of the Utilitarian Jeremy Bentham (1748–1832) and the conservative philosopher and poet Samuel Taylor Coleridge (1772–1834) must be combined in order to function authoritatively:

> In every respect, the two men are each other's 'completing counterpart': the strong points of each correspond to the weak points of the other. Whoever could master the premises and combine the methods of both would possess the entire English philosophy of his age. (Mill, 1980: 102)

Written several years after the deaths of Bentham and Coleridge, Mill is speaking of the books and other publications they left behind, of course. In contrast to the Renaissance version of self-fashioning as the reader's ab-

---

9   Though Jean Francois Marmontel's autobiography is a vitally important book in John Stuart Mill's self-fashioning since it saves him from committing suicide, it functions as a short-lived authority and model for John Stuart Mill in merely jump starting his new project of self-fashioning where individual books are given a much reduced role (145).

sorption of the book, Mill here emphasises the active role of the reader. The reader must first "master" and "combine" their works if they are to manifest themselves as a powerful authority that, in turn, unites in the reader a unified perspective, i.e. "the entire English philosophy of his age". Significantly, he refrains from writing a book that does just that. In fact, books that successfully do this are hypothetical ones:

> If a book were to be compiled containing all the best things ever said on the rule-of-thumb school of political craftsmanship, and on the insufficiency for practical purposes of what the mere practical man calls experience, it is difficult to say whether the collection would be more indebted to the writings of Bentham or of Coleridge.

Moreover, such hypothetical books of authority and power are necessarily collectively authored. They are compendium-like compilations enumerating "all the best things ever said". After my very brief sketch of what I've called the multi-volume, inclusive authority of the book that replaces the sixteenth-century notion, I move on and consider the second of the two books of unique importance in relation to the autobiographer's self, i.e. *On Liberty*.

On Liberty

The *Liberty* functions in a very different manner from the *Traités*. Where the latter was outlined as an absolute power responsible for the creation of Mill's first unified self (a unified self it was incapable of upholding, though), the *Liberty* is presented as the product of his second unified self – a self which needs an authoritative sign since it, too, has been shattered. This particular emotive function of the *Liberty* is constructed in several interconnected moves: first, absolute power and authority in questions of self-fashioning is transferred from books to human beings, more particularly, to Harriet Taylor Mill;[10] secondly, unity is established between the selves of John Stuart and Harriet; thirdly, it is emphasised that her death signified the destruction of his second unified self; fourthly, the *Liberty* is outlined as their joint creation and, moreover, as a privileged sign of their merged selves.

---

10 In 1830 John Stuart Mill met Harriet Taylor, who was married to John Taylor. They married in 1851, three years after his death.

The *Autobiography* constructs Harriet Taylor Mill as the final instance of an absolute power in the story of Mill's self-fashioning. In the first part of the *Autobiography*, which is based upon the First Draft and dating from the winter of 1853–54,[11] she appears in an impersonal and almost divine manner. In the preface-like first paragraph, where Mill outlines his reasons for writing his "memorial" (5), she is referred to as "the one to whom most of all is due, one whom the world had no opportunity of knowing". Later, comparing her to Thomas Carlyle (1795–1881), whose "influence as a social prophet and critic, and […] prestige as historian, were enormous during his lifetime" (Drabble and Stringer, 1990: 93), and himself, she is outlined as "one greatly superior to us both – who was more a poet than he, and more a thinker than I – whose own mind and nature included his, and infinitely more" (Mill, 1981: 183). The main function of this reluctance to identify her by name or gender is not to conceal her social identity[12] but to reveal her real worth as an almost omniscient being. The sixth chapter elaborates on her virtually superhuman emotional, spiritual, and intellectual powers (193–199). For instance, she is compared to Percy Bysshe Shelley (1792–1822), "the poet of volcanic hope for a better world" (Drabble and Stringer, 1990: 514): "In general spiritual characteristics, as well as in temperament and organisation, I have often compared her, as she was at this time, to Shelley: but in thought and intellect, Shelley, so far as his powers were developed in his short life, was but a child compared with what she ultimately became" (Mill, 1981: 195).

After Harriet Taylor Mill has been constructed as a practically absolute authority, her powers are related specifically to the fashioning of Mill's self[13] and the creation of his writings. Speaking of the praise he has received "for the greater practicality" (197) which characterises his books in contrast to those of other theorists, he concludes: "the writings in which this quality has been observed, were not the work of one mind, but the fusion of two, one of them as pre-eminently practical in its judgments and perceptions of things present, as it was high and bold in its anticipations for a remote futurity"

---

11 For the history of the composition of the *Autobiography* see Robson and Stillinger 1981a: xviii–xxx.

12 Contemporary readers were no doubt able to identify the person of whom Mill is speaking as Harriet Taylor Mill. From its beginning their relationship was a social problem because of her marriage to John Taylor.

13 Zerilli also argues that "[Harriet] Taylor is introduced to the reader as part of the theorist's [Mill's] second birth: a reinvention of self […] that released Mill from the prison of his ratiocinative utilitarian education" (1992: 195).

(197–99).[14] This idea of a fusion or merger between the figure of absolute power and Mill is developed in the part of the *Autobiography* which originally concluded the Early Draft written in 1853–54. Here John Stuart Mill claims that the early 1850s saw "the most important events of [his] private life" (247). In particular he is speaking of his marriage to "the lady whose incomparable worth had made her friendship the greatest source to me both of happiness and of improvement" – a marriage which, moreover, he regards as "adding to the partnership of thought, feeling, and even writing which had long existed, a partnership of our entire existence". Marriage, then, is constructed by the autobiographer as the consummation of a process of self-fashioning. In friendship and ultimately in marriage, two separate selves are merged by the formation of a "partnership" which unifies the individual selves.[15] Thus, Harriet Taylor Mill is constructed as a particular kind of authority. She is of "incomparable worth" and "her friendship" is conceptualised as "the greatest source" of his "happiness and improvement". But the idea of partnership constitutes an important modification of the notion of authority by suggesting that processes of reciprocity and sharing are involved.

---

14 Later, the sixth chapter likens her powers to those of his father: "In the power of influencing by mere force of mind and character, the conviction and purposes of others, and in the strenuous exertion of that power to promote freedom and progress, he left, as far as my knowledge extends, no equal among men, but one among women" (213). While I don't want to belittle the power of James Mill over his son, I want to maintain that in the *Autobiography* the father is never depicted in a role similar to Harriet's, i.e. that of fashioning Mill as a unified self.

15 I agree with Susan Bell, who argues that Mill "did not look for opposite poles or complementarity in male and female qualities" (1990: 90). Instead, the *Autobiography* forms a part of the "counter-tradition" studied by Joseph Allen Boone, which, among other things, established "a 'likeness' between mates in defiance of accepted hierarchical and dichotomised notions of sexual identity, or [...] allowed the existence of complex differences between men and women not automatically reducible to gender stereotyping" (1987: 12). A very good example of this can be found in the rejected leaves of the Early Draft where Mill indicates that his "object of [...] admiration" (Mill, 1981: 623) should be like and unlike him at the same time: "[...] the object of my admiration should be of a type very different from my own; should be a character pre-eminently of feeling, combined [...] with a vigorous and bold speculative intellect. Fleishman has argued that Mill equated the self with process and that the "*Autobiography* becomes an embodiment of Mill's self [...] in being persistently animated by the principle of change, transition, anticipation [...]" (1983: 153). However, I want to suggest that stability is equally important to Mill's notion of self. His marriage does constitute an end point, i.e. a completion of their "partnership," in many ways, while it also forms the basis of "improvement". Certainly, as becomes apparent in the following, Mill's self is unmoored by the death of his wife. I suggest that the *Autobiography*, at least in part, is Mill's attempt at containing and stabilizing his self after his wife's death.

The *Autobiography* emphasises that the death of Harriet Taylor Mill in 1858 shattered his second unified self. In his 1861 revision of the Early Draft, he tries to detail the effects of the loss of his wife on his unified self:

> For seven and a half years that blessing was mine; for seven and a half only! I can say nothing which could describe, even in the faintest manner, what that loss was and is. But because I know that she would have wished it, I endeavour to make the best of what life I have left, and to work on for her purposes with such diminished strength as can be derived from thoughts of her, and communion with her memory. (247)

The passage is marked by images which fashion Mill's self as a diminished or reduced one as the result of her death. The "blessing", i.e. the partnership of their "entire existence" including their "partnership of thought, feeling, [...] writing" outlined above, is dissolved. His powers of speech, his physical and mental strength, are impaired or weakened. And his hopes for the future are diminished. In this way, outlining the devastating effects of her present absence, also helps to communicate her vital importance for their partnership and his unified self before her death.

The three paragraph continuation of the Early Draft, which Mill also wrote in 1861, elaborates on his sense of having been shattered by her death and outlines his attempts at maintaining a sense of their self-fashioning partnership:

> Since then, I have sought for such alleviation as my state admitted of, by the mode of life which most enabled me to feel her still near me. I bought a cottage as close as possible to the place where she is buried, and there her daughter (my fellow-sufferer and now my chief comfort) and I, live constantly during a great portion of the year. My objects in life are solely those which were hers; my pursuits and occupations those in which she shared, or sympathized, and which are indissolubly associated with her. Her memory is to me a religion, and her approbation the standard by which, summing up as it does all worthiness, I endeavour to regulate my life. (251)

Unity with his deceased wife and with his former self has become a project where he tries to achieve the greatest degree of closeness with her physically and mentally. By living as closely as possible to her grave, by living with her daughter, by adopting "objects" and "pursuits and occupations" which either "were hers" or "which are indissolubly associated with her", he attempts to recuperate her, his union with her, and his own past unified self. This involves her recreation as a traditional authority and model. Her memory becomes his "religion". Similarly, "her approbation" becomes the regulator of his self.

The attempt to maintain a sense of unity with his wife and his former self also motivates the construction of the *Liberty* as a particularly privileged sign. Mill deals with the *Liberty* in four instances in the last chapter of the *Autobiography*. The first example is found in the three page continuation of the Early Draft from 1861:

> During the two years [1856–1858] which immediately preceded the cessation of my official life, my wife and I were working together at the *Liberty*. I had first planned and written it as a short essay, in 1854. It was in mounting the steps of the Capitol, in January 1855, that the thought first arose of converting it into a volume. None of my writings have been either so carefully composed, or so sedulously corrected as this. After it had been written as usual twice over, we kept it by us, bringing it out from time to time and going through it *de novo*, reading, weighing and criticizing every sentence. Its final revision was to have been a work of the winter of 1858/59, the first after my retirement, which we had arranged to pass in the South of Europe. That hope and every other were frustrated by the most unexpected and bitter calamity of her death – at Avignon, on our way to Montpellier, from a sudden attack of pulmonary congestion. (249)[16]

The passage attempts to foreground the emotive function of the *Liberty* by outlining the peculiar composition history of the *Liberty*. First, the position of the addresser is fleshed out. Although Mill is presented as the originator of the *Liberty*, the structure of the discourse, which emphasises the years 1856–1858, illuminates the collaborative nature of the composition. The *Liberty*, we are to understand, was the result of that partnership in all areas of life which the *Autobiography* mapped out earlier. Similarly, the final sentence indirectly highlights the expressive function. While it testifies to Mill's feeling of hopelessness in the face of her death, it also creates the *Liberty* as a sign of hope. More particularly, the *Liberty* signifies their past hope for its completion and by extension their shattered hopes in general. Secondly, the passage emphasises that, although the *Liberty* was carefully composed and revised, it remained unfinished. As it stands, it is a draft of a whole that was envisioned by them, but remained unrealised since the act of final revision was precluded by her death. While this weakens the referential and conative functions of the work – one cannot really rely on a draft to

---

16 It has been remarked that the actual composition history of the *Liberty* was slightly different from the one outlined in the *Autobiography* (Robson 1977: lxxx–lxxxv).

convey facts objectively and effectively to the addressee – its draft-like status tends to strengthen the relation to the addresser. Like a fragment, e.g. Coleridge's "Kubla Khan", the *Liberty* intimates the addresser's vision first and foremost. As a sign of their past partnership, as a sign of the whole they envisioned, but never completed, and as a sign of the hopes they entertained before they were shattered, the purpose of the above passage, then, is to highlight the relationship between the *Liberty* and its addresser, the position of collaboration and partnership, unifying John Stuart Mill and Harriet Taylor Mill.

Years later, in the part of the *Autobiography* written in 1869–1870, Mill, at the age of 63, returned to the *Liberty*, claiming that it

> [W]as more directly and literally our joint production than anything else which bears my name, for there was not a sentence of it that was not several times gone through by us together, turned over in many ways, and carefully weeded of any faults, either in thought or expression, that we detected in it. It is in consequence of this that, although it never underwent her final revision, it far surpasses, as a mere specimen of composition, anything which has proceeded from me either before or since. With regard to the thoughts, it is difficult to identify any particular part or element as being more hers than all the rest. The whole mode of thinking of which the book was an expression, was emphatically hers. But I also was so thoroughly imbued with it that the same thoughts naturally occurred to us both. That I was thus penetrated with it, however, I owe in a great degree to her. (258–59)

Again the discourse focuses on the expressive function of the *Liberty*, outlining the collaborative nature of the position of the addresser. What matters is the fact that the *Liberty* was the outcome of a careful, though not finalised, process of composition and revision that ought to be understood *literally* as their "joint production". Moreover, their collaboration formed a union of their "thoughts" which blurred their individual contributions. Similarly, though the particular mode of thinking is identified as hers, it is emphasised that Mill was "imbued" and "penetrated" with it to the extent that their mental processes became identical and dissolved the difference between them. Considering the first sentence's emphasis on the non-figurative nature of their "joint production," Mill's use of metaphors becomes highly conspicuous as if he were literally saturated and permeated with the particular mode of thinking in question. However, in contrast to the first example, this passage suggests that the *Liberty* is a sign of relatively high referential and conative value because of the unique construction of the addresser. It is emphasised that the *Liberty* outdoes his other work in terms of "composition," i.e. it renders "the thoughts" in the most effective manner possible taking truth and audience into the question.

Further, in the paragraph immediately following the above, he elaborates on the relationship between the emotive and referential aspects of the work, between the position of partnership characterising the addresser and the cognitive value of the *Liberty*:

> The *Liberty* is likely to survive longer than anything else that I have written (with the possible exception of the *Logic*), because the conjunction of her mind with mine has rendered it a kind of philosophic text-book of a single truth, which the changes progressively taking place in modern society tend to bring out into ever stronger relief: the importance, to man and society, of a large variety in types of character, and of giving full freedom to human nature to expand itself in innumerable and conflicting directions. (259)

The union of their minds has made the *Liberty* into a sign of "a single truth". This mutually constructed "truth," moreover, is essentially visionary in nature since it is only gradually becoming visible in the changes that modern society undergoes.

The fourth and last time the *Liberty* is mentioned, Mill writes:

> After my irreparable loss one of my earliest cares was to print and publish the treatise, so much of which was the work of her whom I had lost, and consecrate it to her memory. I have made no alteration or addition to it, nor shall I ever. Though it wants the last touch of her hand, no substitute for that touch shall ever be attempted by mine. (261)

First of all, he outlines his actions after her death, more particularly, the fact that he printed, published, and consecrated the *Liberty* to her because of her important part in the work. Secondly, he emphasises the fact that the published "treatise" is an unedited version, which doesn't tamper with the original, which is marked by her touch/ presence. The fact that he mentions his 1859 consecration of the *Liberty* to her suggests a context for understanding his attention to that particular book in the *Autobiography*. His purpose of dealing with the unique nature of the addresser of the *Liberty* could be to strengthen and elaborate on the claims he makes in his dedication:

> To the beloved and deplored memory of her who was the inspirer, and in part the author, of all that is best in my writings – the friend and wife whose exalted sense of truth and right was my strongest incitement, and whose approbation was my chief reward – I dedicate this volume. Like all that I

have written for many years, it belongs as much to her as to me; but the work as it stands has had, in a very insufficient degree, the inestimable advantage of her revision; some of the most important portions having been reserved for a more careful re-examination, which they are now never destined to receive. Were I but capable of interpreting to the world one half of the great thoughts and noble feelings which are buried in her grave, I should be the medium of a greater benefit to it, than is ever likely to arise from anything that I can write, unprompted and unassisted by her all but unrivalled wisdom. (Mill, 1977: 216)

As it stands, unmediated by the *Autobiography*, it is difficult not to regard the dedication as an example of hyperbole. But against the background of that work, the outline of Harriet Taylor Mill as his authority, his friend, his wife, and, most importantly, his co-author of the *Liberty* and many other writings becomes a familiar one. I am not suggesting that Mill dealt intensively with the *Liberty* in order to smooth out an earlier rhetorical blunder by a recently bereaved husband. Rather the *Autobiography* calls attention to the fact that the *Liberty* was the last sign of his second unified self and that the last four lines of the dedication accurately sum up his sense of being a shattered, useless, hopeless self that merely lingers on.[17]

Conclusion

In this essay I have outlined the relationships between books and selves in Mill's *Autobiography*. Drawing upon Greenblatt's notion of the printed book as a self-fashioning power, I have shown how the autobiographer first embraces and then departs from that notion in the story of the rise and fall of his first unified self. Although the conative function of books and their effects on readers are problematized by him, books and selves remain interrelated, nevertheless. The *Autobiography* foregrounds the emotive function of the *Liberty*, casting it as a sign of Mill's second unified self, which con-

---

17 I disagree, then, with Glassman's notion that the *Autobiography* ultimately exhibits "a living character, gravely troubled but indominably resilient, wonderfully creative, and heroically healthy" (1982: 213). Similarly, I do not agree with James McDonnell, who concludes: "For Mill was a man 'made', not just by his father, but by himself to an unusual extent and with unusual success. The definitive expression of that 'self-making' is his Autobiography [...]" (1977: 783). Rather, it is in the *Liberty* we find Mill's strong and successful self. a similar point is made by Jerome Buckley, who has argued that, in the *Liberty*, "[...] Mill fashions a strong authorial self and conveys in effect a clearer, "truer" impression of his force of character than appears anywhere in the last part of his actual self-history (1990: 231).

sisted of a merger between Mill himself and his wife – a merger that was dissolved by her death.

The conative function of books remains an important topos in fiction and non-fiction alike. I want to conclude by mapping out two examples of opposite interpretations of books as forms of self-fashioning power. My first example is found in Tony Harrison's poem "Book Ends". Here books are presented as terrible agents of estrangement erecting barriers within the family, more particularly, between the son, "The 'scholar'", (2000: l .7) and his working-class father. After his mother's death, the speaker is sitting together with his father in silence before the fire in the manner they used to do thirty years ago. However, in the absence of his mother, who likened "the pair of" (l. 5) them to "Book ends", no one is there "to tell us we're alike!" (l. 12). Consequently, the speaker is forced to conclude: "Back in our silences and sullen looks, / For all the Scotch we drink, what's still between's / Not the thirty or so years, but books, books, books" (ll. 14–16). A much sunnier image of books is developed in Jeanette Winterson's essay "The Psychometry of Books":

> Brought up without books, my passion for them was, if not directly forbidden, discouraged. At that time I knew nothing of First Editions and their special lure but I associated books with magic. Their totemic qualities aroused me and I believed that to possess them was power. In the difficult years of an evangelical childhood, which is and is not *Oranges are not the only fruit*, I used books as Bram Stoker uses holy wafers, to mark out a charmed place and to save my soul.
>
> Save my soul from what? From ordinariness, from habit, from prejudice, from fear, from the constraints of a life not chosen by me but strapped unto my back. How to make my burden fall? Through Books. Language caught and made to serve a master. Ariel across time and space. (Winterson, 1996: 122)

Here, too, books function by creating distance to one's surroundings. But in contrast to Harrison, Winterson regards their effect as a liberating one. Harrison and Winterson are reminders of the fact that, although the rise of new media during the twentieth century meant tough competition for books and other forms of printed material, and although self-fashioning now seems to be very much in the hands of television, cinema, video, and, last but not least, the internet, books are still considered powerful agents in relation to the self. At least by those who write them.

References

Bell, Susan Groag (1990) "The Feminization of John Stuart Mill". *Revealing Lives: Autobiography, Biography, and Gender*. Susan Groag Bell and Marilyn Yalom, eds.. New York: State University of New York Press

Boone Joseph Allen (1985) *Tradition Counter Tradition: Love and the Form of Fiction*. Chicago and London: The University of Chicago Press

Buckley, Jerome (1990) "John Stuart Mill's 'True' Autobiography". *Studies in the Literary Imagination*. Vol. 23. No. 2. 1990. pp. 223–31

Chartier, Roger (2002) "Labourers and Voyagers": From the Text to the Reader". *The Book History Reader*. David Finkelstein and Alistair McCleery, eds. London and New York: Routledge

——. (1989) "General Introduction: Print Culture". *The Culture of Print: Power and the Uses of Print in Early Modern Europe*. Roger Chartie, ed. Trans. by Lydia G. Cochrane. Princeton, New Jersey: Princeton University Press

Drabble, Margaret and Jenny Stringer (eds.) (1990) *The Concise Oxford Companion to English Literature*. Oxford and New York: Oxford University Press

Fleishman, Avrom (1983) "Mill's *Autobiography*: Two Deities". *Figures of Autobiography: The Language of Self-Writing in Victorian and Modern England*. Berkeley and London: University of California Press

Glassman, Peter (1982) "'Who Made Me?': The *Autobiography* of John Stuart Mill". *Prose Studies*. Vol. 5. No. 2. 1982. pp. 193–214.

Greenblatt, Stephen (1980) *Renaissance Self-Fashioning: From More to Shakespeare*. Chicago & London: The University of Chicago Press

Hall, Stuart (1994) "The Question of Cultural Identity". *The Polity Reader in Cultural Theory*. Cambridge: Polity Press

Harrison, Tony (2000/1978) "Book Ends". *The Norton Anthology of English Literature*. Vol. 2. Seventh edition. M.H. Abrams and Stephen Greenblatt, eds. London and New York: W.W. Norton and Company

Jakobson, Roman (1988) "Linguistics and Poetics". *Modern Criticism and Theory: A Reader*. David Lodge, ed. London and New York: Longman

Jones, W.T. (1975) *A History of Western Philosophy. Vol. IV. Kant and the Nineteenth Century*. Second edition, revised. New York & Chicago: Hartcourt Brace Jovanovich, Inc.

McDonnell, James (1977) "'A Seasoning of Awakening': An Analysis of Chapter Five of Mill's *Autobiography*. *Modern Language Review*. Vol. 72. No. 4. pp. 773–783

McKenzie, D.F. (1982) "Printing in England from Caxton to Milton". *The New Pelican Guide to English Literature. Vol. 2. The Age of Shakespeare*. Boris Ford, ed. Pelican Books

Mill, John Stuart (1981) *Autobiography and Literary Essays*. John M. Robson and Jack Stillinger, eds. Toronto and Buffalo: University of Toronto Press

——. (1980) *Mill on Bentham and Coleridge*. (With an introduction by F.R. Leavis). Cambridge and New York: Cambridge University Press

Robson, J.M. (1977) "Textual Introduction". John Stuart Mill. *Essays on Politics and Society*. J.M. Robson, ed. University of Toronto Press: Toronto and Buffalo

Robson, J.M. and Stillinger, J. (1981a) "Introduction". John Stuart Mill, *Autobiography and Literary Essays*. J.M. Robson and J. Stillinger, eds. University of Toronto Press: Toronto and Buffalo

——. (1981b) "Appendix B. Mill's Early Reading (1809–22)". John Stuart Mill, *Autobiography and Literary Essays*. J.M. Robson and J. Stillinger, eds. University of Toronto Press: Toronto and Buffalo

Winterson, Jeanette (1996 [1995]) "The Psychometry of Books". *Art Objects: Essays on Ecstasy and Effrontery*. Vintage.

Dickens and Kipling: Two Good Victorians

JØRGEN RIBER CHRISTENSEN

Modernity may well be one of the best descriptions of the Victorian Period, this despite nostalgic Victoriana in television series and heritage films. Viewed in this way aspects of the Victorian Period suddenly become updated instead of outdated. Technological and communicative changes of the period are at least as pervasive as present-day changes. Take the development of the communication and traffic system in Britain in the only eight years from 1844 to 1852 as reflected in the two maps of the railway system.

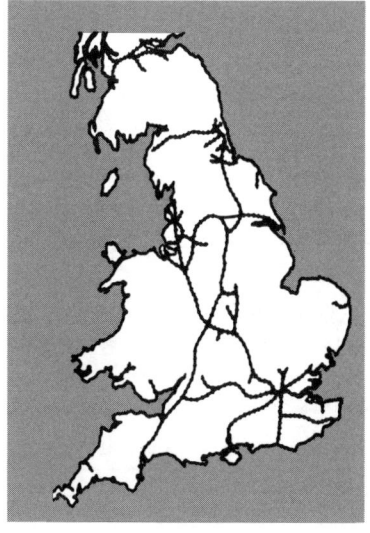
Railways in 1844

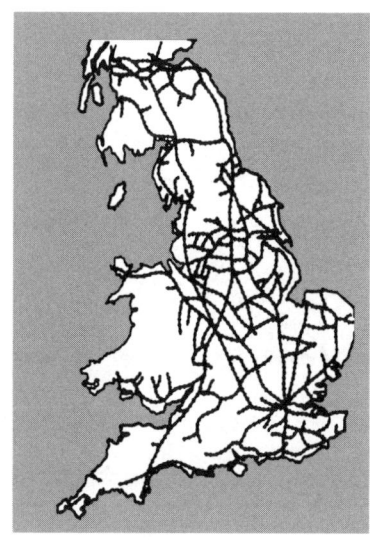
Railways in 1852

Or a view of the development of industrial production shows the same expansive pattern of economic and also social changes. Expansion to a larger world was not only there internally in Britain. Abroad the Empire opened the world at large to the British, as a simple map of the British Empire will show:

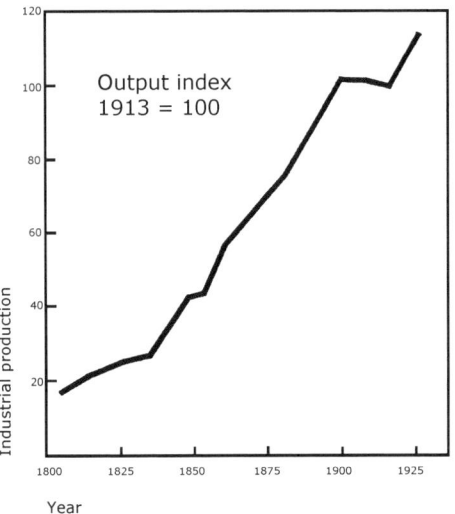

British industrial production during the 19th century

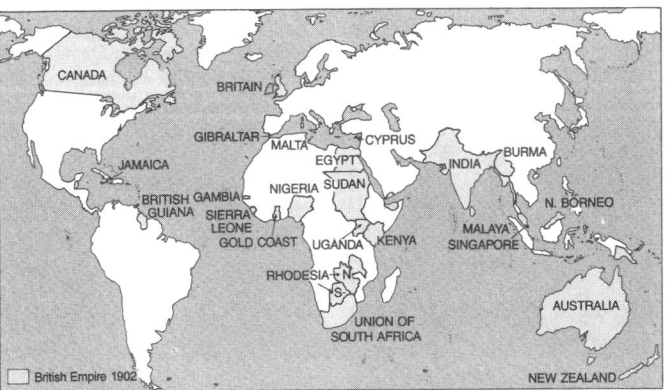

The British Empire 1902

How did concerned writers react to the changes at home and the changes abroad? At home Charles Dickens (1812–1870) described the new industrial and urban mass society with its social problems. In this essay his short ghost story "No. 1 Branch Line: The Signal-man"[1] from *Mugby Junction* (1866) will be related to the issues of technology, progress and modernity in the light of the narrative structure of the short story.

The Signal-man.

Townley Green's illustration for "The Signal-man"

Rudyard Kipling (1865–1936) responded to the geographic and imperialist expansion abroad in texts such as "Recessional" (1897) and "The White Man's Burden" (1899). Here a reading of his short story "Lispeth"[2] (1886) will focus on Kipling's view of imperialist responsibility, and the point will be made that Kipling reversed the traditional Victorian male quest romance in an attempt to inform his readers of aspects of colonial behavior, and that Kipling's views of colonialism and its consequences differ with regard to the public and private spheres.

Charles Dickens: "No. 1 Branch Line: The Signal-man"

The short story "The Signal-man" is a ghost story in which a rather anonymous narrator tells the story about the strange occurrences related to the death of a railway employee, a signal-man. The narrator visits the shed of the signal-man in a deep cutting, and he is told by the signal-man about an apparition that has appeared twice near a warning light. Each appearance of the apparition is followed by a tragedy, and after the

---

1   Dickens wrote "The Signal-man" for the Christmas number of *All the Year Round*.
2   "Lispeth" was first printed in the Lahore newspaper *The Civil and Military Gazette*.

third appearance the signal-man himself is run over by a train. The signal-man has, however, already told the narrator that he has been forewarned by the specter that something horrible was going to happen. The narrator, who is retired and at his leisure and only presented with a few words[3], visits the signal-man three times, each visit incrementally adding to the signal-man's own story. The first visit is dominated by a description of the setting. The setting is overcoded in the sense that it not only creates repulsion in the narrator because of its deep and damp nature, but even more so because of the symbolic value added to it. The railway cutting, which after all is a wonder of new technology, is described as an underworld, a Hades. The narrator feels that he "had left the natural world", and the mouth of the tunnel is "barbarous, depressing and forbidding". The place "had an earthy, deadly smell". (Dickens, 1911: 191)

Summit tunnel, Manchester and Leeds railway, A.W. Tait

In the context of this short story the symbolic description of the setting has the function of creating suspense. It is interesting to compare the narrator's conception of this railway setting with contemporary pictorial renderings of similar scenes. Despite topographical likenesses these are not nearly as somber as Dickens' description would have it. The fascination caused by grand engineering, which is perceptible in the prints, has been modified in Dickens' short story so that the almost sublime in the technological scenery has been inversed from awe to fear. The depiction in the short story of the railway cutting is transmitted to the narrator's conception of the signal-man himself, so that the narrator wonders whether the

---

3   The narrator is only presented as "a man who had been shut up within narrow limits all his life, and who, being at last set free, had a great interest in these great works [the railway]" (Dickens 1911: 191). However, from the context of the other short stories in "Mugby Junction" it will be known that the narrator is Young Jackson, who has just retired as the head of Barbox Brothers.

signal-man with his "fixed eyes and the saturnine face [...] was a spirit, not a man" (191). The narrator is then introduced to the signal-man's job functions in his little box or cabin. The work is characterized by strict routine and by the newest technology such as "a telegraphic instrument with its dial, face and needles" (192) and an electric bell, which the signal-man has to reply to at all times. The signal-man remarks that this bell causes him anxiety, and the narrator notices that the signal-man during their conversation "twice broke off with fallen colour, turned his face towards the little bell when it did NOT ring" (193). He does not confide in the narrator why it is so, however, but promises that if the narrator makes him another visit, he will try to tell him. The uncanny feeling is intensified when the narrator takes his leave "(with a very disagreeable sensation of a train coming behind me)" (193), and the signal-man wonders why the narrator called out "Halloa! Below there!", when he first came, and if these words were conveyed to the narrator in any supernatural way.

After the uncanny atmosphere has been established in the first visit, the next or second visit makes it clear that both visits are part of a narrative frame around the signal-man's own story. The signal-man has been warned by a specter standing at the mouth of the tunnel under the danger signal's red light, and six hours later a railway accident took place with dead and wounded. Six months later he again saw the specter, and the same day a young lady had died in a train compartment near the box. Now the signal-man has again seen the specter a week ago, and the specter rings the signal-man's little bell. The bell has even rung during the narrator's first visit, though only the signal-man could hear it. The narrator seeks to explain the occurrences as coincidences, and he also finds a reason in the mind of the signal-man: "It was the mental torture of a conscientious man, oppressed beyond endurance by an unintelligible responsibility involving life" (200). So to the narrator the specter may seem to be a materialization or rather a projection of the stress caused by the railway employee's job. The narrator succeeds to some degree in calming the signal-man, and he decides to come back the next evening to persuade the signal-man to come with him to see a doctor. On his return the next day the narrator sees from the top of the embankment what the signal-man has told him he had seen on several occasions: a man standing in the same position as the specter waving in the same way. For a moment the narrator shares the signal-man's horror in the belief that he too has seen a ghost. What he has seen is bad enough. It is the reconstruction of the accident that has just killed the signal-man. He has been cut down by a train. The driver has used the very words and the same gestures as the specter had used to warn the signal-man off the tracks, and the signal-man had become paralyzed.

Even though the narrator all the way through the story has tried to be rational and to explain the ghostly appearances as coincidences and as symptoms of a stressed worker, he cannot help pointing out in the final paragraph of the short story the amount of coincidences, and their similarities are curious. Even though the narrator is the detached and rational spectator to the scene and the scenery and a critical listener to the signal-man's story he has in the end been emotionally drawn into what has happened, though not to the extent that he really believes the signal-man's ghost story. As such he may partially be a representative of the reader.

The question, which the reader may ask during the reading of the short story, is basically whether the specter is real or not? Is the narrative of the signal-man to be trusted? These are the very questions that the narrator has asked himself. Here the narrative structure, which embeds the narrative of the signal-man inside the narrator's frame story, is crucial. In a reading of "The Signal-man" Ewald Mengel (Mengel, 1983) has analyzed this narrative structure, and Mengel's finding is that the reader accepts the narrator's story at face value, particularly because of the narrator's reluctance to let himself be drawn into the supernatural interpretation of the events and his repeated attempts to explain everything in a rational way, such as when he attributes the specter to be the consequence of an overworked and stressed mind. This is a psychological explanation, which contains a societal critique, and as such it has thematic importance. The reader accepts the frame story, but is doubtful as to the embedded story. When the two merge, as they do in the final visit when the signal-man has been killed, the reader is forced to carry his or her acceptance of the frame story into an acceptance of the embedded story. The narrator himself is prepared to admit that the two narrative levels have merged:

> Without prolonging the narrative to dwell on any one of its curious circumstances more than on any other, I may, in closing it, point out the coincidence that the warning of the Engine-Driver included, not only the words which the unfortunate Signal-man had repeated to me as haunting him, but also the words which I myself – not he – had attached, and that only in my own mind, to the gesticulation he had imitated. (Dickens 1911: 203–204)

The narrative structure, which is rather complicated in a short story of only 13 pages, in itself becomes an argument to accept that something supernatural took place down the railway viaduct. With the acceptance of the supernatural occurrences as real the impact of the societal critique may seem to be weakened to the point of demanding more lunch breaks for signalmen as the specter is tied to the signal-man. But an inclusion of the symbolic value of the setting in an understanding of these aspects will expand the idea of the supernatural in an individual case to a conception of the railway technology to something daemonic. As the railway more than any other contemporary technology was an emblem of modern industrialism, Victorian industrial society as such is criticized in this short story for being inhuman and having hellish and demonic qualities. So when one asks the question why has Dickens chosen to describe modern technology such as the railway and electricity with classical and ancient emblems of death, the answer given is that modern technology and its social consequences (methods of work), are not really to be regarded naively as simply progress, but progress with serious human costs.

The Staplehurst Railway Accident

In 1857 and 1858 Dickens' family life disintegrated. He had met a young actress, Ellen Ternan, and Dickens separated from his wife. A public scandal followed, though Ellen Ternan was practically left out of it, and Dickens set her up in a small house. In June 1864 Dickens, Ellen Ternan and her mother narrowly escaped death when they were involved in a railway accident at Staplehurst where ten people were killed and 50 injured. The accident weakened Dickens' already failing health, though his behavior at the scene of the accident was exemplary and considerate. He climbed out of his first-class compartment that was hanging by its couplings from a bridge at an angle over the river Beult, helped the Ternans out, and then proceeded to help the injured and the dying. He received a piece of plate in gratitude from the railway company, and he was able to stay out of the public inquest that followed, so that his relationship with Ellen Ternan remained a secret from the public.

The anxiety remained, and Peter Ackroyd relates in his Dickens biography that "travelling became for him the single most distressing activity" (Ackroyd, 1996: 1017), just as Dickens' relatives describe how the Staplehurst accident told on him more and more:

> [M]y father's nerves never really were the same again [...] we have often seen him, when travelling home from London, suddenly fall into a paroxysm of

fear, tremble all over, clutch the arms of the railway carriage, large beads of perspiration standing on his face, and suffer agonies of terror. We never spoke to him, but would touch his hands gently now and then. He had, however, apparently no idea of our presence; he saw nothing for a time but that most awful scene (1017).

Dickens at the Staplehurst railway accident in 1864

Dickens' own anxiety and paroxysms of fear caused by the railway accident may have been one of the sources for the descriptions of the signal-man's reactions and behavior in "The Signal-man"; but Dickens transformed a personal experience into a much wider social critique, and it may be noticed that already in *Dombey and Son* from 1846–48 he described the railway as a destructive and deadly force.

Todorov, Hesitation, and "The Signal-man"

The narrative structure and the thematics of "The Signal-man" are part of a whole. Both seek to convey a critique of industrial and technological progress. It is significant that the form of this critique is a ghost story. The genre designation ghost story must, however, be seriously qualified as the incremental drive of the narrative and its suspense is based on one single question: "Is the ghost really there?" The reality of the ghost or specter may be compared to the state of mind that Dickens himself got into after the Staplehurst accident. "He had, however, apparently no idea of our presence; he saw nothing for a time but that most awful scene" (1017). Here Dickens' imagination took over from reality. The same sense of hovering between reality and hallucination, or to put it more precisely, of moving between reality and hallucination is the basic narrative structure of the short story, which consists of visits from the sane and rational world of the narrator down to the possessed underworld of the railway. In the reader's reception of the action and symbolism of the short story there is the same wavering sense of cognitive dislocation, and it is this dislocation on which the effect of the short story rests. The dislocation of cognition is also the dislocation of industrial progress from the socially rational and humanely beneficial.

Cognitive dislocation and uncertainty are not the best descriptive terms of ghost stories and of the horror genre as such. Rather, a brief definition of the horror genre based on Sigmund Freud's essay "The Uncanny" (Freud, 1985: 335–376) would be that the crucial element of a horror story is the return of the repressed in some supernatural form. In "The Signal-man" the existence of this supernatural entity is doubtful and it is questioned all the way through the short story. This insecurity, questioning and hesitation in the narration and the reception are the terms that Tzvetan Todorov uses to describe the genre the fantastic:

> In a world that is indeed our world, the one we know, a world without devils, sylphides, or vampires, there occurs an event which cannot be explained by the laws of this same familiar world. The person who experiences the event must opt for one of two possible solutions: either he is a victim of an illusion of the senses, of a product of the imagination – and laws of the world then remain what they are; or else the event has indeed taken place, it is an integral part of reality – but then this reality is controlled by laws unknown to us. Either the devil is an illusion, an imaginary being; or else he really exists, precisely like other living beings – with this reservation, that we encounter him infrequently.
>
> The fantastic occupies the duration of this uncertainty. Once we choose one answer or the other, we leave the fantastic for a neighbouring genre, the uncanny or the marvellous. The fantastic is that hesitation experienced by a person who knows only the laws of nature, confronting an apparently supernatural event. (Todorov, 1975: 25)

"The Signal-man" corresponds to Todorov's definition of the fantastic genre: "The fantastic is that hesitation experienced by a person who knows only the laws of nature, confronting an apparently supernatural event" (25). Both the signal-man himself and the narrator are part of the rational and technological world of modernity. Yet, Dickens in his rich and excessive narrative style manages to invert the two characters' connection to this world order. The signal-man, who is an integrated part of modern technology, is after some hesitation most ready to opt for the supernatural understanding of the events, whereas the narrator, who has retired from his career within the same technological world, is the more hesitant of the two. This graded duplication of Todorov's hesitation is thematically significant. The closer one seems to be to the modern railway, the more prepared one will be to accept it as supernatural and demonic. Evil, so to speak. So by inflecting Todorov's hesitation Dickens manages to stress the message of his short story.

In his poetics of the fantastic Todorov prescribes three conditions to be fulfilled for a text to belong to the genre. These demands are tied to the reader's reception. The first condition is that a realist world picture must be established in the text that is acceptable to the reader, so that it becomes a precondition of the consequent hesitation with regard to understanding the events in the text as either natural or supernatural. Secondly, the reader's hesitation must also be a character's hesitation, so that there is a shared ground and that the reader identifies with the character. In this connection Todorov points out that this hesitation is not only a receptive and narrative category. The hesitation must also be foregrounded so that it becomes a theme of the text. This thematic understanding of the hesitation is continued in the final condition. The reader must reject poetic or allegorical interpretations of the events. In other words, the hesitation is tied to the level of the action more than to the level of the enunciation of the action (33).

"The Signal-man" fulfils Todorov's three conditions about the reception of the fantastic. The world of the narrator that circumscribes the world and the story of the signal-man is safely realist and rational, and the reader's hesitation is not only shared by one character. It is actually shared by both the narrator and the signal-man, and the characters repeatedly voice the hesitation. Todorov's hesitation is a temporal category. Hesitation as such means to pause in a decision-making process, and Todorov's third condition that the reader must reject an allegorical or poetic understanding of the events shows this temporal course, as the short story itself with its initial symbol-laden description of the viaduct setting gradually moves from this metaphorical level towards a down-to-earth acceptance of the reality of the specter in its own right.

In "The Signal-man" Dickens has given a complex narrative and aesthetic form to a societal critique of working conditions in modernity. The Age of Steam and the railway are recurring themes in Dickens' works. In "The Signal-man" the railway is used as a vehicle for a fundamental societal critique. Dickens also wrote journalistically[4] about the railway, but without this kind of societal critique. Dickens left it to the narrative disguise of the fantastic to express so radical a critique as a way of making this fundamental critique palatable and acceptable to his large reading audience.

Rudyard Kipling

In George Orwell's essay "Rudyard Kipling" from 1942 Orwell says about Kipling:

> During five literary generations every enlightened person has despised him, and at the end of that time nine-tenths of those enlightened persons are forgotten and Kipling is in some sense still there...
> Kipling *is* a jingo imperialist, he *is* morally insensitive and aesthetically disgusting. (Orwell, 1986: 45)

And Orwell goes on to defend Kipling. Orwell himself had colonial experiences as may be seen from his other essay "Shooting an Elephant" (1936) and his novel *Burmese Days* (1934).

The line "Or lesser breeds without the Law –" in Kipling's poem "Recessional" (Kipling, 1999: 478) from 1897 is often quoted as an expression of Kipling's view of the colonized peoples as second-rate, and this facile and wrong reading of the "lesser breeds" places the white Anglo-Saxon male at the top of an evolutionary hierarchy. Orwell says about the "lesser breeds":

> This line is always good for a snigger in pansy-left wing circles. It is assumed as a matter of course that the 'lesser breeds' are 'natives', and a mental picture is called up of some pukha sahib in a pith helmet kicking a coolie... (Orwell, 1986: 46)

---

4 For instance in "Railway Dreaming", "Fire and Snow", "An Unsettled Neighbourhood", and "Railway Strikes".

The line from "Recessional" in fact refers to the Germans or perhaps the Italians as colonizers that do not abide to any "Law" or to any sense of responsibility towards the colonized peoples. The poem is a denunciation of power politics, and it is a denunciation of colonialism as an economic affair. Kipling's attitude is not economic. It is moral, and therefore the language and stylistic register of the poem is biblical. Yet "Recessional" is also an acceptance of colonialism as such, and our response as enlightened persons to Kipling will be ambivalent, though it should not just be negative and without nuances as the reading here of a few of his colonial texts aims to demonstrate. To Kipling colonialism is a question of moral responsibility, which the British and other European colonial powers should practice. Kipling is the good Victorian concerned with the responsibility and burden of the Empire abroad in much the same way, as Dickens was concerned with the consequences of industrialism at home.

Two years after "Recessional" Kipling wrote his best-known poem "The White Man's Burden" (Kipling, 1999: 479), and having read this title one's immediate response is a question: "Oughtn't it to be 'The Black Man's Burden'?" The answer to this question must be carefully contextualized. To Kipling and to his contemporaries from conservatives to Karl Marx[5] it was a common belief that Europe had reached the highest stage of civilization. As it was the case with the expansion of the railway system in Britain where the railway became the emblem of modernity, the spread of the railway in Asia was used as a direct expression of development, and Orwell remarks that it is instructive to take a look at a map of Asia and compare the railway system of India to that of the surrounding countries. Kipling's point with his poem is as the title says that it is a burden to Europe to colonize, and the immediate function of "The White Man's Burden" is that the USA ought to help carry this burden, so Kipling sent it to Theodore Roosevelt, who became president soon after. Roosevelt's response to the poem is a reminder that Kipling may have been politically naïve. Though he saw colonialism as a moral responsibility, colonialism and imperialism are also political and economic exploitation. Roosevelt wrote about the poem that "it was rather poor poetry [...] but that it was good sense from an expan-

---

5 Karl Marx writes in an article in *The New York Daily Tribune*, 8 August 1853, "The Future Results of the British Rule in India": "England has to fulfill a double mission in India: one destructive, the other regenerating – the annihilation of old Asiatic society, and the laying of the material foundations of Western society in Asia" (Marx 1973: 320).

sionist point of view" (Roosevelt in a letter to Senator Henry Cabot Lodge, *History Matters*, 2006: http).

"Lispeth" and Kipling

A central theme in early Kipling is the meeting between East and West. In "Recessional" and in "The White Man's Burden" this meeting is of a general, ideological and political nature. In the short story "Lispeth" (Kipling, 1897) from 1886 this meeting is at a personal and fictionalized level, and it is of a melodramatic nature. Not only "Lispeth", but also many of the short stories in *Plain Tales from the Hills*, e.g. the unforgettable "Beyond the Pale", as well as the novel *Kim* (1901) add to an overall treatment of this theme.

Charles Dickens' experiences with the Staplehurst accident were part of the personal background for the creative process in writing "The Signalman". In Kipling's case his personal or biographical involvement with Anglo-Indian relationships is of importance, too. Kipling's life shows a duality where his identity seems to belong to two worlds. He was born in Bombay in 1865. His father was a teacher at an art school and then director of the Lahore Museum. When six years old Kipling was sent to England to be educated. In 1882 he went back to India, and he became a journalist at *The Civil and Military Gazette* in Lahore. After the successful publication of *Plain Tales from the Hills* he went to England in 1889 as a literary celebrity, and later in his life he lived for a period in the USA, and he traveled in South Africa. In India Kipling, who had a dark complexion, liked to disguise himself as an Indian and go to the Indian neighborhoods and bazaars. He identified with Indians, especially with traders and the Indian petit-bourgeoisie. This split in his identity and his love for India and Indians might have led to an insoluble conflict and animosity towards colonialism; but the opposite was the case. Kipling managed to unite his love for India with the system of colonialism: the love of India demanded colonial responsibility. The British have a moral obligation to improve life for the Indians, and they must follow a moral code. This does not mean that the relationship between the British colonizers and the Indians was an easy one. Again at the personal level, Kipling experienced conflicts also to do with morals, but morals of a less ideological kind. What would happen if an Englishman fell in love with an Indian, or an Indian fell in love with an Englishman? There is the mystery of the *Mother Maturin* manuscript. Kipling wrote at least some part of a manuscript for a novel called *Mother Maturin* (Wilson, 1979: 62–63). The novel was never published, and this manuscript is lost, perhaps destroyed by Kipling himself. It was the story of a young Englishman's love for an Indian woman, possibly a young prostitute included in a spy story about an old Irish woman, who had an opium den in Lahore (Lycett, 1999: 103). The short story "Lispeth" explores both the passionate love between an Indian woman and an Englishman; but at the same time this love story is embedded in the larger moral obligation of the colonizer towards the colonized. In "Lispeth" it is the Indian woman, who is the subject and heroine of the story, and it is her love, which is the passionate one. Already here, one can see a pattern of inversions, where not only gender roles, but also colonial roles are inversed.

"Lispeth" has a verse prelude in which the theme and the action of the short story are presented in religious terms. The prelude is signed by "The Convert", who criticizes Christianity, to which she has been converted, for coldness, and she states that she will go back to her own old religion. The young and orphaned girl Lispeth is brought to the house of a missionary couple. Here she grows into a goddess-like young woman, who because of her beauty and character cannot just become a servant girl in the house: "Lispeth had a Greek face – one of those faces people paint so often, and see so seldom […] you would, meeting her on the hillside unexpectedly, have thought her the original Diana of the Romans going out to slay" (Kipling, 1897: 2). Lispeth is intelligent and independent. She reads all the books in the house, and her physical strength is equal to her mental strength for she rescues an unconscious young Englishman, who has had an accident in the hills. He is an explorer, who has been hunting for plants and butterflies. She falls in love with him during his convalescence in the missionary station. He toys with her feelings, promises her marriage, and then leaves her to go to England to his fiancée. When Lispeth is told this after some time of lies on the part of the missionaries, she goes native again:

> She took to her own unclean people savagely, as if to make up for the arrears of the life she had stepped out of; and in a little time, she married a wood-cutter who beat her after the manner of *paharis*, and her beauty faded soon. (8)[6]

"Lispeth" is heavily didactic. The story is narrated with an ironic distance to the missionaries and their stereotypical attitudes towards Indians and morality. Lispeth herself is depicted according to ancient Greek ideals, and

---

6 Lispeth does not quite disappear. Later in *Kim*, she has a cameo role as an old, alcoholic woman, the exotic Woman of Shamlegh.

as such she is presented as being close to the foundation of European civilization. The flaw of the British is that they cannot cope with the moral demands made to them as colonizers. The missionaries are ignorant and dishonest, and the young British explorer is at best irresponsible. All seem devoid of morals. The short story is not simply a naïve stereotypical praise of the qualities of Indians. Lispeth is battered by her Indian husband, and she becomes an alcoholic. The aim of "Lispeth" is to educate its Anglo-British and British readership as it demonstrates how not to behave in a colony, and how not to regard colonized people.

The Victorian Quest Romance

A literary genre was developed that reflected the imperial expansion and its consequences for the British male. In the Victorian quest romance the often Darwinist clash between cultures forces the white man to define his gender role in a changing and expanding world. The Victorian quest romance is shorter and more action-packed than the traditional, domestic three-volume Victorian novel. Its generic plot structure is that a group of men depart for unknown places on a double quest. There is the public quest for knowledge, science or wealth, and there is the quest for personal development. The narrative structure is the one also found in folk tales and many myths: at home - out - home. One of the crucial themes is male friendship as a safe haven in a world that is not safe any more. This means that women are simply excluded from the quest world, or that women are excluded from the realist level of this world so that women become mysterious and mythical beings. Some examples of the Victorian quest romance are: R.L. Stevenson's *Treasure Island* (1881), Rider Haggard's *King Solomon's Mines* (1885) and *She* (1887), Conan Doyle's *The Lost World* (1912) and Kipling's *The Man Who Would Be King* (1888), *The Jungle Books* (1894–5) and *Kim* (1901).

The short story "Lispeth" is not unrelated to the Victorian quest romance. In "Lispeth" the typical male quest hero is diminished almost beyond recognition. He has become the young British man hunting for butterflies, who is so clumsy climbing the hills that he knocks himself unconscious, only to be found and carried home by the physically stronger Lispeth. His public quest for scientific knowledge fails, and his private quest for personal knowledge does not seem to leave a trace in him, as the only thing he can do is to lie to his rescuer before going home to marry his fiancée. There is no development in this male mind. Lispeth herself, on the other hand is more interesting, though her quest for personal fulfillment is unsuccessful, too. She is almost permitted inside this male genre. But her role is ambiguous. She is both a resourceful person, but she is also described with some of the characteristics of women in the Victorian quest romance. Lispeth is mythologized like Rider Haggard's She. She is described as a Greek or Roman goddess; but when Kipling locates her solidly within a specific colonial context, he inverses the quest romance structure. The woman, who is also native, becomes the main character. Her almost super-human qualities are then moved from the mythological realm to the colonial one, and Kipling demonstrates that there is no room for such qualities here. Kipling has re-gendered the quest structure to criticize the imperial system that created the Victorian quest romance in the first place.

Colonialism in the Private and the Public Sphere

One of the other short stories in *Plain Tales from the Hills*, "Beyond the Pale", takes the message of "Lispeth" one step further. This short story is together with "Lispeth" part of a group of stories about the (sexual) relationship between British men and Indian women. The others are "Yoked with an Unbeliever" and "Kidnapped", both from *Plain Tales from the Hills*, and also "Without Benefit of Clergy" from *Life's Handicap* (1891). The style of these short stories is first of all characterized by an almost imperceptible irony that gradually becomes satire directed against hypocrisy and lack of respect for Indians, and there is no room for sentimentality whatsoever, as it may be seen in the fate of Lispeth. In "Beyond the Pale" a segment of Indian society is revealed as sadistic, cruel and almost unbelievably suppressive towards women, and in "Without Benefit of Clergy" a mother whose daughter has just died is so greedy that she does not mourn her daughter's death: "In her anxiety to take stock of the house-fittings forgot to mourn" (Kipling, 1987: 33). Lispeth has no real home or culture of her own. Neither the missionaries nor her own people provide any solutions to her divided identity and existence. The unsymmetrical mixture of cultures produced by the colonial situation has only costs to her. "Yoked with an Unbeliever" again has the theme of marriage between an Indian woman, "Dunmaya, the daughter of a Rajput ex-Subadar-Major of our Native Army" (Kipling, 1897: 52), and Philip Garron, a young man sent out to "this mysterious 'tea' business near Darjiling" (49). In contrast to "Lispeth" the third-party British woman involved here is not anonymous:

> When the Gravesend tender left the P. & O. steamer for Bombay and went back to catch the train to Town, there were many people in it crying. But the one who wept most, and most openly, was Miss Agnes Laiter. She had reason to cry, because the only man she ever loved – or ever could love, so she said – was going out to India; and India as everyone knows, is divided equally between jungle, tigers, cobras, cholera, and sepoys. (48)

As already this first paragraph shows "Yoked with an Unbeliever" is even more ironic than "Lispeth". The narrator distances himself from Miss Agnes Laiter with embedding the description of her attitude to both love and India within phrases such as: "so she said" and "as everyone knows", and Miss Laiter does not only weep the most, she weeps "most openly". Philip Garron does not receive a very sympathetic treatment from the narrator either, nor from Miss Laiter, who a little later marries another man home in England. Philip Garron then marries Dunmaya, who "in spite of her reverence for an Englishman had a reasonable estimate of her husband's weaknesses" and who "became, in less than a year, a very passable imitation of an English lady in dress and carriage" (53). However, Agnes Laiter's husband soon dies, and she goes out to India to find Philip and to marry him, only to find him already married to Dunmaya, and the narrator's closing words are sympathetic to this Indian woman: "Dunmaya is making a decent man of him; and he will ultimately be saved from perdition through her training" (54).

"Kidnapped" again employs irony to describe a colonial marriage. In this case it is between Peythroppe and Miss Castries with "what innocent people at Home call a 'Spanish' complexion" (143), i.e. a Eurasian. As the title of the short story indicates the solution to this problem is that colonial society uses violence, as Peythroppe is simply kidnapped for seven weeks and brainwashed by his friends and superiors to break his promise to marry Miss Castries. Kipling's satire is not only directed against this racist societal suppression. There is also the theme of arranged marriages in "Kidnapped". The opening lines of this short story are an ironic criticism of Hindu arranged marriages; but this European criticism is turned against itself. If ever there was an arranged marriage, then it was Peythroppe's future one:

> So Peythroppe came to his right mind again, and did much good work, and was honoured by all who knew him. One of these days he will marry a sweet pink-and-white maiden, on the Government House List, with a little money and some influential connections, as every wise man should. (147)

"Beyond the Pale" has lost the light use of irony found in the other short stories within this group. Instead of only irony, symbolism is used as a narratorial response to societal colonial suppression and to its consequent psychological and bodily repression. "Beyond the Pale" with its few pages is about the impossible and passionate love affair between the British Trejago and his little Bisesa, who is only 15 years old – and a widow. Trejago goes beyond the pale, as he likes to stray into the innermost Indian parts of his town, where he meets Bisesa. They fall in love, and they have to suffer the punishment, as the opening of this short story foreshadows:

> A man should, whatever happens, keep to his own caste, race and breed. Let the White go to the White and the Black to the Black… This is the story of a man who wilfully stepped beyond the safe limits of decent everyday society, and paid for it heavily…He took too deep an interest in native life; but he will never do so again. (186)

Bisesa loses both of her hands and Trejago is wounded in the groin by a spear. This wound in an allusion to the wounding and killing of Adonis in Greek mythology. Adonis was in love with Aphrodite, the goddess of love, and he was killed by a boar that gored him. Bisesa and Trejago had only been able to communicate through the bars of a little window, as Bisesa is imprisoned within her family's house. "Without Benefit of Clergy" from *Life's Handicap* is practically a companion piece to "Beyond the Pale", as it may be read as an alternative outcome of this story. What would married life inside the native house have been like? John Holden has a secret, native wife, Ameera. They get a child. The child dies from a fever, and later Ameera dies from cholera. Just like Trejago John Holden has absolutely nowhere to go with his grief. The theme of this short story is again the ill-fated meeting between two cultures, and it may together with the other short stories here help to define Kipling's attitude to colonialism more precisely and in a more nuanced manner, than if only the more known poems were taken into account. As it is expressed in the poems Kipling is in favor of colonialism in *the public sphere*. In *the private sphere* colonialism only brings misery and sorrow. In the public sphere the utilitarian task of colonialism is accepted in "Without Benefit of Clergy": "The Government, which had decreed that no man die of want, sent wheat" (Kipling, 1987: 31), and the British colonial administrators die heroically as they try to relieve the epidemic of cholera: "There were gaps among the English, but the gaps were filled. The work of superintending famine-relief, cholera-sheds, medicine-distribution, and what little sanitation was possible, went forward because it was so ordered" (31). These lines echo the lines in the "The White Man's Burden": "Take up the White Man's Burden [...] Fill full the mouth of famine, And bid the sickness cease" (Kipling, 1999: 479). In the private sphere of the colonial situation in "Without Benefit of Clergy" the discourse of a fatal cultural clash is expressed symbolically, for instance in the last two pages' description of the rain washing away the interracial home; but Ameera is allowed to express openly and critically the differences between her own position as a native woman and the position of British women.

The colonial power discourse is gendered. It was not allowed to take the form of an Indian man wooing an Anglo-Indian or British woman. Kipling did not go this far in his criticism of the consequences of colonialism in the private sphere. Yet he did go very close to it in one of the short stories in *Plain Tales from the Hills*, "Miss Youghal's Sais". Strickland falls in love with Miss Youghal; but her parents will not allow the match. As many of Kipling's characters Strickland likes to go Fantee. He dresses up like an Indian and mixes with the Indians. To get near Miss Youghal he disguises himself as a sais (a native groom), and he courts her. In this way there is a love affair between an Indian man, though he is a fake, and a British woman. At the same time Youghal's disguise allows Kipling to show his readers what life is like from the other side of the cultural barrier. "Miss Youghal's Sais" is more subversive in the colonial context than the other critical short stories in *Plain Tales from the Hills*.

Rudyard Kipling was, like many of his characters, caught between two cultures. This dilemma and contradiction he sought to turn into the positive ideology of the obligation – or burden – of the Europeans to better the conditions for the less advanced peoples. The expression of this view was stated directly in the two poems "Recessional" and "The White Man's Burden", which are political proclamations. The clash of cultures where one suppresses the other has its human victims. It is in Kipling's fictional works, such as the short stories discussed here, that Kipling like Dickens became concerned, and it is here that an ethical judgment and condemnation of colonialism and imperialism became intense and human.

References

Ackroyd, Peter (1996/1990) *Dickens*. London: Minerva

Christensen, Jørgen Riber (2000) *Charles Dickens CD–ROM*. Aarhus: Systime

Dickens, Charles (1911) *Christmas Stories*. Vol. II. *The Centenary Edition of the Works of Charles Dickens* in 36 Volumes. London: Chapman & Hall

——. (1997) *Selected Journalism 1850–1870.* Harmondsworth: Penguin

Fraser, Robert, *Victorian Quest Romance* (1998) Northcote House: Writers and Their Works

Freud, Sigmund (1985) "Das Unheimliche". First printed in *Imago* 5, 1919. "The Uncanny" in Freud, Sigmund *Art and Literature.* Harmondsworth: *The Pelican Freud Library*. Vol. 14.

History Matters. *The US Survey Course on the Web* [http://historymatters.gmu.edu/d/5478/] – last consulted Jan. 2006

Kipling, Rudyard (1897) *Plain Tales from the Hills*. Edition de Luxe. *The Writings in Prose and Verse of Rudyard Kipling*, I. London: Macmillan

——. (1987) *Selected Stories*. Ed. by Sandra Kemp. London: Dent, Everyman Classics

——. (1999) *Rudyard Kipling*. OUP: The Oxford Authors

Klingender, Francis D. (1972) *Art and the Industrial Revolution*. Frogmore: Granada Publishing

Lycett, Andrew (1999) *Rudyard Kipling*. London: Weidenfeld & Nicholson

Marx, Karl (1973) *Surveys from Exile*. Harmondsworth: Penguin

Mengel, Ewald (1983) "The Structure and Meaning of Dickens' 'The Signalman'". *Studies in Short Fiction.* Vol. 20 pp. 271–280

Orwell, George (1986/1942) "Rudyard Kipling". *Decline of the English Murder and Other Essays*, Harmondsworth: Penguin

Todorov, Tzvetan (1975/1970) *The Fantastic A Structural Approach to a Literary Genre*. N.Y.: Cornell University Press

Wilson, Angus (1979/1977) *The Strange Ride of Rudyard Kipling*. Harmondsworth: Penguin

Poetic Means for Social Ends:
Reading Positions in Modernist Interwar Poetry

JESPER TRIER GISSEL

Within the sphere of modernist studies, it has almost become customary to discuss the obvious problem inherent in the term itself. The term 'modernism' seems to denote a poetics which is 'modern', meaning 'contemporary'. Such a poetics would necessarily exist in a continuous flux, constantly moulding itself to fit the needs of its constantly changing social context. Nevertheless, such an interpretation of the term appears stubbornly to persist in reading it in strict accordance with its semantics. When applied to art, modernism is not simply an advocacy for new ideas. It is a term defining a mode of art which, from ca. 1890 to 1930, struggled consciously to restore the bond between humanity and the rapidly advancing technological, industrial, and societal changes which it encountered around the turn of the century.

This article is intended to provide some general insights concerning modernism as a cultural phenomenon and to demonstrate these from a brief discussion on reading positions in modernist poetry from the period between WWI and WWII. The essay will focus exclusively on two of the most prominent writers of the period, namely Thomas Stearns Eliot and William Butler Yeats. As will be apparent through the article, Yeats and Eliot differ radically in their approaches to the problem of modernity. And it is the endeavour of this essay, on the one hand, to highlight the differences between Eliot and Yeats with a point of departure in their respective poetic treatments of reading positions, and on the other, to discuss how the two can still be considered part of the same artistic and cultural tendency. In other words, the article will, by comparing two conspicuously different modernist poets, attempt to illuminate some basic modernist characteristics.

Notice that the article limits itself to discussing the 'early' Eliot up until 1922 and Yeats in the 1920s (his 'fourth period' (Abrams, 1962/1993: 1862)). However, initially the article will present some general observations on modernism and briefly discuss the impact of WWI with regard to the sphere of poetry.

Around 1900, Europe was decidedly the world's dominant economical and political power. It was the hey-day of imperialism and, with the exceptions of Japan and America, the world was largely under the rule of the European empires. By 1900 the British Empire alone stretched over one quarter of the globe's land surface and counted 400 million inhabitants. And, hardly surprisingly, this domination gave the Europeans a firm belief in the cultural and racial superiority of the white races of Europe (Bradbury and McFarland, 1976/1991: 58–62).

In spite of the mounting tensions between the major powers in Europe, the pre-war years in England were characterized by a feeling of ease and security if one belonged to the upper class or the substantial middle-class which had emerged during the Victorian period (if one belonged to the working class the feeling was more one of poverty and the various inconveniences this affected). At the time, it was those belonging to middle-class which were the primary consumers of art and therefore also to some extent dictated artistic taste. This dominant middle-class still adhered to the artistic modes of the nineteenth century and was highly critical towards the massive artistic experimentations and philosophical upheavals which had been instigated in Europe during the 1880s and which may be regarded as the advent of modernism. It seems that the comfortable position which had been attained by the middle class in its struggle to gain foothold above the working class was not to be disturbed by any form of commotion within any sphere. The position of the middle class was still quite new and throughout its materialization it had exhibited a still growing awareness of its own position establishing a culture, an art, and a mode of Christian worship of its own. Any attacks on these categories which served as the ideological foundations of the middle class were treated as threats to its position. And, accordingly, modernist experimental art remained a peripheral phenomenon in its early years reaching only a very limited audience, often considered depraved bohemians or worse.

Modernist art, as we understand it today, did not gain foothold as a dominant cultural phenomenon until after WWI. Initially, the war was considered a minor conflict and, by many, expected to be over by Christmas. In some instances the declaration of war was even greeted with cheers (Bradbury and McFarland, 1971/1991: 61). However, as we know, the war grew vastly beyond the initial expectations and, when it ended in 1918, it left a Europe which was radically different from the one it had seized four years previously. The security and ease which had prevailed in the pre-war years was gone and modern society's potential for chaos and destruction had been disclosed. It was this potential which had been sensed, addressed, and even embraced by philosophers such as Nietzsche and artists such as Duchamp and Alfred Jarry. The war had revealed the relevance of these modernist artistic experimentations, paving the way for modernist art to enter dominant culture and manifest itself as a genuine cultural response to contemporary modernity.

The period from 1880 and up towards WWII was characterized by an art which to a hitherto unseen degree tested the limits and conventions of what was considered proper and wholesome. The cultural capitals, and especially Paris, became the cradle of what has since been known as the 'avant-garde'. One of the main features of this self-proclaimed avant-garde was rebellion against everything which was regarded as conventional and proper. The bourgeoisie was considered shallow and hypocritical and their preferred art a result of, and an aiding factor in, this shallowness and hypocrisy. In effect, the avant-garde assaulted the bourgeoisie on all fronts in the form of art and happenings which occasionally bordered on terrorism.

The avant-gardists felt an immediate need for social upheaval and their art reflected this need in abundance. Most famous is probably Duchamp's sculpture *Fountain by R. Mutt* (1917) which is simply a signed urinal on display. It is easy to see how this 'sculpture' constitutes a provocation of basically any preconception about what is in good taste and what art is; the subject matter is purposely obscene and producing it required no artistic skill whatsoever. This is not the place to scrutinize this avant-garde 'masterpiece' in any further details. It is mentioned here simply to provide an idea of the artistic milieu in Europe at the time. Not all avant-garde artistic revolts were as extreme as Duchamp's *Fountain*. However, its characteristics include irrationality, infantilism, and primitivism, and the period fostered probably the most pronounced and radical artistic revolution ever to have taken place.

In England, nonetheless, all this radicalism never really reached the extremes which could be observed in Paris, Rome, Berlin, Bucharest etc. There may be a number of explanations for this. One is suggested by Poggioli in his *The Theory of the Avant-Garde* (1968), namely that there was a difference between continental Europe and Anglo-America regarding their relation to tradition and their tradition for novelty and surprise (8). Whatever the reason, the prominent British artists of the period engaged in the problem of modernity with less radical means. Britain did present a number of artistic radicals (e.g. the Vorticist movement) but the poets and authors rising to public fame and critical acclaim (especially after WWI) were to a large degree associated with a group of writers known as the 'high modernists'.

With the poet Ezra Pound as a sort of 'anchor-person' the group counted renowned artists such as Virginia Woolf, James Joyce, T.S. Eliot, and W.B. Yeats. The high modernists were not a group in the traditional sense. In fact, the only true common denominator seems largely to have been personal acquaintance with Ezra Pound and a firm belief in the power of poetical brilliance. As will be evident later, these modernists' artistic and theoretical production often varies quite distinctly, and especially Yeats exhibits many views on poetry directly conflicting even with Pound's. Nevertheless, as we shall see, Yeats addresses the same problems as the others and with a very different but still conspicuous complexity and technical brilliance. He thus emerges as highly valuable in illustrating the rich variety of the modernist endeavour.

The interwar period became the period in which the high modernists entered as the dominant writers of the Anglo-American art-scene. To the modernist artist, modern society's main characteristic was chaos and WWI was considered a result of the spiritual imbalance in Europe in the years prior to the war. In effect, WWI played a major part in the art of the years succeeding it by becoming a symbol of what was wrong with modern society. Apart from Europe's proven potential for horrific acts of war, scientific, technological, and societal progress had caused former hierarchical structures to deteriorate. In particular the loss of religion as the dominating authority (on life, the universe, and everything else) left modern man in a meaningless spiritual wasteland. Consequently, the spirituality of modern man was considered almost catastrophically out of tune with his actual physical and societal context. He no longer had any means of dealing with life since 'truth' was now dictated from a rational, scientific authority which presented only facts and no comfort or moral guidance. And it was only natural to regard the war as a symptom of this modern lack of moral guidance and spiritual imbalance.

Consequently, the principal characteristic of modernist poetry became a conscious dealing with the gap perceived to exist between modern man and modern society. Technological and societal progress had superseded man's spiritual development and the high modernist poets made the restoration of balance between the two their personal quest. From this perspective, it is hardly surprising that modernist poets frequently emphasized the poet/reader relationship in their work. Since the endeavour emerged as a spiritual 'training' or 'teaching' of modern man, it follows naturally that the artists developed an idea of art's position in relation to its public and, hence, also their own function in this regard.

The modernist era, and the interwar years especially, presented a unique climate for art to prove its worth. And several modernist poets lunged at the opportunity to inaugurate art as the one thing which could train modern man to encounter the chaos perceived to surround him. We will now turn to Yeats and Eliot. Through a presentation of some basic characteristics of their respective poetics, the essay will present their ideas of the reader's position vis-à-vis the poem, art, and society in general and discuss how they each approach the task of teaching the public how to cope with its contemporary world.

It should be quite obvious that the nature of the modernist ambition as described above precipitates a high level of involvement in spheres beyond the artistic. The modernist artist can in fact partly be characterized by his insistence that art did not simply reflect its contemporaneity; it had the power, if not the obligation, to influence its readers and, on a broader scale, society as such. Nevertheless, as mentioned, modernist artists rarely shared the same ideas of how and what the public should be taught. T.S. Eliot and W.B. Yeats represent two very different stances of modernist thinking and writing and we will now turn to examining the two poets', in some regards, even contrasting modernist projects.

Metaphorically, Eliot's poetics can be classified as 'scientific'. As can be observed in his theoretical work, Eliot was extraordinarily focused on what is factual and frequently advocates what he coins 'an escape from emotion'. Occasionally, he even employs scientific metaphors as explanatory imagery when presenting his poetic ideals. The perhaps most readily conceivable example of his use of scientific imagery can be found in his "Tradition and the Individual Talent" (1919). Here, he explains the position of the poet in relation to truth and imagery as that of a 'catalyst', meaning that, ideally, the poet should fuse language and truth into poetry without revealing any signs of his own personality in his work[1].

Apart from hinting at Eliot's affiliation with the terminology of natural science, the metaphor also reveals a number of the most important facets of his early poetics. As mentioned above, the catalyst metaphor illuminates Eliot's call for an impersonal poetics. In Eliot's renowned phrase, he coins the sublime poetic expression an 'objective correlative' (Eliot, 1932/1999: 145). Basically, the term expresses the ideal that poetry should be able to invoke the same feeling in any recipient regardless of his or her background. Utopian as this ideal may seem, Eliot actually held that instances of such objective correlatives may be found in some of Shakespeare's work. But he was also keenly aware that Shakespeare's social and historical context differed radically from his own and, in effect, Shakespeare's poetic strategies could not simply be copied. They needed to evolve and be made relevant to whichever context they would emerge. And, since Eliot found himself in an increasingly complex and modern society, poetry should produce "various and complex results" (Eliot 1932/1999, p. 289). In other words, society evolves and so should poetry in order to correspond to it.

A further implication of Eliot's catalyst metaphor is that it connotes the peculiar notion that 'truth' and 'language' are inherently bound together (an idea which can be linked to Wittgenstein's early philosophy such as presented in his *Tractatus* (1921/1922)). To contemporary readers, even the notion of 'truth' emerges as highly problematic in itself. Nevertheless, just as science produces truth through facts, so Eliot considered language a 'perfect' construct and, in the hands of the capable poet, an authoritative mediator of objective truth. This conviction is what constitutes the 'quasi-religiousness' of Eliot's poetry. Eliot's work exhibits a strong sense of 'inherent truth' or 'epistemological closure' which resembles religious faith. Eliot's poetics is, so to speak, based on the conviction that the world 'makes sense', that it works according to a specific pattern or 'essence' which, in itself, contains transcendent 'truths' about, e.g. moral conduct. This 'essence' is what the capable poet may reveal and teach to the masses and he thus assumes a function resembling that of a clergyman or priest. In this

---

1 Eliot explains how 'catalyst' is the chemical term for a component which triggers a reaction between two other components without itself either changing or leaving traces of itself (Eliot, 1932/1999: 18).

way, Eliot perceives truth inherent in language. If the poet attains the pure 'objective correlative' he will inevitably be mediating truth.[2]

The result of Eliot's insistence on objectivity is an analytically highly demanding poetry. Even though Eliot's poetry expresses strong views on e.g. ethics and moral, these subjects are never addressed directly since they must emerge as objective, rather than as Eliot's own. An example of this is *Sweeney Among the Nightingales* (1918/1919).

In this poem, the reader is presented with a bar-scenario in a language loaded with suggestive connotations of murder and gothic horror (most prominently perhaps in Eliot's reference to Poe's *The Raven* (1845) l. 7). The bar-crowd seems to complement the atmosphere by emerging as a particularly depraved gathering of people, most notably 'Apeneck Sweeney' (l. 1) and his two apparently drunk female companions. Nevertheless, nothing interesting or even remotely dramatic happens and the reader is left with suggestions of a murder without knowing whodunit or even who it was 'dun' to (ll. 35–38 allude to the murder of Agamemnon in Greek myth). The immediate suggestion is that Sweeney's female companions are plotting to do away with him. Nevertheless, this suspicion cannot be proven, and only through meticulous analysis is the reader able to discover how it seems to be depravity itself (personified in Sweeney and his companions) which is plotting to do away with common decency, ultimately represented as an innocent passive bystander "the silent man in mocha brown" (l. 17).

The poetic strategy at work here is that the reader is lured into drawing his own conclusions. It is suggested by the poem that, if the reader is able to solve the puzzle, he must also recognize the danger of depraved behaviour and, hence, have discovered the poem's 'objective' message. This analysis is of course a vast simplification but it serves to demonstrate how Eliot's poetry 'proves' its points by involving the reader in the process of separating right from wrong. The reader is invited to judge the situation himself, but he will not arrive at a satisfactory conclusion before he has taken every aspect into account. He has thus been 'taught', not only to separate right from wrong, but also always to consider every aspect in order to draw the

---

2   In relation to these observations concerning the quasi-religious aspects of Eliot's work consider e.g. his positioning of the poet in opposition to the "practical and active person" in "Tradition and the Individual Talent" (Eliot, 1932/1999: 21).

'right' conclusions. And Eliot has thus 'disguised' the poem's message as objective/inherent rather than his own.[3]

Lastly, it should be emphasized that the poem's message goes far beyond decent behaviour. Thus, it is no coincidence that the 'victim' is a passive bystander. Eliot's ideas of dealing with a depraved society are characterized by the insistence that man does have an obligation to confront the problems of his society. If he remains passive, he will be done away with by what he should have dealt with immediately.

From this analysis, Eliot's poetry does not seem provocative or radical in any sense and he may in fact probably be considered the most conservative poet within the British modernist paradigm. However, *Sweeney Among the Nightingales* is also definitely less provocative in its address to the public than some of his earlier other poems. *The Love Song of J. Alfred Prufrock* (1917) contains so many indications of cross-dressing, voyeurism, and perverse sexual conduct that, initially, critics openly declared that Eliot must be an insane and deeply perverted individual. However, the provocations seem to fade from Eliot's work and, therefore, we can observe his tendency to increasingly trying to reach his public rather than, as with the avant-garde, continuously distancing himself from it through provocation. We are, in Eliot, dealing with a seemingly honest (however often rather patronizing) endeavour to teach the public. And, indeed, when his famous and infamous poem *The Waste Land* was published in 1922 it became an instant bestseller despite its highly complex structure (which probably made the poem completely inaccessible to most readers).

Yeats' project is radically different. Where all essentials in Eliot's poetry are veiled as a result of his objective poetics, Yeats' seems much straighter to the point regarding his religious or mystic convictions. He openly declared his belief in ghosts and spirits and went so far as to publish his personal 'bible' titled *A Vision* in 1925. It is not of any immediate relevance here to venture an in-depth account of this highly complex work, which postulates 28 incarnations or phases of man and is based on the relations between 'will', 'creative mind', 'mask', and 'body of faith'. Presently, the interest lies in Yeats' own perception of its production.

As Yeats explains in his introduction, the work on *A Vision* was initiated by Yeats's wife's attempts at automatic writing and her talking in her sleep.

---

3   In connection with *Sweeney Among the Nightingales*, it is interesting to note how the 'whodunit-atmosphere' seems complimented by Eliot's insistence on the analytic praxis as 'fact-finding' (Eliot 1932/1999: 31. "The Function of Criticism").

Yeats believed that, in both conditions, spirits or ghosts spoke through her and he held that the rest of *A Vision* was written with the aid of such spirits (Yeats, 1925/1974: 8–25). The extent to which Yeats is reliable in this account and his frequently proclaimed belief in ghosts is of course debatable. It has been suggested that *A Vision* merely constitutes a useful manual for Yeats' imagery and symbols, a, for Yeats, convenient or even 'easy' way of presenting an ordered reality which was more apt for poetic treatment than the real world (Sidnell, 1996: 111). Nevertheless, in spite of this not entirely implausible idea (which could find support in the lengthy and subtly ironic introduction to *A Vision*), it seems that approaching Yeats on his own terms presumes a recognition of Yeats' sincerity when engaging in matters of spirituality. The alternative emerges as a simplification in itself of Yeats and his work, committing an error similar to the one of its accusation. Hence, Yeats will here be treated, as Sidnell suggests, namely as a "spiritualist pseudo-poet" (Sidnell, 1996: 10), as a spiritualist who happened to be a poet.

Accordingly, Yeats's positioning of himself in relation to his social context resembles that of Eliot. In the absence of a clerical authority, a poet institutes himself as mediator of truth. Nonetheless, Yeats simply assumes this role rather than advocating it as a 'new' function or task for poetry in general. His truth is not poetically based and therefore the poet is not necessarily the mediator of truth. It should be noted that, even if Yeats's position, as analysed here, is not necessarily an ambition on behalf of poetry in general, he did express an immense belief in poetry's influential power. In 1936, he commented on the European political situation at the time:

> Communist, Fascist, nationalist, clerical, anti-clerical, are all responsible according to the number of their victims. I have not been silent; I have used the only vehicle I possess – verse. If you have my poems by you, look up a poem called *The Second Coming*. It was written some sixteen or seventeen years ago and foretold what is happening […] This will seem little to you with your strong practical sense, for it takes fifty years for a poet's weapons to influence the issue. (Marcus, 2001: 177–178)

In association with the present discussion, it is imperative to note, how Yeats puts himself first. *He* has opinions which *he* expresses in poetry. For Yeats, poetry is a tool rather than, as with Eliot, an elevated sphere of potential objective truth. A comparison between Eliot's essays and Yeats' *A Vision* is a highly complex task, especially in terms of deixis. Here, it is sufficient to observe how the poets place themselves in the positions of elevated spiritual guides. And both Yeats and Eliot can thus be shown consciously to adhere to a quasi-religious poetics, albeit, with a conspicuous difference in project.

Additionally, the quotation shows how Yeats maintains that he has foretold the mounting tensions of the 1930s in Europe and, thus, the quotation displays little doubt concerning Yeats's faith in poetry's influential power. Yeats's confidence in poetry is very similar to Eliot's. Nevertheless, Yeats seems to address his issues much more unswervingly and, hence, his status as a modernist is readily conceivable. He openly engages in the problems of his age by means of his position and abilities as a poet.

From a contemporary perspective, Eliot's project would probably be considered the less far-fetched of the two (most notably due to the lack of ghosts). Nevertheless, this fact makes it all the more interesting that, examining the results of the two respective quasi-religious points of departure, Yeats's ghosts actually appear to conjure up the more digestible poetics. The crucial point here is Eliot's insistence on objectivity. It is highly unlikely that a contemporary reader will accept the notion of a completely objective poetics, and neither does Yeats.

In *A Vision*, he promotes his notion that the world constantly oscillates between subjectivity and objectivity., which he illustrates with his famous gyres (funnel-shaped spirals reaching into each other). According to this theory, one will never conquer the other. To Yeats, pure objectivity or subjectivity is an inhuman and impossible condition. The dynamism of the world is kept alive by the constant struggle between such dichotomies, not by the victory of one over the other.

Interestingly, in connection with this, Yeats makes reference to an earlier prominent 'mystic poet', namely William Blake: "Contraries are positive", wrote Blake, "a negation is not a contrary" (Yeats, 1925/1974: 72). In *A Vision* Yeats also demonstrates how he perceives this flux working in relation to his 28 incarnations or lunar phases, in one of which all people are born. This is mentioned here primarily to provide an idea of the complexity of his system, which continues to puzzle and excite readers with an affinity for the occult. E.g. the internet features a large number of websites dedicated to explaining *A Vision*.

As is obvious, Yeats's truth differs radically from Eliot's even if it is the product of a similar urge to order a chaotic reality. Eliot wanted to teach society about objective truth through poetry. Yeats presents a complex system which explains the composition and dynamics of the world. But the system in itself offers no guidelines on moral conduct. Such guidelines are present in *A Vision* but they are not inevitable truths ratified or 'proven' by the system. They are comments on how man may deal with each phase or incarnation. The descriptions of each phase thus contain information about the right and wrong way of 'living' the phase (being "out of phase" or "true to phase"). And it is from these descriptions that Yeats's ideas of morals emerge. In contrast to Eliot, they are simply printed directly and are not veiled as the inevitable consequence of poetic purity and epistemological closure.

Not surprisingly, the respective moral ideals of Eliot and Yeats also differ significantly. Again, this is not a topic to be discussed at great length but it is definitely noteworthy how Eliot's moral ideal exhibits a strong resemblance to a Christian moral code (against excessive drinking and depraved behaviour as shown in *Sweeney Among the Nightingales*). Consider also how Eliot's ideals must be striven for, just as a devoted Christian must constantly strive towards a saint-like purity through restrictions. With Yeats, such ideals are not present. Where Eliot attempts to move poetry to a purer level of objectivity, thereby motivating a move in society towards a higher level of moral, Yeats describes a system of the world which is constant. The individual is not called upon to purify himself. Man inevitably lives his phases and can only seek to make the best of his situation. Being "true to phase" is not a utopian undertaking. Nonetheless, in an ideal world everybody should be true to phase and, hence, Yeats does in some form employ what must be regarded a utopian undertaking.

Since Yeats's project is not poetic but 'religious/philosophical', his project does not govern his poetical method to the same extent as with Eliot. Rather, as discussed above, Yeats's message emerges in the form of content (hence the previous classification of Yeats as a 'spiritualist pseudo-poet'). Naturally, this results in a very different poetry. A luminous example of this can be found in Yeats's previously mentioned poem *The Second Coming* (1921) (Yeats, 1933/1952: 210–211).

The title itself is a direct reference to Yeats's notion of continuous flux between contraries (e.g. subjectivity and objectivity). The world moves towards one extreme, but at some point the movement reverses and the movement is then repeated towards the opposite. The world thus functions as a repetitive pattern and *The Second Coming* refers to a nearby reversal of this movement, an approaching radical change. The initial three lines present the idea that something is wrong, that something has gotten out of hand ("Things fall apart; the centre cannot hold" l. 3). The poem then establishes the scale and nature of the problem ("Mere anarchy is loosed upon the world" l. 4) and the following four lines present a frightening and bloody image which it is impossible not to connect with the historical context of post WWI. Especially, if one considers Yeats' early draft of the poem in which lines 5–6 read "The Germans are […] now to Russia come/ Though every day some innocent has died" (Bloom, 1970: 318) which, in the final version was changed to "The blood-dimmed tide is loosed, and everywhere/ The ceremony of innocence is drowned". Yeats's inspiration for the poem seems definitely rooted in the horrors of the war. However, Yeats chose the more dense sustained metaphor of the bloody tidal wave. Potentially this was also done in order to liberate the poem from contemporary historical anchorage and thus ensure a more generalized aim of the poem's message.

The second stanza initiates with an exclamation of the hope that the tide is about to change, that "The Second Coming is at hand" (l. 10). The words themselves seem to motivate a vision of the long awaited revelation and lines 11 to 20 are dedicated to describing it. The vision is that of a Sphinx which is awoken and the poem thus seems to suggest that Christianity (or perhaps rather the society it has spawned) is in for substitution by ancient religions. This new religion, personified in the Sphinx, carries a number of connotations of cruelty, and its followers are indicated to be nothing less than vultures (l. 18).

From line 18 to 22 the poet speaker digresses from the vision and turns to contemplate its consequences. The poet speaker deduces that the image was of a near future and the sphinx emerges as an image of an inevitable force which will soon rise in some form or other (the concluding question of the poem (ll. 21–22) emphasizes the indefinite nature of this inevitable force).

Initially, the feeling evoked is one of fear and uncertainty and it is possible that the reader will interpret the vision as pro-Christian. Nevertheless, the concluding lines of the poem seem to blur this notion. Apparently, the "rough beast" must reach Bethlehem in order to be born. This strange statement serves somehow to draw a parallel between the sphinx and Christ. Therefore, the indication seems to be that Christ and the sphinx inhabit similar qualities. The information about the sphinx appears negative and frightening, but it is provided by a poet speaker who simply recognizes a massive force but does not understand it. The sphinx is described to the reader by a voice of ignorance. This is especially prominent in that the poet speaker never uses the term 'sphinx' but simply describes a creature which could not possibly be anything else ("somewhere in the sands of the desert" (l. 13), and "the shape of a lion and the head of a man" (l. 14)). The sphinx is new and, as of yet, a mystery of tremendous power. The same may be said of Christ at the beginning of his 'reign' before Christianity rose as a dominant factor in western civilisation. And thus it seems that the Sphinx and Christ are subjected to the same overall tendency, namely being contraries who will inevitably substitute each other with certain intervals (in *A Vision* Yeats even provides a time table displaying how his phases work in relation to historical time (266)).

Hence, it seems that the poet speaker has reached a state where he can recognize the chaos of his own 'Christian' contemporaneity. Christianity has progressed to a state where it is in dire need of substitution, it has gone out of hand (also illuminated by the poet speaker being unable to recognize the sphinx, meaning that he has completely lost touch with preceding religious traditions). The poet speaker expresses the final stage of 'pure Christianity' before it, as a consequence of the inevitable dynamic of the world, must fall into decline.

As is obvious, Yeats's ideas on Christianity and its 'replacement' could be discussed at great length. (Bohlman (1982: 178–179) makes a great effort at interpreting the replacement as a Nietzschean reality) However, the focus here is primarily to show how Yeats's and Eliot's respective philosophical orientations result in two significantly different poetics. As the analysis above shows, Yeats's subject matter is addressed directly. The poem does call for a certain amount of interpretation but the main topic is launched immediately and then treated through a three-section structure (problem (ll. 1–10) – vision (ll. 11–17) – understanding (ll. 18–22)). Interpretation leads to a deeper and more profound understanding of Yeats's vision, but it is not necessary in order to grasp the general idea of the poem. Eliot's poem remains almost enigmatic until a thorough investigation has taken place, even drawing a parallel between the 'victim' ('the silent man in mocha brown') and an analyst satisfying himself with the explanation that Sweeney's companions are plotting against him (they "Are suspect, thought to be in league" l. 26). The inadequate reader is 'murdered' by the poem.

Nevertheless, Yeats's straightforwardness does not exclude the presence of a 'poet-truth-recipient' model. The poet speaker of *The Second Coming* may in fact be regarded as a poet. The question of whether or not this poet is identical with Yeats must rest with the individual critic. However, it seems indisputable that the poem expresses a personal vision or epiphany on the part of Yeats, since the poet speaker refers directly to Yeats's rather idiosyncratic terminology ('*Spiritus Mundi*' l. 12) and world image (l. 1).

Therefore, when this essay has previously suggested that the voice of the poem was 'ignorant' due to its failure to recognize the sphinx as a sphinx, it should be added that this also serves to establish a feeling of immediacy, fear, and wonder. Not analysing what he sees and concluding that it is a sphinx, the poet speaker simply conveys his immediate impressions then and there, whereby he pulls the recipient as close to the poet speaker's feelings when encountering the vision as possible. The passage becomes an image of his feeling of wonder, uncertainty, and powerlessness, a versification of near speechlessness standing before the inevitable turning of the tide. Notice also how the 'purity' of the passage (meaning its immediacy and lack of interpretative effort) conveys a feeling of one side being 'missing'. There is an abundance of one thing (the overwhelming feeling encountering the vision) but a complete lack of ability to convey an interpreted or rationalised version of it. The poet is standing where one force has completely prevailed over the other and is about to begin its demise.

In this way, Yeats's choice of imagery and technique serves to illuminate, not only the poet's, but also the recipient's place in the poem. By accentuating the immediacy and overwhelming nature of the vision, Yeats establishes the poet's role as mediator and the importance of the vision to the reader. Yeats involves the reader by letting him or her 'experience' the vision and interpret it for himself. Accordingly, Yeats has, in a manner similar to Eliot's, involved the reader in the process of interpretation. However, Yeats's peculiar technique causes the reader to automatically engage in the interpretative process. Few readers would not recognize the sphinx for what it is and determining it becomes the first step in disclosing the deeper levels of the poem. So, where *Sweeney Among the Nightingales* inevitably 'loses' a vast amount of its readers due to its complexity, *The Second Coming* actually seems to invite and even prompt the reader to seek a more profound understanding.

From this discussion, it is obvious that both Eliot and Yeats consciously entered the struggle to align modern man with his contemporaneity. The two poets share a profound confidence in the power of their art and, despite their considerable poetic differences, they can both be shown to attempt to activate their readers by incorporating them in their poetic structures. Furthermore, both poets position themselves as the mediators of each their idea of inherent truth. And, especially in the case of Eliot, it was possible to determine a correlation between his philosophy/truth and his poetics, since his ideal of objectivity transcended to all aspects of his work, both poetic and theoretical.

We may then ask if the same relationship is present in Yeats. This question is more problematic. Nevertheless, we may close in on an answer by pointing to the freedom Yeats is allowed by not sharing Eliot's idea of truth and poetry inevitably being interlinked. In terms of subject matter, *The Second Coming* is not representative of Yeats's entire poetics. It is the result of a reaction to a specific problem encountered at the time. Naturally, Yeats also constantly circles the subject of inherent truth, but the mere fact that he allows himself to be visible as the poet behind the verse shows how he is less limited by his philosophy/truth than Eliot. Whereas Eliot's poetics presumes that he will always, to some degree, be addressing the major issue of inherent truth, Yeats is more at liberty to address whatever issue he wishes. However, as this essay has shown, they both partook in the same effort to train the modern European to meet the challenges of his contemporaneity.

References

Bloom, Harold (1970) *Yeats*. London: Oxford University Press

Bohlman, Otto (1982) *Yeats and Nietzsche*. New Jersey: Barnes and Noble Books

Bradbury and McFarlane (1976/1991) *Modernism; A Guide to European Literature 1830–1930*. London: Penguin

Eliot, Thomas Stearns (1920/1997) *The Sacred Wood*. London: Faber and Faber

———. (1936/1963) *Collected Poems 1909–1962*. London: Faber and Faber

———. (1951/1999) *Selected Essays*. London: Faber and Faber

Kirschner and Stillmark (1992) *Between Time and Eternity*. Amsterdam – Atlanta: Rodopi

Marcus, Philip L. (2001) *Yeats and Artistic Power*. NY: Syracuse University Press

Sidnell, Michael J. (1996) *Yeat's Poetry and Poetics*. London: Macmillan Press

Williams, Louise Blakeney (2002) *Modernism and the Ideology of History*. Cambridge: Cambridge University Press

Yeats, William Butler (1925/1974) *A Vision*. London: Macmillan Press

———. (1961/1974). *Essays and Introductions*. London: Macmillan Press

Imagining Ireland:
The Cultural Space of the Irish Free State

Lene Yding Pedersen

Seamus Deane has suggested that in the first decades of the 20th century Ireland became a new "cultural space" (Deane, 1994: 140). The first decades of the 20th century also witnessed the establishment in 1922 of the Irish Free State. In this essay I will discuss some of the connections between a new cultural space and a new nation in the Irish context.

In order to do that I will focus on the literary movement known as the Irish Revival or the Celtic Renaissance, the status of the Irish and the English Languages, and the 'cultural standards' set by the new political authorities as seen in the Censorship of Publication Act of 1929. These three aspects are central for the understanding of the cultural space of the Irish Free State. There are of course other aspects that could be discussed in this connection and which may be said to underlie those matters that I discuss: for instance issues concerning the social and economic conditions of the Irish Free State and the role of the Catholic Church.[1] While acknowledging that the general 'backwardness' of the authorities in the 1920s may have had to do with the social and economic conditions of that time, and that the Censorship Bill of 1929 was related to the new status of the Catholic Church, I have not included these issues in my discussion.

As a framework for my discussion I will consider Benedict Anderson's concept of the nation as an imagined community. Anderson is primarily interested in the general underlying styles of how nations are imagined

---

[1] For a good introduction to the social history of Ireland, see Terence Brown (1985).

and the conditions that make such imagining possible. His focus is, in other words, on "the grammar of nations". What I will do in this essay is to look at the *specific* ideational and thematic contents of such imagining in a particular nation at a particular point in history.

Imagined Communities

In his book *Imagined Communities* Anderson provides the following definition of the nation: [I]t is an imagined political community – and imagined as both inherently limited and sovereign (Anderson, 1991: 6).

What is most significant about Anderson's definition is that the nation is seen as an 'imagined' community. In Anderson's theory 'imagined' refers to the fact that "the members of even the smallest nation will never know most of their fellow-members, meet them, or even hear of them, yet in the minds of each lives the image of their communion" (6). In other words, a nation relies on the fact that a group of people *consider* themselves to form a nation (and behave as if they formed one), and an imagined community is therefore based on its population's self-interpretation. A nation is therefore an imagined construct. According to Anderson, all communities are 'imagined' in this way.[2]

If we then turn to a particular nation we can look at the specific ways and styles in which that community is imagined. Then we see what distinguishes this community. In relation to the Irish Free State we must consider the style(s) in which the new nation was imagined, and who imagined what. Furthermore, we will have to consider people whose ways of imagining an Irish national community differed so much from the majority of the members of that community, that we can no longer assume that they really consider themselves part of it. (This point is not central in Anderson's theory of the nation, but, I believe, follows naturally from it.)

Anderson defines the nation as imagined as both "limited" and "sovereign". By limited he refers to the idea that even the largest of nations have "finite, if elastic, boundaries, beyond which lie other nations" (7). Implied

---

2   Anderson is not the only one to think of nations and nationalism in this way. In *Postnationalist Ireland: Politics, Culture, Philosophy* (1997) Richard Kearney refers to a particular understanding of nationalism as a "hermeneutic construct". Kearney quotes Liah Greenfeld's argument from *Nationalism – Five Roads to Modernity* (1992) that national identity is determined by self-interpretation, that is, with the view which the members of the nation in question have of themselves: "If a particular identity does not mean anything to the population in question, this population does not have this particular identity" (Greenfeld qtd. in Kearney, 1997: 198, n. 20).

in this part of the definition is the understanding that a nation (partly) defines itself negatively; it is *this* nation not *that*, and *this* nation is imagined differently from *that* nation. In the case of the Irish Free State the new nation and the way it was imagined had to show both domestic identity (that which is supposedly particularly Irish) and international difference (that which separates the Irish from the British and/or the European).

That a nation is imagined as "sovereign" is a consequence of the time in which the concept was born. "[T]he concept was born in an age in which Enlightenment and Revolution was destroying the legitimacy of the divinely-ordained, hierarchical dynastic realm" (7). Up through the 17th and 18th centuries the automatic legitimacy of sacral monarchy was questioned in Western Europe, leading to the establishment of nation-states. The dynastic realm which characterized the "political" system of earlier times was hierarchical and centripetal (populations were subjects not citizens as pointed out by Anderson). In the modern conception of the nation "state sovereignty is fully, flatly, and evenly operative over each square centimetre of a legally demarcated territory" (19). For the Irish Free State this meant that it was no longer to be ruled from London and that it could make its own laws without anyone from the outside interfering. Generally, this was seen as a positive and liberating turn. However, some people saw a danger in this because they feared that the sovereignty of the new state could be 'misused'. This misuse would mean that Ireland – in its search for ways of imagining itself – would become detached from the rest of Europe and the world. We shall see examples of that in the discussion of censorship below.

Finally, Anderson defines the nation as a "community". He says, "regardless of the actual inequality and exploitation that may prevail in each, the nation is always conceived as a deep, horizontal comradeship. Ultimately it is this fraternity that makes it possible, over the past two centuries, for so many millions of people, not so much to kill, as willingly to die for such limited imaginings" (7). The nation is here defined not as a political entity or a territory but a community relying on comradeship and fraternity. To speak of nations in terms of communities stresses the active roles of its members and – again – the ways in which they consider themselves part of such communities. That there have been innumerable killings and deaths for the imagined community of Ireland is beyond doubt, but this is not what we will be concerned with here. In relation to the Irish Free State as an imagined community we shall look at the ways in which different groups of its members each in their own ways imagined their community.

And we may ask the question whether it is the same community they imagined.

According to Anderson nationalism cannot be understood in the light of self-consciously held political ideologies, but by aligning it with the large cultural system that preceded it (12). Nationality, nation-ness and nationalism are cultural artefacts of a particular kind. Anderson links the possibility of imagining the nation to changes within three cultural conceptions concerning, first, the religious community, second, the dynastic realm, and third, the apprehension of time.

Anderson suggests that the imagined communities of nations that appeared towards the end of the 18th century has to be thought of in relation to the decomposition of religious communities and dynastic realms – two cultural systems that were as self-evidently plausible in their time as nationality is today (12). Furthermore he suggests that we must consider a change in the apprehension of time. This new apprehension of time is based on a conception of simultaneity. It is "marked not by prefiguring and fulfilment, but by temporal coincidence, and measured by clock and calendar" (24). "So deep-lying is this new idea that one could argue that every essential modern conception is based on a conception of 'meanwhile'" (24, n.34). This conception of time made the imagining of nations possible because the imagined community of a nation involves the simultaneous existence of large number of individuals. To explain this change Anderson discusses two forms of imagining which first appeared in Europe in the 18th century: the novel and the newspaper. "For these forms provided the technical means for 're-presenting' the kind of imagined community that is the nation" (25). By including the novel and the newspaper Anderson establishes a connection between a particular apprehension of time, certain *ways* or *styles* of imagining, and the nation.

According to Anderson the "old-fashioned novel" relies on the idea of "meanwhile". The characters in a novel are embedded in 'societies' "of such firm and stable reality that their members (A and D) can even be described as passing each other on the street, without ever becoming acquainted, and still be connected" (25). These societies are the imagined world conjured up by the author in the reader's mind (26). The characters themselves can be largely unaware of the other characters and what they do *simultaneously* – it is only the reader who can see all the acts at once. The formal structures of the novel therefore offer the space of a community.³ This is a situation which mirrors that of the nation as an imagined community:

> The idea of a sociological organism moving calendrically through homogeneous, empty time is a precise analogue of the idea of the nation, which also is conceived as a solid community moving steadily down (or up) history. An American will never meet, or even know the names of more than a handful of his 240.000-odd fellow Americans. He has no idea of what they are up to at any one time. But he has complete confidence in their steady, anonymous, simultaneous activity. (Anderson, 1991: 26)

Likewise, Anderson analyzes the newspaper as a cultural product. To the question of what it is that connects the various stories in a newspaper, Anderson suggests that obviously most of them happen independently without the actors being aware of each other or of what the others are up to. In this respect the newspaper relies on the same conception of "meanwhile" as the novel does, and Anderson speaks of the "novelistic format of the newspaper" (33). The linkage between the various stories is not only based on chance but derives from two sources: first, calendrical coincidence, and second, the relationship between the newspaper, as a form of book, and the market. The date at the top of the newspaper provides the first essential connection. The fact that newspapers, like books, are objects that were reproduced in very large numbers makes Anderson consider them the first modern-style mass-produced industrial commodity (34). Just as the stories in the newspaper are connected through their calendrical coincidence, so the reading of the newspaper is largely coincidental. There is an almost precisely simultaneous consumption (imagining) of the newspaper in the sense that it is read on this day and not that. And even though the specific reader of the newspaper reads his newspaper in silent privacy, he is still aware that exact replicas of his own paper are, at largely the same time, being consumed by many other people, "of whose existence he is confident, yet of whose identity he has not the slightest notion" (35). This makes Anderson conclude, "What more vivid figure for the secular, historically clocked, imagined community can be envisioned?" (35)

In Anderson's argument there is a formal *analogy* between the space-time presumed by the old-fashioned novel and newspapers and the imag-

---

3 In a critical essay on Anderson's theory Jonathan Culler stresses the fact that it is the formal *structure* of the novel and not a specific national *content* that links the novel to the imagining of nations – even though Anderson in his own analyses focuses on novels with a particularly 'national' plot (Culler, 1999: 20–39).

ined community of a nation. Likewise, the community of readers of a novel or a newspaper is a *model* for the imagined community of a nation. The old-fashioned novel which Anderson speaks of is the novel of the 17th and 18th centuries. These were also the centuries in which nations emerged. However, the Irish Free State emerged at a different point in history, and the cultural space of the Irish Free State was constructed at a time when the structural forms of the novel underwent some dramatic changes. Later on in this essay I shall return to this idea of an analogy between the formal structure of the novel and the nation. Before that, we must look at some of the ways and styles of 'imagining' the nation that formed the cultural space of the Irish Free State.

The Irish Revival/The Celtic Renaissance

Anderson sees the nation as an imagined construct based largely on narratives, myths and symbols. He argues that nationalism was a needed style of imagining as religious belief lost its grip on men's minds:

> Disintegration of Paradise: nothing makes fatality more arbitrary. Absurdity of salvation: nothing makes another style of continuity more necessary. What then was required was a secular transformation of fatality into continuity, contingency into meaning. As we shall see, few things were (are) better suited for this end than an idea of nation. (Anderson, 1991: 11)

Nations always loom out of an immemorial past and at the same time they glide into a limitless future.

The second half of the 19th century in Ireland witnessed an 'Irish Revival' or a 'Celtic Renaissance', and in 1893 the Gaelic League was founded. In this revival there was s strong focus on Celtic myths and folktales. The Irish revival marked an increasing awareness of a Celtic identity as distinct from the English. In relation to this, the Revival acknowledged a Celtic literary past which was seen as the true foundation for a contemporary Irish literature. In 1893 W.B. Yeats published *The Celtic Twilight*, a collection of Irish folktales. By collecting and focusing on folk tales and legends (which were primarily oral and therefore in danger of being forgotten), Yeats emphasised what he saw as the need to establish a tradition of Irish literature expressing what would be the basis for an Irish cultural identity.

In Anderson's book we find the issue of the past and its importance discussed in the essay "Memory and Forgetting" (187–206). In his discussion of the curious paradox that nations rely on their members remembering things they at the same time have to have already forgotten, Anderson introduces the idea of the biography of nations. The biography of nations relies on a nation's continuity. This continuity is lost from memory and since it cannot be remembered, it has to be narrated. The biography of nations is in other words a story of a nation's *identity*. This identity (like the biographies of modern persons) is based on a huge modern accumulation of documentary evidence. Anderson mentions photographs, birth certificates, diaries, report cards, letters, medical reports and the like as documentary evidence of a modern person (204). Regarding the nation, Anderson focuses on violent deaths ("exemplary suicides, poignant martyrdoms, assassinations, executions, wars, and holocausts") and emphasizes that "[…] to serve the narrative purpose, these violent deaths must be remembered/forgotten as 'our own'" (206).

If we return to Yeats, we can see his *Celtic Twilight* as an example of documentary evidence and the focus on Celtic myths and folktales as an example of 'reshaping' the imagination towards a national conception of 'Irish', where Celtic culture is seen as Irish and therefore 'our own'. Yeats may be said to add a new kind of documentary evidence to the existing ones of historical facts. There is no reason to believe that the ancient Celts considered themselves Irish in the national sense of the word, but by including them in the Irish literary past, a continuity concerning the national biography of Ireland is constructed. "Yeats's gesture implies that the Irish might have no history without writing, no history without a narrative that would record that history, no history without the recording of narratives, tales, of the Irish folk" (Plug, 1999: 136).

In this passage from the story "By the Roadside" from *The Celtic Twilight* we see some of the connections between history and identity, stories and language:

> Then some of the other men stood up and began to dance, while another lilted the measure they danced to, and then somebody sang *Eiblin a Rúin*, that glad song of meeting which has always moved me more than other songs, because the lover who made it sang it to his sweetheart under the shadow of a mountain I looked at every day through my childhood. The voices melted into the twilight, and were mixed into the trees, and when I thought of the words they too melted away, and were mixed with the generations of men. Now it was a phrase, now it was an attitude of mind, an emotional form, that had carried my memory to older verses, or even to forgotten mythologies. (Yeats, 1959: 138)

Yeats here links the Irish song to both a personal and a national past which looms out of a prior mythology (for a detailed analysis of passage, see Plug). There is therefore a temporal continuity all the way 'back' from the temporally indeterminate forgotten mythologies, over a generational, cultural history of "the generations of men" and the narrator's personal history (his childhood) to the present moment. And it is language itself that establishes this continuity. The voices and the words of the song dissolve into past and at the same time they also bring the past into the present. They become ways of 'remembering' or 'imagining' the continuity between present and past. This gives language a function which is different from 'just' representing things and events already existing. It is language itself which constitutes the mixing and melting of present and past, of personal and cultural, of place and time, of history and myth.[4]

The passage from *The Celtic Twilight* illustrates some of the ways in which the 'twilighters' of the Irish Revival were imagining a national identity based on myth, history and language. In his famous essay on "The Celtic Element in Literature" Yeats writes:

> All folk literature has indeed a passion whose like is not in modern literature and music and art, except where it has come by some straight or crooked way out of ancient times. Love was held to be a fatal sickness in ancient Ireland, and there is a love-poem in the *Love Songs of Connaught* that is like a death cry. (Yeats, 1961: 180)

This passage shows Yeats's dedication to the past and its literatures and his scepticism towards modern literature and art. What is wrong with most of modern literature, in Yeats's view, is that it lacks the "passions and beliefs of ancient times" (185) as well as its myths (Yeats speaks of "the fountain of Gaelic legends" (186). Without this element, literature will be nothing but "a mere chronicle of circumstance, or passionless fantasies, and passionless meditations" (185). To Yeats the past on which the Irish identity rests is more of a mythological past than a historical past. Let us look at one of Yeats's own poems to see how this view on Ireland and its past is thematized.

---

4 In my discussion of the continuity between the past and the present I focus only on the "memory" part of Anderson's discussion of "memory and forgetting". By doing that I am aware that I leave out what is really the most interesting point in his essay, the *connection* between memory and forgetting.

THE FISHERMAN

Although I can see him still,
The freckled man who goes
To a grey place on a hill
In grey Connemara clothes
At dawn to cast his flies,
It's long since I began
To call up to the eyes
This wise and simple man.
All day I'd looked in the face
What I had hoped 'twould be
To write for my own race
And the reality;
The living men that I hate,
The dead man that I loved,
The craven man in his seat,
The insolent unreproved,
And no knave brought to book
Who has won a drunken cheer,
The witty man and his joke
Aimed at the commonest ear,
The clever man who cries
The catch-cries of the clown,
The beating down of the wise
And great Art beaten down.
Maybe a twelvemonth since
Suddenly I began,
In scorn of this audience,
Imagining a man
And his sun-freckled face,
And grey Connemara cloth,
Climbing up to a place
Where stone is dark under froth,
And the down turn of his wrist
When the flies drop in the stream:
A man who does not exist,
A man who is but a dream;
And cried, 'Before I am old
I shall have written him one
Poem maybe as cold
And passionate as the dawn.'
(1919)

This poem may be seen as presenting an opposition between the past and the present, where the fisherman can be read as a personification of ancient or original Ireland, in contrast to whom the present is personified by "the craven man", "the witty man" and "the clever man". The fisherman is wise and simple in contrast to the others, who are craven and insolent (second half of the first stanza). In a sense the fisherman *is* traditional Ireland in that he appears as a part of it. The line "In grey Connemara clothers" (repeated in the second stanza) connects the fisherman to Irish topography (Connemara is in the Western rural part of Ireland). He is silent as the breaking dawn in contrast to the representatives of contemporary modern Irish society, who are loud and rude.

An interesting thing about the fisherman is that he is not real, so we have a contrast not only between ancient and original Ireland and contemporary modern Ireland but also one between image and reality. The fisherman "does not exist" and "is but a dream", and yet he is the poet speaker's alternative to the reality of the second half of the first stanza. Furthermore, and connected to this point, the fisherman comes to illustrate the function of art and literature for the construction of national images. The word that connects the fisherman's existence to the poet speaker is "imagining" (line 28). The poet speaker can "still see" the fisherman, and as an imagined image he *does* exist. The resolute decision in the closing lines of the poem, where the poet speaker promises to write the fisherman a poem, reflects on the poem so far: This is exactly what he has done. Imagined in and through the poem the fisherman does exist, despite the description of him as a man who does not exist and who is but a dream. And what is more, he also exists to the readers of the poem.[5]

The image of ancient and traditional Ireland which is seen in this poem is an example of one of the ways a symbol (or a myth) may function as a way of imagining a nation. It functions as a means of establishing continuity with the past and thereby making it meaningful. The poem also thematizes how art, literature and language play an active part in the process of imagining in that it provides images that the readers of the poem may identify as 'theirs'. Furthermore it suggests a way of being modern which differs from the kind of modernist art and literature which Yeats attacks in the above quote about folk literature vs. modernist art and literature: this poem is perhaps an example of the "except" in that quote (note also that the poem the poet speaker promises to write is *passionate* (closing line) and that passion is one of the things that modernist literature apparently lacks).

The Irish Revival was an important part of the move towards the establishment of the Irish Free State, and Brown suggests that the Celtic League had been perhaps *the* most vital and best-supported cultural movement of the three decades preceding the establishment of the Irish Free State. It had been a nursery for active members of Sinn Féin and the Irish Volunteers of 1916 at the same time as its ideology had a general accept and support in the country at large (Brown, 1985: 39).

This means that we have here a cultural movement which at the same time pushed Ireland towards its modern statehood while also pulling it backwards towards its past. By gathering and cataloguing literary, documentary evidence of Ireland's cultural history, the Celtic revivalists wanted to revive the history of the Irish by re-remembering the 'forgotten' generations and myths. The way of doing that was to focus on Irish art (stories and songs), as Irish art alone was considered able connect the present to both its past and its future. In this way the Irish Revival constructed a space

---

5   I wish to emphasize that this allegorical reading of Yeats's poem is incomplete and does not do full justice to the poem. The purpose here is only to indicate how a symbol or myth may function as a way of imagining a nation in and through literature.

within which a national identity was thematized, and we can therefore see it as a way or style of 'imagining' Ireland.

Language

One of the main aims of the Gaelic League was to spread knowledge of and interest in the Irish language and thus to revive the language. During the 19th century this language was almost eradicated, partly as a result of a "national school" system prohibiting the speaking of Irish, partly as a result of the emigration that followed the Irish Famine of 1845–48. Yet the process of a language shift from the indigenous Irish language to English had been going on since the 17th century. The language shift can be explained both as a result of the fact that English had been the language of opportunities and higher standards of living, and because of immigration from the Irish-speaking parts of the country (Kuha, 1996). In other words, the gradual language shift from Irish to English was based on pragmatic purposes and demographic changes as well as an imposed English policy. In 1926 there were only 257.000 Irish-speakers altogether in the Gaeltacht (the Irish-speaking parts of the country where 80 % or more of the population claimed knowledge of Irish) and the breac-Gaeltacht (the partly Irish-speaking parts of the country where 25–79 % of the population claimed knowledge of Irish) (Brown, 1985: 49).

In the Irish Free State the Irish language was made, officially, the first language of the state. This language was (and is) a minority language which the majority had ceased to speak, and in order to 'revive' Irish as a vernacular language, a radical language policy was initiated in the early 1920s. The most important aspect of this was an attempt to 'Gaelicize' the educational system. This Gaelicization meant that all teachers leaving training colleges should have a knowledge of Irish (no appointments were offered to people who lacked proficiency in Irish); school inspectors were requited to study Irish; and in primary schools all teaching in the first two grades should be in Irish; all singing should be in Irish; the teaching of history and geography should be in Irish; and one hour a day should be spent in direct language acquisition (Brown, 1985: 42).

The language policy of the 1920s failed for several reasons that need not detain us here (see Brown 40–50), and Irish has never become the dominant language in use in Ireland. English is still dominant, albeit a particular Irish kind of English (Hiberno-English). What is interesting when we want to examine the different ways of imagining the community of the

Irish nation in the first decades of the century is *why* the Irish language was given such a high priority.

According to The Gaelic League, Gaelic equalled rurality, purity, and authenticity while English equalled urbanity, decadence and vice (Kearney, 1997: 6). So in order to establish a cultural space and a new national literature free of the things related to the English language, the new nation should base itself on the Irish language. This means that as a language Irish had a strong *symbolic* function. When discussing language and identity Kuha makes a distinction between the communicative and symbolic functions of a language, between "language as a tool for communication and language as a symbol of groupness" (Kuha, 1996: 107). Whereas the learning of the English language in earlier centuries may be seen as the learning of a language with a primarily communicative function (even though it is easy to see that the imposing of English on the Irish *by* the English has an equally important symbolic function), the attempted revival of the Irish language was mainly based on its symbolic function (there was no communicative *need* for Irish as everybody spoke English).[6]

The symbolic function of the Irish language in the new state may be understood in the light of Anderson's definition of the nation as "limited", which means that a nation partly defines itself negatively. The new status of Irish as the official first language of the Irish Free State signalled most of all international difference, or more correctly, difference from England. The domestic identity concerning the Irish language was not just *there* and it had to be revived through a language policy (a policy which the majority agreed on, according to Brown). Paradoxically this part of the Irish domestic identity had to be taught. Furthermore a language provides concrete cultural products such as literature, and the knowledge of Irish would provide an access to the "forgotten" cultural heritage that was inherent in Irish art and literature and which was emphasized by the Celtic Revival. Language therefore also functions as a means for establishing the continuity a national biography relies on.

Yet there are others ways of explaining the dissatisfaction with English felt among the Irish than the 'moral' one advocated by the Celtic League. In his novel *A Portrait of the Artist as a Young Man* James Joyce has his main character, Stephen, reflect on the English language of the Dean, who is an

---

6   Kuha here makes a comparison to the successful revival of Hebrew. This success was based on the communicative need for a common language in the new state of Israel, which had a linguistically heterogeneous population.

Englishman. (Joyce was very suspicious of the Celtic League and its ideology and referred to the Celtic Twilight in *Finnegans Wake* as the "cultic Twalette"):

> – The language in which we are speaking is his before it is mine. How different are the words *home*, *Christ*, *ale*, *master*, on his lips and on mine! I cannot speak or write these words without unrest of spirit. His language, so familiar and so foreign, will always be for me an acquired speech. I have not made or accepted its words. My voice holds them at bay. My soul frets in the shadow of his language. (Joyce, 1960: 189)

Joyce did not want the revival of the Irish language, and he did not consider Irish an alternative to English. But as is apparent from the quote above, Joyce did not feel at home in the English language either.

It has been suggested that Joyce's linguistic inventiveness functions as a way of estranging the English language in a way that destabilizes the imperial authority of English (Corcoran, 1997: 3). Joyce's English, perhaps in particular in *Finnegans Wake* (1939), was a new kind of English which was both familiar and strange. Crudely speaking, Yeats may be seen as representing a traditionalist, nationalist kind of literature whereas Joyce may be seen as representing the urban, European modernist, stylistic revolutionary literature (Brown, 1988: 77–90). Both are important when we consider the cultural space of the Irish Free State – the difference between them is that Yeats saw Ireland as something that was to be reconstituted in writing, whereas Joyce saw it as being constituted for the first time in writing, as also Deane points out.

In addition to Yeats and Joyce, who have been described as "the points of inevitable return" in any writing on Irish literature (Graham, 2001: 54), we should also consider the writings of Flann O'Brien when discussing both the importance of the 'original Ireland' and the Irish vs. the English language for the cultural space of the Irish Free State.

Flann O'Brien was a Celtic scholar and contrary to Yeats and Joyce he actually wrote in Irish. Despite his knowledge of and active use of the Irish language and his dealing with the 'original Ireland' in some of his novels, O'Brien is more correctly to be associated with Joyce than with Yeats – Kearney groups him with "cosmopolitan modernists" such as Joyce, Beckett, and McGreevy (Kearney 1997: 113). (For a more detailed and subtle discussion of the relationship between O'Brien and Joyce see Keith Hopper's 1995 book on Flann O'Brien.) O'Brien's novel from 1941 *An Beal Bocht* (translated into English in 1973 as *The Poor Mouth*) describes the fictive community of "Corkadoragha" situated in the Gaeltacht. According to the preface to the first edition the goal of the novel is that "a little report on the people who inhabit that remote Gaeltacht should be available after their times and also that some little account of the learned smooth Gaelic which they used should be obtainable" (O'Brien, 1993: 7). Yet even before we begin reading the story we realize that this is not the kind of praising description of the unspoiled original Ireland that we saw in Yeats's "The Fisherman". According to the translator of the novel, "putting on the poor mouth" in Gaelic and in Anglo-Irish dialect means "making a pretence of being poor or in bad circumstances in order to gain advantage for oneself from creditors or prospective creditors" (5). The image we get of the 'original' rural Ireland in this novel is a satire of the one we find in the Celtic Revival. Through irony and hyperbole O'Brien provides a counter-image of rural Ireland which assaults the national sentiments of the Irish Revival. In this novel the people of Corkadoragha are constantly eating potatoes in little dark houses while the rain is pouring down outside, and words such as "hard times", "poverty", "drunkenness", "spirits" and "potatoes" are repeated endlessly. This underlying ironic image of the Irish is seen in these lines where the Old-Fellow comments on the English government's decision to pay two pounds a skull for every child that speaks English instead of Gaelic:

> Trying to separate us from the Gaelic they are, praise them sempiternally! I don't think there'll ever be good conditions for the Gaels while having small houses in the corner of the glen, going about in the dirty ashes, constantly fishing in the constant storm, telling stories at night about the hardship and hard times of the Gaels in sweet words of Gaelic is natural to them. (O'Brien, 1997: 35)

Here O'Brien uses the stereotypical image of the Gael in an ironic way through the hyperbolic description of them: they are constantly fishing, it is constantly storming, and the stories they tell themselves are about the (constant) hardship and hard times of the Gaels. When the Old-Fellow hears of the inspector who is in the area counting the children and testing the quality of their English, he provides a further aspect to the image of the Gail through his saying that "there is no cow unmilkable, no hound untraceable, and, also, no money, which cannot be stolen" (35), which reminds us of the title of the novel. The problem for the Old-Fellow is that in his house there is only one child. To solve the problem (and to get the money from the English government) 11 piglets are dressed up as youngsters because, as the Old-Fellow says, "they have vigorous voices, even though their dialect is unintelligible to us. How do we know but that their conversation isn't in English" (36). The inspector (who is an aged crippled man without good sight and who "cared not a whit for the Gaels – no wonder" (37)) arrives and concludes that all is fine and well.

This little story illustrates both O'Brien's ironic and satiric attitude towards both the glorification of the Gaels and the English language policy (and the English language itself, which becomes indistinguishable from the noises of piglets). But neither story nor irony ends here. After the inspector has left the house, the Old-Fellow realizes that there is one piglet missing. It turns out that this piglet (still dressed up) has met a gentleman from Dublin who is extremely interested in Gaelic and who therefore – in Irish Revival fashion – travels the area of Corkadoragha in order to collect the folklore of ancient times (42–43). After the piglet stumbles into a dark house where this gentleman is trying (by means of bottles of spirits) to make some old fellows speak, the following happens:

> […] the gentleman's heart leaped when he heard a great flow of talk issuing from that place. It really was rapid, complicated, stern speech – one might have thought that the old fellow [the piglet] was swearing drunkenly – but the gentleman did not tarry to understand it. He leaped up and set the machine [a gramophone] near the one who was spewing out Gaelic. It appeared that the gentleman thought the Gaelic extremely difficult and he was overjoyed that the machine was absorbing it; he understood that good Gaelic is difficult but that the best Gaelic of all is well-neigh unintelligible. (O'Brien, 1997: 44)

Here it is the Gaelic language which is the object for O'Brien's irony. This language is presented as something quite exotic in the eyes of the gentleman – the more difficult and unintelligible the language, the better. This ironic description of the Gaelic language is taken one step further when we realize that the gentleman takes his gramophone to Berlin, where "[t]hese learned ones said that they never heard any fragment of Gaelic which was so good, so poetic and so obscure as it and that [sic!] were sure there was no fear for Gaelic while the like was audible in Ireland. They bestowed fondly a fine academic degree on the gentleman […]" (44–45).

The Poor Mouth thematizes both the Irish Revival's understanding of rural Ireland as the 'real' Ireland and the attempt to 'revive' the Irish language. It ridicules not only what was thought to be the original people of Ireland but also the scholars interested in them and their stories and language. Furthermore, O'Brien's own use of the Gaelic language parodies the styles of certain Gaelic authors (according to the translator's note). All in all, the novel presents a satire of the Celtic Revival and the Gaelic League. By 'reviving' rural Ireland and the Irish language in this ironic way, O'Brien rejects the ideology of the Revival 'from within'.

At the same time O'Brien may be seen as a representative of the new kind of English both familiar and strange mentioned in relation to Joyce. O'Brien's novel from 1939, *At Swim-Two-Birds*, (written in English) is a strange piece of fiction in which Irish myth (most notably in the figure of Sweeny, who is a figure in Irish literature going back to the ninth century) clashes with modernism (for instance through Joyce's influence on O'Brien's writing) and (post)modern metafiction (this is a novel about a writer writing a novel about a writer writing a novel whose characters end up revolting against their author). In this novel we find another way of 'using' the Irish past and mythology than the one favoured by the Celtic Revival. Here the legendary Sweeny meets with cowboy westerns in a clash of 'high' literature and pulp fiction. We also find O'Brien's own translation into English of the Irish Sweeny material, and the interesting thing in this connection is the way in which this text is juxtaposed with other texts and self-reflexive critical commentary. Out of this comes a different kind of language and text dealing with both the notions of history and language in a way that breaks with the Gaelic Revival, but which none the less presents a revived kind of (English) language.

Both O'Brien examples are from around 1940, which means that they are written at a time when the Irish Free State had been a fact for over a decade. O'Brien's satirical attitude towards the Celtic Revival must be considered in light of this. O'Brien was born in 1911, and he thus belongs to the next generation of Irish writers following Yeats (born 1865) and Joyce (born 1882). Up through the twenties and thirties it became clear that the Irish Free State did not turn out as some of its advocates had hoped it would some decades earlier. However, O'Brien never left Ireland (as many other writers did), and in 1935 he joined the Irish Civil service. Yet he kept on writing about the Irish. For almost thirty years he wrote a daily satirical column under the pseudonym Myles na Gopaleen for the *Irish Times* called "Cruiskeen Lawn" (which O'Brien began in Irish but gradually turned into English as well) – dealing among other things with the "Plain People of Ireland".

In the Irish Free State the language question was an important issue. The attempt to 'de-Anglicize' and 'Gaelicize' the new State can be seen as an example of the symbolic rather than communicative function that a language also has for a population and its sense of forming a community. Together with the renewed interest in the old language there emerged, with Joyce in particular, a need for a new kind of language, which was influenced by modernist currents in the rest of Europe. This idea of a familiar and strange language became extremely important for later writers such as Beckett, who in the 1950s began writing in French which he later translated 'back' into English (The trilogy *Molloy, Malone meurt, L'innommable/ Molloy, Malone Dies, the Unnamable* is an example of this). Kearney is probably right when he says about the Irish language:

> Nor is it the tongue responsible for making Irish writing one of the world's great modern literatures. Joyce, Yeats, Wilde, Kavanagh, Heaney may be haunted by the Gaelic ghost as their souls 'fret in the shadow of the [English] language' – but it is the English language that they speak and write, albeit in a singularly Irish way. (Kearney, 1997: 6)

That "singularly Irish way" is not defined by Kearney, but it obviously has something to do with the far from evident relationship between language(s) and Irish nationality.[7]

The Censorship of Publication Act 1929

As we have seen above, the revival of the Irish language was a major concern for the authorities as well as the Gaelic League once the Irish Free State was a fact. Another thing the government of the Irish Free State did and which came to influence the emergence of a new national literature/ the cultural space of the Irish Free State was to introduce the 'Censorship of Publication Act' in 1929. This Act was to secure that the new national literature as well as that coming from abroad lived up to certain 'standards'. Publications were banned on three grounds: first, they were "in […] gen-

---

7   As early as 1937–38 Beckett stated his unease with language in general and English in particular. In a letter to a German friend he writes that it is becoming more and more difficult, even senseless, for him to write in English. "And more and more my own language appears to me like a veil that must be torn part in order to get at the things (or the Nothingness) behind it …. Let us hope that the time will come, thank God that in certain circles it has already come, when language is most efficiently used where it is being most efficiently misused. As we cannot eliminate language all at once, we should at least leave nothing undone that might contribute to its falling into disrepute." (Beckett, 1983, 171–72). Beckett's thoughts about language here obviously go beyond the question of language and nationality, and it would take us too far to go into a discussion of it here. Suffice it to say that Beckett probably is the one Irish writer in whose writing the question of language is most radically thematized.

eral tendency indecent or obscene", second, they devote "an unduly large proportion of space to the publication of matter relating to crime", and third, they advocate "the unnatural prevention of conception or the procurement of abortion or miscarriage" (Carlson, 1990: 3–4). Behind this Act was the idea that Irish literature and literature read by Irish readers was to counter the 'decadent' tendencies within the European modernist literature of the time.

Right from the beginning the Act was criticized by both writers and critics. In 1928 both Yeats and George Bernard Shaw published essays protesting against censorship in Ireland, apparently in the hope that they could influence public opinion and thus play an active part in establishing the new Irish cultural space. Both saw a danger in how censorship was to be handled, what art would have to be banned if the Censorship Board followed the words of the Act, and what the broader consequences of it might be. In his essay Yeats focuses his critique and warning on the use of the word "indecent", which was defined as including "calculated to excite sexual passion". To illustrate his point of view, Yeats considers the status of religious paintings of Virgin Mary and concludes:

> The lawyers who drew up the Bill, and any member of the Dáil or Senate who thinks of voting for it, should study in some illustrated history of Art Titian's *Sacred and Profane Love*, and ask themselves if there is no one it could incite to 'sexual passion', and if they answer, as they are bound to, that there are many ask this further question of themselves. Are we prepared to exclude such art from Ireland and to sail in a ship of fools, fools that dressed bodies Michael Angelo left naked, Town Councillors of Montreal who hid the Discobulus in the cellar? (Yeats in Carlson, 1990: 132)

Likewise Shaw considers some of the implications of the Act and point to Ireland's new position both in relation to itself and in relation to the rest of the world. He opens his essay this way:

> It is common to assume that there is nothing people like more than political liberty. As a matter of fact there is nothing they dread more. Under the feeble and apologetic tyranny of Dublin Castle [the centre of British administration in Ireland] we Irish were forced to endure a considerable degree of compulsory freedom. The moment we got rid of that tyranny we rushed to enslave ourselves. (Shaw in Carlson, 1990: 133)

Here Shaw suggests that instead of liberating its citizens, the Irish Free State actually enslaves them by denying them 'indecent' publications. Not only does the Act affect and influence the lives of the Irish people in their own nation; it also influences the status of the new Irish in the world around it. Shaw ends his essay with these words:

> The moral is obvious. In the nineteenth century all the world was concerned about Ireland. In the twentieth, nobody outside Ireland cares twopence what happens to her. If she holds her own in the front of European culture, so much the better for her and for Europe. But if, having broken England's grip of her, she slops back into the Atlantic as a little grass patch in which a few million moral cowards are not allowed to call their souls their own by a handful of morbid Catholics, mad with heresyphobia, unnaturally combining with a handful of Calvinists mad with sexophobia (both being in a small and intensely disliked minority of their own co-religionists) then the world will let 'these Irish' go down their own way into insignificance without the smallest concern. It will no longer even tell funny stories about them. (Shaw in Carlson, 1990: 138)

Instead of the moral panic and the general cowardice of the Irish people, Shaw here suggests that Ireland should be *part* of modern European life. The alternative, as he saw it, was that Ireland would become an isolated nation living in a previous century. In other words, Shaw points out the dangers for the Free State to live too much in the past without paying attention to the changes in the modern world around it.

Shaw's concern here illustrates the balance between Ireland, on the one hand, being a sovereign nation with domestic identity and international difference, and, on the other hand, part of a modern world. If the Irish imagined their community only in terms of "the heresyphobia of morbid Catholics" and the "sexophobia of mad Calvinists", they would isolate their nation from the rest of the world. And the cultural space of such a nation would be insignificant to the rest of the world.

Despite the very critical tone in these essays both writers seemed to hope that what they said would be taken seriously by the political authorities or by the public. They present the view that the cultural space of the Irish Free State was still to be defined – or in the process of being defined – and that their opinions mattered and may make a difference.

Up through the thirties writers became more cynical about the effectiveness of protesting against censorship in Ireland, and the fighting spirit of the earlier protests gave way to increasing bitterness and alienation. Liam O'Flaherty was the first writer writing in both English and Irish to have his work banned. This happened in 1930. In 1932 O'Flaherty wrote in *The American Spectator* about the sad conditions in Ireland and how the censorship of books prevented the Irish people from reading anything that might "plant the desire for civilization and freedom" (O'Flaherty in Carlson, 1990: 140). Just as Shaw predicted, the censorship act has influenced the status of Irish culture both within the country and abroad: "And so tortured Ireland, which a few years ago asked for and received the sympathy of the world's intellectuals, now shows herself as a surly, sick bitch biting the hand that fed her" (O'Flaherty in Carlson, 1990: 140).

Samuel Beckett had three of his works banned in Ireland (*More Pricks than Kicks* (1934), *Watt* (1953) and *Molloy* (1954). In 1935 Beckett wrote a cynical essay on "Censorship in the Saorstat" in which he ridicules the Act and the men behind it.[8] In this essay Beckett attacks the narrow-mindedness not only of these "deputies and senators" but also of the Irish population at large (Beckett in Carlson, 1990: 142–143).

> Such is the cream of a measure that the Grand Academy of Balnibarbi could hardly have improved on. Even if it worked, which needless to say it does not, it would do so gratis, an *actum agere* regardless of expense. For the Irish are a characteristic agricultural community in this, they have something better to do than read and that they produce a finished type of natural fraudeur having nothing to learn from the nice discriminations of Margaret Sanger and Marie Carmichael Stopes, D.Sc., Ph.D., F.R.S. Litt., etc. Doubtless there is something agreeable to the eye in this failure to function to no purpose, the broken handpump in the free air station. (Beckett in Carlson, 1990: 145)[9]

Whereas O'Flaherty had some faith that the Irish people, if they were made aware of their own condition, would again appreciate "beauty and amorousness", Beckett here displays a much more sinister view on that issue. The only good thing about the Irish censorship and the censorship board is that they ensure the sale of at least *some* copies in Ireland, "assuming, as in reverence bound, that the censors would have gone to bed simultaneously and independently with the text, and not passed a single copy of the work from hand to hand, nor engaged a fit and proper person to read it to them in assembly." This irony is further emphasized by Beckett's idea of the Register of Prohibited Publications as an advertising list:

---

8   Though written in 1935, this essay was not published until 1983.
9   Balnibarbi is an island in Jonathan Swift's *Gulliver's Travels* from 1726. In Chapters 5 and 6 we hear of the Grand Academy of Lagado (the metropolis of the island). This academy employs scholars dedicated to projects for extracting sunbeams out of cucumbers, for reducing human excrements to its original food, for building houses by beginning at the roof, and other absurdities.

> The Register of Prohibited Publications is a most happy idea, constituting as it does, after the manner of Boston's Black Book, a free and permanent advertisement of those books and periodicals in which, be their strictly literary status never so humble, inheres the a priori excellence that they have annoyed the specialist in common sense. I may add that it is the duty of every customs official in the Saorstat to exhibit on demand this Register to the incoming mug. (Beckett in Carlson, 1990: 144)

The cultural space described in Beckett's essay has very little to do with the intentions of the intellectuals of the late 19th century. At the same time it shows a bitter-humorous or tragic-comical view on Irish culture which is not only a description of the cultural space but also a part of it. We find it in Flann O'Brien's *The Poor Mouth* as well. The satirical (O'Brien) and alienated (Beckett) views on Irish culture are just as much *part* of that culture as they are comments on it.

There is no doubt that censorship had a great influence on the cultural space of the Irish Free State – as Brown points out, censorship is a cultural fact in 20th century Ireland (Brown, 1985: 60). It had an effect on both Irish writers (some of whom, like Beckett, left the country and went into a kind of voluntary exile) and the Irish reading public:

> For Foley [a librarian from County Clare in the 1920s] the greatest crime perpetrated by censorship was not the undoubted injury done to Irish writers, not the difficulty experienced by educated men and women in getting hold on banned books, but the perpetuation of cultural poverty in the country as a whole, left without the leaven of serious contemporary literature. (Brown, 1985: 61)

If we look at the importance of the Censorship of Publican Act from an Andersonian point of view we can say that together with the language policy it functioned as a specific way of 'ordering' the imagining of the Irish community. The community imagined by the authorities was based on high moral (and the Catholic Church understanding of such) and the 'original' pure Ireland (and its language). Yet this image did not appeal to all in the Irish community, and the self-interpretation of some members of the community did not correspond to this image. These writers (of whom many had their books banned) formed a kind of dissident image of Ireland which was a different way of imagining the community. If we use the novel as an image in the way that Anderson does, we can say that perhaps the characters did not feel that they were part of the same (national) plot anymore. Compared to the Celtic twilighters these writers formed a less optimistic image where alienation and distance replace comradeship and fraternity. And the question is whether we can keep on insisting on the sense of community and its reliance on comradeship that Anderson's theory relies on in relation to these writers. To answer this question it is important to keep in mind that in Anderson's theory the formal structure of the novel as a figure for the imagined community offers "the space of a community", but there is nothing benign or democratic about it, as also Culler points out (Culler, 1999: 24). In his chapter on "Official Nationalism and Imperialism" Anderson shows how nations may show the same tendencies to impose a certain version of nationalism on a nation as the one we see the Empire have.

A Community without Unity?

As I have tried to show in this essay so far, the cultural space of the Irish Free State was constructed through various, at times contradictory, ways of imagining Ireland. I have pointed out some of the differences between the Celtic Revival and the Modernist currents; between the morals of the Catholic Church and some prominent writers and critics; between the status and function of the English language and the Irish language. And I have tried to explain this cultural space in the light of Anderson's theory of imagined communities. There is, however, one thing I think we must consider in relation to Anderson, here at the end of this discussion of the cultural space of the Irish Free State. Anderson's analysis of novels as a force for imagining national communities relies on "the old-fashioned novel" (Anderson, 1991: 25). Anderson does not define this kind of novel, but Culler defines it as a set of novels which

> Consist[s] of narratives where the narrator is not a character in the story (or at least is not confined to what a character might know). Most significantly (and this is why Anderson speaks of the 'old-fashioned novel') the narrative is not filtered through the consciousness or positions of a single observer. What is excluded is the limited point of view that developed in the novel during the course of the nineteenth century. (Culler, 1999: 23)

Perhaps we should turn to the kinds of novels that Joyce, O'Brien and Beckett wrote in order to explain how the cultural space of the Irish national community was imagined. These modern novels have neither the 'omniscient reader' nor the all-encompassing narrator of the old fashioned novel. Instead of seeing this as a 'fault' or a limitation in relation to imagined communities, we may consider Culler's idea that such narratives may be read as attempts to imagine "a community without unity, or what Jean-Luc Nancy calls a 'communauté désoeuvrée': community as spacing rather than fusion, sublation, or transcendence" (Culler, 1999: 32). In such an imagined community there would be a focus on difference and singularity. It is not within the scope of this essay to explore the idea of a community without unity in any great depth, but the idea of such a community leaves us with this general question: how divided and fragmented can a community be and still be a community? And the more specific one: If the cultural space of the Irish Free State was an 'imagined Ireland' characterized by difference and singularity, what does that do to the very notions of 'Ireland' and 'Irish'?

Bibliography

Anderson, Benedict (1991) *Imagined Communities: Reflections on the Origin and Spread of Nationalism* (revised and extended ed.). London and Netw York: Verso

Beckett, Samuel (1983) "Censorship in the Saorstat". *Banned in Ireland: Censorship and the Irish Writer*. Julia Carlson (ed.) (1990) Athens: University of Georgia Press

——. (1983) *Disjecta: Miscellaneous Writings and a Dramatic Fragment*. London: John Calder

Brown, Terence (1985) *Ireland: A Social and Cultural History, 1922 to the Present*. Ithaca and London: Cornell University Press

——. (1988) "Yeats, Joyce and the Irish Critical Debate". *Ireland's Literature: Selected Essays*. Mullingar, Ireland: The Lilliput Press

Carlson, Julia (ed.) (1990) *Banned in Ireland: Censorship and the Irish Writer*. Athens: University of Georgia Press

Corcoran, Neil (1997) *After Yeats and Joyce: Reading Modern Irish Literature*. Oxford and New York: Oxford University Press

Culler, Jonathan (1999) "Anderson and the Novel". *Diacritics*. Vol. 29 No. 4. Winter 1999. pp. 20–39

Deane, Seamus (1994) "The Production of Cultural Space in Irish Writing". *Boundary 2*. Vol. 21. No. 3. Autumn 1994. pp. 117–44

Graham, Colin (2001) *Deconstructing Ireland: Identity, Theory, Culture*. Edinburgh: Edinburgh University Press

Greenfeld, Liah (1992) *Nationalism – Five Roads to Modernity*. Cambridge, Mass: Harvard University Press

Hopper, Keith (1995) *Flann O'Brien: A Portrait of the Artist as a Young Postmodernist*. Ireland: Cork University Press

Joyce, James (1960) *A Portrait of the Artist as a Young Man* (1916). England: Penguin Books

Kearney, Richard (1997) *Postnationalist Ireland: Politics, Culture, Philosophy*. London: Routledge

Kuha, Tuija (1996) "The Significance of Language for Irish Identity". Anders Ahlqvist et al. (eds.) *Celtica Helsingiensia*. Commentationes Humanarum Litterarum 107

O'Brien, Flann (1993) *The Poor Mouth*. London: Flamingo Modern Classic

Plug, Jan (1999) "The Specular Nation: Yeats's Myth of the Irish". *The Centennial Review* Vol. 43. No. 1. Winter 1999. pp. 135–158

O'Flaherty, Liam (1932) "The Irish Censorship". *Banned in Ireland: Censorship and the Irish Writer*. Julia Carlson (ed.) (1990) Athens: University of Georgia Press

Shaw, G. Bernard (1928) "The Censorship". *Banned in Ireland: Censorship and the Irish Writer*. Julia Carlson (ed.) (1990) Athens: University of Georgia Press

Yeats, W.B. (1928) "The Censorship and St. Thomas Aquinas". *Banned in Ireland: Censorship and the Irish Writer*. Julia Carlson (ed.) (1990) Athens: University of Georgia Press

—. (1959) *Mythologies*. London: The Macmillan Press Ltd.

—. (1961) "The Celtic Element in Literature" (1897). *Essays and Introductions*. London: The Macmillan Press Ltd.

"Small, but exalted":
Otherness in Nella Larsen's Novels

Bent Sørensen

In the field of cultural text studies a number of methodological approaches are available. In this particular essay the approach is to see the fate of one writer as the result of a specific historical and cultural situatedness. Nella Larsen's own biography and her literary works can both be read as social and cultural texts, situating themselves in a particular socio-cultural context: The Harlem Renaissance. The themes she discusses in her literary works are specific to a racial and gendered discourse, and her own fate is readable as a text which is also marked by the dynamics of racial and gendered belonging and (fear of) exclusion. Complicating this dynamics of race and gender negotiations are economic and class related pressures on Larsen to achieve a means of living as a professional writer, pressures which ultimately led to her being silenced as an artist.

    The essay that follows is therefore necessarily prefaced by a number of small chapters giving the prerequisites for understanding Nella Larsen. These chapters give, first, a biographical sketch of Larsen's mixed, and to some extent obscure, origin and background. Here the focus will be on the issues of race and ethnicity, and to some extent on class and economic issues. Second, a brief introduction to the social construct of The Harlem Renaissance will be given, where this group of writers, artists and social thinkers will be discussed as a force to be reckoned with in the USA of the 1920s. The third, longer, introductory chapter will be of a more theoretical and methodological nature, and it will present the notion of difference discourses as a tool for understanding and analyzing texts in the widest sense of the word. The article will then move on to looking more closely at Nella

Larsen's literary works in order to illustrate how these three frames add new layers of understanding to our readings of her fictional texts, as well as the text of her life. The readings will focus in particular on her first novel, *Quicksand* (and especially on those portions of it that are set in Denmark), but will also briefly discuss her second novel, *Passing*, and the concept of negotiating racial belonging that is known as "passing (for white)". Finally the essay will look at how Nella Larsen lost her foothold in the socio-cultural group of her choice, and how she was effectively ostracized from this position of belonging or cultural sanctuary.

Biography

Nella Larsen's biography is still not fully clarified. Despite the exhaustive work by Thadious M. Davis in her 1994 biography of Larsen, and forthcoming supplemental and corrective work by George Hutchinson, there are still areas of her life that are uncharted and obscure. Some of these obscurities are deliberately created by Larsen herself or by her parents and other family members, some are unintentional in the sense that they are due to lack of sources or corruption of source material over the several decades that have passed since Larsen's death. As the main topic of this essay is the figuration of belonging, the issues of greatest immediate interest are those of roots, heritage and race. In Larsen's case it is necessary to distinguish as sharply as possible between her own manufactured accounts of her origins and heritage, those stories created and disseminated by her relatives and friends, and those that are a matter of public (and to some extent verifiable) record. What remains after all three types of accounts are collated can be seen to be Larsen's mixture of heritages: West Indian, Danish, and African-American. What also remains clear is that she ultimately felt no real sense of either diasporic or native belonging to any one of these heritages.

At birth Nella Larsen was apparently named neither Nella, nor Larsen. In fact, neither of her parents went by the name Larsen, either. According to Davis, the child was "born Nellie Walker, on April 13, 1891, in Chicago" (Davis, 1994: 3), registered at birth as 'coloured', and listed as the child of Peter Walker and Mary Hanson Walker. These names indicate a Danish – or at least Scandinavian – belonging on the mother's side, but none on the father's. Certainly, baby Nellie's status as 'colored' is most likely due to a genetic contribution from Walker's side. A few years later, however, Peter

Walker changed his name to Larson (or Larsen), which indicates a Scandinavian heritage on his side of the family as well. The name change seems to coincide with Walker/Larsen's rise in employment status, namely his getting a job as a tram conductor, which positions at the time were reserved for 'whites' only (30). One might therefore speculate that Walker was passing for white, and conveniently backed his claim of racial (white) identity up with a Scandinavian sounding name. Therefore Davis further speculates that the presence of a coloured child in a now, seemingly, all-white family was an inconvenience and potentially a liability in terms of financial opportunities. Nellie was then perhaps sent away to an institution to be raised outside the family unit. She certainly did not figure in the census rosters for a number of years as belonging to the Larsen household, unlike a later child (Anna) born to the couple, who was listed as 'white' and as the household's sole child.

These 'facts' are all puzzled out by meticulous archive research by Davis, but remain curiously gappy. The most obvious lack is that there are no extant photos of any of the family members, neither of the parents nor any of their two children. The earliest photographs of Nella reproduced in Davis' book are from her high school year (1908) and her time at nursing school (1915). These pictures, as all later photos of Larsen, show an African-American woman whose skin appears too dark for her to be able to pass as white in most contexts. While there thus is reason to believe in Davis' claim that Nella may have been sent off by her family because of her skin colour, there are no actual records of where she might have spent her missing years, and the theory remains speculative. However, Nella Larsen herself has greatly contributed to the confusion about her early years, partly by giving a – to say the least – sketchy account of her childhood (actually altering her birth year to make herself two years younger), and partly by publicly putting out several mutually conflicting stories to 'explain' her roots and heritage.

According to one of these stories, Larsen claims a Danish West Indian heritage for her father, suggesting that he was a light skinned Negro from the Caribbean island of St. Thomas (now part of the Virgin Islands), and that her mother was a Danish immigrant. In other statements she claims an even 'whiter' heritage for her father by leaving out the reference to his colour, and adding "all his people live in Denmark", thus perhaps suggesting that these relations were white enough to pass, even in a white monoculture such as Denmark in the early part of the 20th century (See Davis,

1994: 26 for these references). None of these claims have yet been verified, and Davis at least has found no record of Danish relatives of Walker/Larsen. Nella Larsen also liked to occasionally claim that she herself was born in the Virgin Islands and raised in the jungle. Several historians of the Harlem Renaissance have accepted these stories as factual and perpetuated these errors by including them in their articles and books.

Another of Larsen's claims is that as a young person she visited Denmark and spent time with her mother's relatives. This would explain her knowledge of the geography of Copenhagen and of Danish language and customs, which figure prominently in several chapters of her novel *Quicksand*. If that book is read autobiographically, it may also be argued that Larsen drew upon her factual knowledge and used her experience of life in her actual family in her descriptions of life in the fictive Dahl family. Davis did not find independent sources that could confirm Larsen's visit to Denmark, but several of her earliest publications describe Danish games and riddles that Larsen seems to have had first hand knowledge of. If, however, her mother indeed was Danish by birth, Nella could also conceivably have learned these things as a child at home in Chicago. Larsen also claimed to have at least reading competence in Danish, and was paid to read a Danish novel her publishers were considering for translation. However, the actual snippets of Danish in *Quicksand* seem slightly odd for a native speaker of Danish, and contain spelling mistakes ("frøkken" for "frøken" (Miss), "Amielenborg Palace" for "Amalienborg Palace", etc.). Not until 1997 did research by George Hutchinson appear that uncovered records of Larsen having made at least one, and possibly two separate Atlantic passages, and the article in which Hutchinson presents his findings does not give all the details one might expect. As yet no record of her having studied at the University of Copenhagen, as she claimed to have, has surfaced. The extent of her actual connections to Denmark remains unclear, at least until George Hutchinson in his forthcoming biography of Nella Larsen (2006) presents more conclusive evidence.

Thus, with all the conflicting stories put about by Larsen herself, and the lack of primary source evidence, such as interviews with her family in the USA or Denmark, little is known with any certainty about Larsen's life before she entered high school and eventually went on to nursing school. These events are amply documented by her school records. It was during her adolescence and early youth that she finally changed her first name to Nella, after experimenting with several spellings, including "Nellye". In this period she also established the spelling "Larsen" of her last name, and she consistently used the Larsen name for the rest of her life, although often in combination with her married name. In 1919 she married a research physicist, Elmer Imes, thus securing for herself some financial security and a place in the black middle class as long as that marriage lasted. The marriage was in many ways a prerequisite for Larsen's writing career, and coincided in time with the very brief span of years during which Larsen actually considered herself an author and was able to function as one. After an acrimonious divorce from Imes in 1933, Nella Larsen was left to fend for herself, and she spent the rest of her life working as a nurse.

However, marriage and financial security were not the only prerequisites for Larsen's artistic life. Without a cultural and intellectual environment into which she could fit, she might never have become a published writer. Such an environment was in place in New York City in the 1920s, namely the so-called Harlem Renaissance. The Renaissance was not only a rebirth of African-American culture in the freer socio-cultural surroundings of New York's black neighbourhood, but also a personal rebirth for writers such as Nella Larsen.

Harlem Renaissance

As a writer Larsen found a possible peer group to understand herself through – The Harlem Renaissance. The label 'renaissance' is one of several that can be given to a historically situated creative and cultural circle ('generation' or 'school' are others), and the study of such groups as productive and receptive bodies is different from and more complex than the study of individual authors. An example of such a study is the book *The Harlem Renaissance: Hub of African-American Culture, 1920 – 1930* by Steven Watson, who quotes W.E.B. Du Bois, "the eminent African American intellectual", as having said: "The history of the world is the history not of individuals, but of groups" (Watson 1995: ix). Watson's book, while introductory in nature and occasionally prone to errors, is a good example of the interdisciplinary scope required in cultural text studies.

The other part of the label "Harlem Renaissance" of course refers to the geographical location of this "hub", namely the predominantly African American populated part of New York City, Harlem. This is significant for several reasons. First, Harlem was (and is) a very small geographical entity, but one closely connected with the rest of the world's greatest metropolis, NYC. Thus Harlem offered both intimacy and sanctuary for its racially uniform inhabitants, and an open connection to the white dominated world of patrons, publishers and people with almost unlimited economic resources. Second, the northernness of Harlem should be emphasized. New York, Illinois and other Northern states offered a goal for internal migration of the African-American population in the early decades of the 20th century, primarily due to the presence of large cities with employment opportunities in these states, but also due to more liberal race legislation and integration practices in these states, compared to the American South.

For a brief time, roughly coinciding with the decade between the end of WW I and the Wall Street crash of 1929, Harlem was a promised land of opportunity of all kinds for black Americans and immigrants from other parts of the world, who created a large number of diasporic presences in the City. For artists and writers the time was right for the creation of a cultural circle of importance – a platform for publication and dissemination of both art products (books, plays, pictorial art etc.) and manifestos of cultural politics (for instance concerning racial education and 'uplift').

In this climate writers such as Claude McKay (a West Indian immigrant), Countee Cullen (who may have migrated from the South, but who obscured his origins like many of his peers), and Langston Hughes (born in Missouri) wrote, published and socialized. All three were poets, first and foremost, although Hughes wrote in all genres and in terms of publications is the most important of all Renaissance writers. Here they found financial and artistic potential which they negotiated into literary careers of some importance. Intellectual figures such as Du Bois and Alain Locke used these opportunities to create a debate on racial destiny vs. education and uplift for African-Americans. Patrons of the arts virtually adopted black writers and supported their careers financially and in creating publishing contacts.

The number of male writers and artists far exceeded the number of women involved in the renaissance, but perhaps the most enduring figure of all the people associated with the Renaissance was a woman. Her name was Zora Neale Hurston (born in Florida, but trained and educated in New York City as Barnard College's only black student at the time), and she has recently been the centre of attention for academics and creative writers alike – not least thanks to the work of reinstatement into the literary canon, done on her behalf by best-selling African-American novelist Alice Walker. Apart from Hurston only two female novelists are remembered today as integral to the Renaissance, Nella Larsen and Jessie Faucet.

Thus, it was in this hotbed of creativity and intellectual challenges that Larsen found the opportunity to fashion herself as a writer. There were outlets for short non-fiction pieces and stories in the numerous magazines in circulation at the time, and ultimately mainstream publishing houses such as Alfred Knopf were open to 'Negro' literature and started publishing novels by the Renaissance writers. This would not have happened without the extensive networking going on under the Renaissance label, which involved a complex structure of patronage, friendships, movements and parties, social and cultural functions (parties in another sense of the word!), awards and prizes of many kinds – or in short a whole critical and cultural public, consumed with an interest in African-American issues.

Though the Renaissance had a short life span in term of years, and stopped being a thriving cultural force of magnitude, when the economic climate took a drastic downturn after 1929, its lasting importance lies in the legacy of texts produced in this circle, and the issues that were raised and dramatized by the texts and lives of its writers, which continued to inform intellectual debates in the USA well into the 1970s.

Difference Discourses

As a tool for situating the concentric circles of topics of interest to us in this essay: Nella Larsen's work, her life, and her participation in a socio-cultural group such as the Harlem Renaissance, we need a general theory that conceptualizes all these dimensions as social texts. Such a theory is set forth in brief terms in the following section.

Formulating the concept of difference discourses marks an attempt to come to terms with a dynamic culture composed of many layers of social text. A dynamic culture, where more and more discourse carrying media have become available, and where more people than ever before have some form of reading competence, requires a dynamic theory of reading such discourses, or social texts. Reading competence should here be understood not merely in the narrow sense of literacy, but in the wide sense of having the tools to engage in various reading protocols for various genres and media – ranging from old-fashioned print media, such as novels, via movies, cartoons, music products, to computer carried discourse types.

Such a diversified media picture, where each medium has a set of specific genres and conventions that are suited for expression through that particular medium, or several specific media, is very difficult to theorize.

Just as there are specific discourse genres that follow specific media, there has been a tendency that theories of the genesis and reception of these genres have been specified narrowly to accommodate readings of these discourse types. We have specified theories for literature, for film and TV, other theories for printed texts that are not literary, or for texts that function only orally, or in specific machine carried contexts.

What we do not tend to have are theories concerning the functions of and reading of discourses in general; theories that historicize developments in text production and reception, yet transcend genre limits. We need to have a trans-generic dissemination theory, because the way we live and function discursively in our society is in communicative totalities. We all understand discourse of many different types in many different communication situations, and most readers relish basking in the multiverse of discourses without the old distinctions between high and low culture, between the canonical and the trashy, between the sacred and the profane.

Such a dynamic theory must be developed in broad strokes before any attempt can be made at hybrid analyses of cultural and literary phenomena in process. The theory has to pay both attention to genetic as well as reception aspects of the textual phenomena, and attention to the historical situatedness of these phenomena. The theory of difference discourses is an attempt at creating such a dynamic, yet general, theory, and a starting point for the discussion of it is definitions of the two parts of the label for the theory: 'difference' and 'discourses'.

The first label element is 'discourses'. It is no longer revolutionary to talk about an extended concept of text, meaning text in the semiotic sense. Semiotics is in fact the only suitable reading method that cuts across all genres to the understanding that all combinations of signs are texts, in that they carry signification, whether this combination of signs is created intentionally or not. All combinations of signs can be read, and everything can be semioticized, i.e. postulated as readable. It does not matter, as such, whether the signs composing the text in question are graphic signs, moving or still images, words, letters etc.

For the purposes of this theory then, let us posit that all texts in a communicative situation, i.e. all readable texts, be termed discourses, allowing us also to talk about a discourse, or about various discourse types. While there are texts that are undoubtedly texts, understood as strings of signs, they may still not necessarily be discursive if they are not placed in a communicative situation, by which I mean having a reader(ship). Such 'unread' or 'unreadable' texts do not figure in the dynamic of the difference discourses which only concerns itself with what one could also term social texts.

Turning now to the other label element: 'Differences' are here to be understood as modes of explanations for phenomena and events. These are invariably structured as pairs of oppositions in the 'cultural' realm, expressed in figures of speech, discursive or narrative structures. (This is familiar territory from Saussurian linguistics and other (post-)structuralist derivatives of this basic dualistic insight.) These 'differences' are traditionally perceived as either biological givens (man vs. woman, for instance) or socially derived invariables (working class vs. middle class, for instance). They are believed to constitute us as subjects and to explain our being in the world. In postmodernity we have gradually come to realize that all these differences are language constructs as well as/rather than (which of the preceding pair you believe in, depends on how radical your perception of 'identity' and 'subject' is) situated givens, and therefore all differences are negotiable in communicative situations.

A very limited catalogue of large, signification-carrying differences can be generated, consisting of the following six discourse differences: age, sex, race, class, nation, and religion. Of course, as all naming is problematic, not all the category names chosen for the differences are unproblematic, but the names used here are recognizable for 20th and 21st century people with some cultural competence and discursive agency.

There may be periods where terms such as 'religion', 'nation', and 'class' are not applicable, but for the 20th century all these are useable as cover terms. 'Class', for all discourse about socially constituted differences; 'nation', as covering all in-group, out-group figurations with relation to topological origin, whereabouts or belonging; 'religion', as covering all issues of spirituality, belief and destiny. The supposedly biologically determined differences take various other identities when discursively placed: for instance, 'sex' differences are usually discoursed about as gender differences, where 'gender' is taken to mean culturally and communicatively significant aspects of our sexuality, and 'race' differences are often nuanced into discourse about 'ethnicity'.

Here it should be reiterated as strongly as possible that all the differences are negotiable, even the supposedly biologically determined ones. These should rather be seen to just have a biological origin that can be used as the base for historicizing and situating them communicatively, i.e. negotiating them in discourse. 'Sex' is, for instance, not an unalterable absolute – as witnessed by transsexual and transgendered identities, and race is not an absolute, clear cut identity – as witnessed by the notion of 'passing (for white)'.

It is now possible to claim that it is exactly when the negotiation of differences takes place that the differences become readable as discursive phenomena and that they generate social texts. They may be presented or present themselves in the following tropes (the examples given are of course far from exhaustive and may not be the most universal ones in all decades of the 20th century):

Age	-	e.g.: young/old, generation
Race	-	e.g.: black/white, primitive/civilized
Sex/Gender	-	e.g.: woman/man, love
Class	-	e.g.: poor/rich, status
Nation	-	e.g.: them/us, foreign/domestic
Religion	-	e.g.: man/God or virtue/sin

All these difference discourses/social texts are readable as embodying narratives of an 'I' and 'The Other' or an 'Other'. The textual representation of 'I' and 'The Other' and the inter-relations between these as textual instances may contain any blend of the above tropes, but in various historical periods and climates one or more difference discourses will be dominant, whereas others are marginalized or potentially excluded from discursivity as 'givens'.

This leads us to introduce the concept of discursive field as an applicable metaphor for this dynamic. The notion of field allows for several difference discourses to co-exist simultaneously, yet also allows for some of them to be more centrally placed vis-à-vis the power structures current at any time, ruling the public discourse sphere. Here the concept of dominant versus marginalized discourses is useful. This latter statement forms the next step in making this theory applicable in the field of text history, by necessarily historicizing the occurrence of discourse types and introducing the variables according to which the dynamics of the model may play itself out.

It should now be apparent that any one textual object can act and inscribe itself in a number of the available difference discourses. One overlap is the one between the generational thematic and the love story, which often will be found in a *Bildungsroman*, another might be the complexities of a novel both about race and gender, as in the case of Nella Larsen's works. In such a case a struggle for dominance of one discourse over the other(s) will ensue, and the outcome of this struggle is ultimately determined by the climate of difference discourses in the larger public sphere, which will decide which discourse any given book/object becomes inscribed in. Therefore Larsen's books can (and have been) read variously as African-American literature and/or as proto-feminist literature. None of these reading protocols are inherently wrong, but merely reduce the complexities of the novels in question to a larger degree than necessary. Such a reductionism may be avoided when the difference discourse theory is applied.

Double Othering: Race and Gender Biases

The operative differences in Nella Larsen's case are primarily the double minority position of race and gender: she was a black woman. She was both othered by the dominantly white literary establishment (there are of course exceptions to this general statement, for instance the white patron of the arts and mentor of many of the Renaissance writers, Carl Van Vechten, who remained a steadfast friend and supporter of Larsen, until she herself broke off contact with him), and by the male dominated black Renaissance (one could cite examples of downright hatred of Larsen, as witnessed by descriptions in Davis's biography (see Davis, 1994: 8 & 357)). Class played a smaller but important role, because of the pressures of financial dependence that the other minority positions forced her to negotiate. Larsen therefore developed a consistent behaviour of alternately 'begging' and 'bullying' in order to gain recognition and/or support that further alienated her from potential supporters. This dynamics of double othering, always with the threat and fear of social deroute and poverty lurking in the background were not only real-life pressures Larsen had to negotiate, but, as we shall see in the following analyses, also surfaced as constant thematic complexes in her literary works.

Quicksand

Larsen's first novel (published 1928) is partly an autobiographical account in the shape of a female *Bildungsroman*, also conforming to the so-called tragic mulatto formula of earlier black literature. (This subgenre of African-American literature tends to be strongly didactic, and often features an ending where the mulatto hero(ine) is 'punished' for a betrayal of destiny by not choosing firmly to belong to one race, specifically the black one.) The heroine of *Quicksand*, Helga Crane, undertakes a journey of character formation. She moves from the rural south, where she is a teacher at an institution for blacks, seems to find a temporary home in Harlem, until disgust with her own race makes her flee Harlem when a magical solution presents itself – namely going to Copenhagen. Her sojourn in Denmark forms the centerpiece of the novel, but ultimately she has to leave Denmark, because she does not conform to the social norms: marriage being the expected and ultimately the only accepted behaviour of a woman. Thereupon she travels back to Harlem ("homesick, not for America, but for Negroes" (Larsen, 1986: 92)), and ultimately back to the rural south, where, ironically, she ends up in the worst case scenario of all her fears, as a wife doomed to endless child births, living in a totally unstimulating, all black, environment, waiting for death while her spirit has already died. She is thus oppressed on behalf of race in the US, oppressed on behalf of gender in Denmark, and always in the background lurks the threat of social deroute, if she deviates from the narrow path of normative behaviour for a coloured woman.

Helga Crane is offered a number of opportunities for happiness, but discards them one by one (usually they present themselves as marriage proposals), as she is restless and unable to accept any form of compromise. She is also tainted by her non-belonging to two races and cultures, the African-American and the Danish, i.e. white. She alternates between hatred and disgust of her blackness, and a superficial pride in being exotic among the pale Danes. Ultimately she realizes that even in Denmark she is being othered by being turned into a show-piece which her Danish relatives, the Dahls, use to create a better platform for their own position in society. This is symbolically expressed in the novel through several metaphors for bondage and slavery. She is being put on display in many ways in Denmark, not least through the way she is dressed and accessorized by her aunt. She is given bracelets that are the figurative equivalent of shackles hinting at a slavery position. She is dressed very colourfully and sexually provocatively, which is figured as a way of prostituting her. Prostitution is here also linked to slavery and seen as the only way in which Helga as a subaltern other can achieve a form of conditional freedom.

Trading a life in the utter poverty of slavery for a life of relative financial ease as a prostitute or a wife is regarded as the best option for Crane by the Dahls, who thus symbolically function as her pimps. Ultimately she becomes a model for a painter who does a portrait of her, showing her as a bad, wicked person, and who yet cannot resist propositioning her, first to be his mistress, and when she refuses that, then to be his wife. The reification of her in the portrait as a temptress and a whore is emblematic of the way that she is seen by the men of the Danish upper middle class circles which the Dahls move in. "A disgusting sensual creature with her features" (89), is how she herself thinks of the portrait, denying that it represents her true self. We as readers are here invited to reflect on whether Helga at this point in her development has a true image of herself, or whether the gaze that others her as a sensual creature in fact sees her more truly than herself.

When she also refuses the offer of marriage she is punished by the Dahls, who find her ungrateful and ultimately take her off the market and urge her to go back to America and try her fortunes there. This means a sacrifice of her sanctuary in an apparently racially unbiased society such as Denmark, but it also means that she is back in an economic situation where she is forced to be self-dependent and self-sufficient. As it turns out, this initiates her slide downward in social and financial terms, ending with her forced marriage to a preacher from the rural South.

While Helga left Harlem for Denmark with "no regret" (63), and after two years leaves Denmark for Harlem "with infinite regret" (93), the reader realizes that Copenhagen has been nothing but a magical interlude in her life, and that the problems of racism, misogyny and class pressures have haunted Helga with equal force in the two cities. Thus what she has tried to escape from in Denmark is waiting for her back in America, and the slavery is only postponed, not avoided as her fate. Denmark is not the promised land it appeared to Helga to be, and her fond childhood memories of Denmark from her first visit there, as a country with "no Negroes, no problems, no prejudice" (55) prove false. These ironies are made very plain when we remember Helga's first impressions of Copenhagen: "how odd and how different to America" (72), but realize in retrospect that it is only on the surface that Denmark is different and that the underlying social pressures are really the same for a coloured woman no matter what nation she lives in. This can be read as the strong feminist and racial message that Larsen has created for the reader of *Quicksand*, and unlike Larsen's contemporary readers we should not let the tragic figuration of the mulatto heroine's life expressed in the last chapters of the novel blur this message.

Passing

In her second novel (published 1929) Nella Larsen explores different strategies of escaping the double othering of race and gender through the strategy of passing (for white) – but similarly to the first novel *Passing* also ends up with the heroine as a victim of envy and hatred.

Irene Redfield and Clare Kendry are the two female main characters, and of the two, Clare represents the type of woman who is willing to sacrifice everything for a chance at personal and social uplift. To achieve her aims Clare exploits the fact that her skin is white enough for her to be able to pass, and this becomes the key to a comfortable middle class life. The price she first must pay is that her new husband, who is unaware of her 'former' life as a coloured person, is a bigot and a racist whose favourite pet name for his wife is "Nig". The irony of this situation is not lost on any of the characters in the book, nor on the reader. Irene, on the other hand, feels trapped in her life, but comforts herself that at least she remains true to her racial destiny as a woman of colour.

In the culmination of the novel, Clare dies as a result of a fall from a high window during a party. It is suggested strongly, but still with some slight ambiguity, that Irene has pushed her to her death, but none of the other characters actually seem to have seen the events unfold, so Irene will not be punished by law for her act. Of course she will then have to live silently with her guilt, which is almost as intolerable an alternative, as it involves a sacrifice of her personal integrity. Irene chooses the lie, and she justifies this to herself as necessary for the protection of her family, and particularly her husband's reputation. However, she also initially justifies the murder of Clare, paradoxically, as an act of protection of Clare: "She couldn't have Clare Kendry cast aside by Bellew [her bigoted husband]" (Larsen, 1986: 239), but in the very next sentence (rendering Irene's thoughts, or internal monologue) the real motive slips through: "She couldn't have her free" (239).

Thus, it is really jealousy of Clare's self-realization that motivates Irene's hatred and her deed. This goes to the core of the problematic of passing (and *Passing*): passing is tempting, because it holds out the lure of uplift, but also dangerous because people who are unable to pass will begrudge you the opportunity. Larsen was, of course, herself painfully aware of the emotions of one who could never pass for white, but rather than identifying her with the murderous Irene, it would perhaps do Larsen's imaginative craft more justice to suggest that she, in her novel, shows the empowered woman, Clare Kendry, as the real heroine, and Irene as the victim for whom we should not feel pity, but rather outrage that she is permitted to extinguish Clare's freedom. (Clare is several times figured metaphorically as a flame, burning (too) brightly: "One moment Clare has been there, a vital glowing thing, like a flame of red and gold. The next she was gone" (239)).

Both Larsen's novels were well received by critics and reading public alike, but criticized for their endings, casting female characters as victims. No one seems to have considered the possibility of deliberate feminist didacticism as a strategy on Larsen's part, yet as we have seen above, the many cases of ironic narration in *Quicksand* and *Passing* make such readings plausible. Larsen's autobiographical role as the victim of discrimination and exclusion from family because of her dark skin colour made her very well acquainted with the economies of victimhood. It is not farfetched to think that she used her novels as a vehicle to communicate the dangers of dark females accepting this victim status and relinquishing the perpetual struggle for recognition despite of otherness of appearance.

"Sanctuary" and Plagiarism: Recognition and Backlash

In 1930, after winning a Guggenheim fellowship to research and write her third novel in Europe, Larsen was hit by accusations of plagiarism in connection with the publication of her short story, "Sanctuary", in the magazine *Forum*. Larsen's Harlem peers quickly began circulating rumours that Nella Larsen had adapted a British short story, "Mrs. Adis" by Sheila Kaye-Smith, and altered only a few of the incidentals of that story in her version. The main change was that the 1922 British story used class as the difference on which the story hinged, whereas Larsen used race. This was particularly expressed in the dialogue, which Larsen turned into black rural dialect. Otherwise both stories featured a strong female protagonist who protects the murderer of her own son out of loyalty to her own peer group, defined in terms of either class or race. This is a strong, but rather melodramatic plot, and one which Larsen later, when she was forced to publicly defend herself against the accusations, claimed was a generic (black) legend told to her many times by her patients and other associates, always as having happened to them personally.

The Guggenheim was supposed to be the highpoint of Larsen's journey towards recognition as a writer, not just a black writer and a woman writer. Her psychology made her fiercely competitive in relation to other women – for example Jessie Faucet, whom Larsen considered the only other female novelist of quality, associated with the Renaissance. This competitive and at times self-promoting behaviour also galled several male intellectuals who lashed out in chauvinistic and patronizing terms against her character which was seen as manipulative and mischievous (See Davis, 1994: 8). The language used in some of the private accusations against Larsen was strongly patronizing and sexist. Harold Jackman, a minor Renaissance author and society gossip writer, was particularly vicious, for example writing to Countee Cullen: "Boy, that gal has used some of the identical words miss Smith uses in her *Mrs. Adis*, and as for the dialogue, little Nell, I'll call her this time, has just changed it to make it colored" (quoted in Davis, 1994: 349). Note here in particular the patronizing diminutives used about Larsen, and how they are specifically gendered in contrast to the male gendering of the recipient of the letter, Cullen, implied (perhaps subconsciously, perhaps jokingly) by the exclamation "Boy".

The accusations against Larsen of plagiarism were apparently well founded, although the scandal was somewhat alleviated by her article defending her writing of "Sanctuary", also published in *Forum*, but the long-term consequences were unnecessarily harsh, since she never again published a work of fiction. Metaphorically speaking, this silencing of a black female author has aspects of a lynching about it, but in this case a lynching perpetrated by her own male peers who shared her race, yet othered her on the basis of her gender – perhaps further motivated by the superior craft she exhibited as a writer.

The Guggenheim scholarship was not retracted, and Larsen spent time in France, Spain and North Africa researching her novel. Her progress reports to the Guggenheim foundation were guardedly positive, but in private letters it was clear that she was seriously worried about finances and the impending dissolution of her marriage to Elmer Imes. After that was finalized by her divorce from him in 1933, her days of financial independence were over, and she was unable to sustain her writing career. The manuscript of the final novel seems to have been left in care of one of her European friends, but is now apparently lost. Larsen was silenced while alive by a combination of gender jealousies, racial circumstances and social pressures. Posthumously she has remained silenced for a long time, due to the neglect and carelessness of her friends and the forgetfulness and lack of respect from her former peers.

Conclusion: A Note on the Title of This Essay

Originally, of course, this essay's title is a quote from the novel *Quicksand* (Larsen, 1986: 67), but the phrase "small, but exalted" can suitably serve not only as a title, but also as a springboard for the conclusion to this essay, for at least the following reasons:

When Larsen's protagonist alter ego, Helga Crane, thinks of herself through this dual metaphor, she is in the midst of re-discovering her self in a new setting. She has that same day arrived in Denmark, been well received by her Danish family and treated like visiting royalty. The pleasure of that day is encapsulated in this ambivalent feeling of Helga's: she is still a small person in the sense that she is not important, wealthy or well-connected, and she is alone in the world in the sense that her belonging is tenuous and uncertain. However, she has the sense that her belonging is about to be redefined and re-affirmed in a Danish context, where she will be thought of as special and unique. This singles her out and exalts her above her peers whom she has already left behind along with the other members of her race back in the USA, and she does not yet understand the perils of such high visibility as would come with the exaltedness of her position.

On the level of the author, Nella Larsen is in a sense a small writer, both because her published out-put is not large, but also because she was largely forgotten for many years. She has, however, of late become exalted because of the increased interest in her specifically (as the subject of one very large biography by Thadious M. Davis, and soon another by Hutchinson), and generally in unearthing African-American literary foremothers (the project of among others Alice Walker and Tony Morrison).

Thus the phrase "small, but exalted" serves as a connector on two analytical levels. It can be read as a metaphor that connects the issue of personal identity with issues of group belonging and identification, cf. the negotiations of the difference discourses Larsen herself and her protagonists were forced to conduct. It also serves to illuminate the efforts of us as readers and analysts of Larsen's life (as social and cultural text) and her works, in the sense that we may conclude that the phrase adequately describes our understanding of Larsen's textual legacy at this point in history.

References

Baker, Houston A. (1987) *Modernism and the Harlem Renaissance.* Chicago: The University of Chicago Press

Balshaw, Maria (2000) *Looking for Harlem: Urban Aesthetics in African-American Literature.* Virginia: Pluto Press, London & Sterling

Davis, Thadious M. (1994) *Nella Larsen: Novelist of the Harlem Renaissance – A Woman's Life Unveiled.* Baton Rouge & London: Louisiana State University Press

Douglas, Ann (1995) *Terrible Honesty: Mongrel Manhattan in the 1920s.* New York: The Noonday Press, Farrar, Straus and Giroux

Hutchinson, George (1995) *The Harlem Renaissance in Black and White.* Cambridge, Mass: Bellknap Harvard

Hutchinson, George (1997) "Nella Larsen and the Veil of Race". *American Literary History.* Vol. 9. No. 2. Summer 1997. pp. 329–349

Larsen, Nella (1986) *Quicksand and Passing.* (Edited by Deborah E. McDowell). New Brunswick, New Jersey: Rutgers University Press

Lewis, David Levering (1979/1997) *When Harlem Was in Vogue.* New York, London: Penguin Books

Watson, Steven (1995) *The Harlem Renaissance: Hub of African-American Culture, 1920–1930.* New York: Pantheon Books

The Production of the Martians

JENS KIRK

> *To introduce difference is to produce time. Hence the importance, in this struggle for life and survival, of the distinctive marks which, at best, aim to identify what are often the most superficial and most visible properties of a set of works or producers. Words – the names of schools or groups, proper names – are so important only because they make things. These distinctive signs produce existence in a world in which the only way to be is to be different, to 'make one's name', either personally or as a group.*
>
> – Pierre Bourdieu

In the recent history of English literature, the notion of the Martian school refers to a number of writers, mostly poets, who were trying to represent the everyday world from unfamiliar perspectives. Craig Raine, Christopher Reid, and David Sweetman are usually regarded as the leading figures of Martian poetry (see, for example, Hamilton, 1994: 343). Generally speaking, the early reception of the Martian poets was characterised by strong disagreements among reviewers and critics on the meaning and value of their writings. According to *Contemporary Literary Criticism*, Raine was recognized as "a clever poet" but faulted "for not addressing human emotions or concerns" (Stine and Marowski, 1985a: 348). Similarly, with respect to Reid, we are told that "Critics generally praised his clever and inventive style; however, some found his poems lacking in depth and in concern for human conflicts" (Stine and Marowski, 1985b: 348). In this essay, I map out the early stages in the reception history of the Martians, roughly speaking between the publication of Raine's *The Onion, Memory* (1977) and James Fenton's "The Manifesto Against Manifestoes" (1983). In contrast to *Contemporary Literary Criticism*, this essay shows that the element of feeling was an important concern to both supporters and opponents of the Martians. Moreover, I argue that the idea of a "Martian School" and related notions such as "Martian poetry" or just "the Martians" were invented and circulated, not just to describe, either endorsingly or accusingly, a contemporary aesthetic phenomenon, i.e. a new direction in English poetry, but also for social or cultural purposes: What was at stake in the early reception of the Martians was the salvation of the social function of poetry as a discourse of feeling.

I

In dealing with the reception history of the Martians, I am dealing with domains which Bourdieu (1993) has labelled the field of cultural production, which includes, for example, the artistic field, the literary field, and the field of production. These fields, according to Bourdieu, form separate social universes having their own laws and constituting "the economic world reversed" (29, 164). The literary field, like the artistic field in general, is governed by the law of "disinterestedness, which establishes a negative correlation between temporal (notably financial) success and properly artistic value" (164). This means that for authors, critics, and other participants in the art world, which per definition does not allow the pursuit of immediate economic profits:

> [T]he only legitimate accumulation consists in making a name for oneself, a known, recognized name, a capital of consecration implying a power to consecrate objects (with a trademark or signature) or persons (through publication, exhibition, etc.) and therefore to give value, and to appropriate the profits from this operation. (75)

By identifying the name of the game in terms of consecration, Bourdieu introduces a religious analogy into his conceptualisation of the artistic and literary fields as the economic world reversed. It is worth pursuing this analogy in order to understand how the field works according to Bourdieu. Like priests, who, for instance, wield the power of consecrating the bread in the Eucharist, artists, art dealers, critics and publishers who have succeeded in making a name for themselves hold powers of consecration, for example, the power of setting apart particular objects or people as very special, noteworthy, valuable, and meaningful. And like priests, whose powers do not really originate in God but in the belief of their congregations, artists, critics, and other members of the art world who have become known names do not really owe their authority to their genius but to the other participants' belief in their genius. This is why, according to Bourdieu,

> The artistic field is a *universe of belief*. Cultural production distinguishes itself from the production of the most common objects in that it must produce not only the object in its materiality, but also the value of this object, that is, the recognition of artistic legitimacy. This is inseparable from the production of the artist or writer as artist or writer, in other words, as a creator of value (164).

Bourdieu's notion of artistic value, then, emphasizes the fact that, in spite of what the participants in the art world may believe, it is a process taking place between people involved in the world of art rather than an entity specific to the work of art and guaranteed by the author's genius. Thus, the responsibility for the generation of "the value of works of art and belief in that value" (78) is a collective one involving not just the author of a work of art, but also its publisher, other writers, publishers, critics, and the public, in short, what he calls the agents and institutions of "the field of production" (78).

According to one commentator, "Bourdieu's *genetic sociology* or *genetic structuralism* [...] combines an analysis of objective social structures with an analysis of the genesis, within particular individuals, of the socially constituted mental structures which generate practice" (Johnson, 1993: 4). With respect to the notion of the field of production this means that Bourdieu understands two things: it is both "the system of objective relations" (78) between the agents and institutions mentioned above, and it is "the site of the struggles for the monopoly of the power to consecrate" (78). Understood as "a system of objective relations" the field of production forms a structured space of opposite positions. Thus, the overall structure of the field is said to rely on the "opposition between the 'commercial' and the 'non-commercial'" or the "'genuine'" (82). This aspect of the field of production displays a spatial structure: "While this opposition can change its substantive content and designate very different realities in different fields, it remains structurally invariant in different fields and in the same field at different moments" (82). Within the 'non-commercial' pole, moreover, Bourdieu identifies an opposition between "consecrated art and avant-garde art, or between orthodoxy and heresy" (83), that is, between producers in "dominant positions" and "the dominated producers" (83). Approached as "the site of the struggles for the monopoly of the power to consecrate", the field of production manifests itself as a dynamic and temporal structure.

> Through the struggle the field is given a temporal dimension. The ageing of authors, works or schools is [...] the continuous creation of the battle between those who have made their names [*fait date*] and are struggling to stay in view and those who cannot make their own names without relegating to the past the established figures, whose interest lies in freezing the movement of time, fixing the present state of the field for ever. On one side are the dominant figures, who want continuity, identity, reproduction; on the other, the newcomers, who seek discontinuity, rupture, difference, revolution. To 'make one's name' [*faire date*] means making one's *mark*, achieving recognition (in both senses) of one's *difference* from other producers, especially the most consecrated of them; at the same time, it means *creating a new position* beyond the positions presently occupied, *ahead* of them, in the *avant-garde* (106).

Bourdieu's agents, then, have only two opposite strategies at their disposal – strategies, including that of the avant-garde – which only make sense relationally and structurally with reference to each other. Thus, the dominant producers "operate essentially defensive strategies designed to perpetuate the status quo" while those who occupy the other pole "have to resort to subversive strategies", for instance, "the 'return to the sources'" (84) strategy.

In this essay my aim is not to map out the field of production regarded as "the system of objective relations," rather, I will be dealing with its manifestation as a "site of the struggles for the monopoly of the powers to consecrate". In the following, then, I examine the production of the Martians, the production of the value of their work and of the belief in the value of their work, resulting from the consecration struggles between the agents occupying the "non-commercial" or "genuine" pole of this particular field. Moreover, I examine why this battle of consecration involved the issue of emotion in particular. This essay does not examine the early discourse concerning the Martians in its totality. Rather, I have selected a variety of printed genres such as literary reviews, critical essays, interviews, award reports, manifestoes, and statements from editors.

II

On 20 October 1978, in an article entitled "Of the Martian School", James Fenton introduced the concept to the readers of the *New Statesman*. More particularly, it was launched in connection with his selection of Craig Raine's "A Martian Sends a Postcard Home" as the winner of the Prudence Farmer Award, and his decision to "create a second prize for the occasion" (520) for "Baldanders" by Christopher Reid. Although Fenton has claimed that the notion was made public "in an irresponsible fit" (1983: 13), and although, for instance, Dana Gioia has claimed that the Martian nickname was intended "playfully" (Stine and Marowski, vol. 32: 354), I want to emphasise that Fenton's readers had several reasons for taking him seriously since he creates an aura of importance around the phenomenon. First of all, by 1978 Fenton had made a name for himself as a poet, political journalist, travel writer, and foreign correspondent. In fact, according to an influential commentator, he was "the most intellectually audacious" (Thwaite, 1985: 123) among the new wave of British poets emerging since 1970. Secondly, his choice of "genre", that is, *The Prudence Farmer Award Report*, which was produced annually by various poets and critics with the purpose of celebrating the best poem published in *New Statesman* during the previous 12 months, bespoke a certain amount of sincerity. Thirdly, his decision to use the *New Statesman*, "a weekly journal of politics, art, and letters" which, according to *The Concise Oxford Companion to English Literature*, "has maintained its policy of 'dissent, of scepticism, of inquiry, of nonconformity'" (Drabble and Stringer, 1991: 397) since its inception in 1913, signified sincerity. Although I am going to return to the issue of playfulness in Fenton's article, I want to conclude that the author, genre, and context associated with the invention of the Martian school manifest a relatively high capital of consecration and imply a relatively strong power to consecrate.

Apart from the combined authority of author, genre, and context, the structure and key concerns of Fenton's Report betray his attempt at inventing the Martian school as a noteworthy player on the English poetry scene and as a recognizable poetics followed by a number of writers. Fenton does this by literally making a name for Raine's poetry, and by considering Raine's poetry in relation to its reception, to other poets, and to itself. Fenton's selection of the Martian tag for the poets in question is, of course, determined by the title of Raine's prize-winning poem "A Martian Sends a Postcard Home". However, Fenton uses the name of the school strategically. By entitling his Report "Of the Martian School", Fenton, from the very beginning, succeeds in creating this group of writers as different from other writers. Moreover, the extraterrestrial epithet of the title suggests that the difference in question is a difference of kind rather than degree. The development of difference is continued within the Report. The first three paragraphs primarily defend Raine from charges forwarded by other reviewers, and, secondly, describe him in contrast to other contemporary poets. But before Fenton's purpose with his article can be fully appreciated, it is necessary briefly to map out the responses Raine's poetry had received before 20 October 1978.

As I pointed out earlier, Raine's poetry was, generally speaking, met by a highly mixed response from his earliest readers. On the one hand, consecrating voices of considerable cultural capital reacted positively: he was awarded Cheltenham Festival Poetry Competition and National Poetry Competition prizes in 1977 and 1978. Moreover, John Osborne, in a full-length article on Raine, described *The Onion, Memory*, as constituting in some respects "a book of poems unrivalled in this country since Sylvia Plath's *Ariel*" (Osborne, 1978: 52). On the other hand, many reviewers of his first book of poetry, while acknowledging the inventiveness of Raine's use of simile and metaphor, nevertheless, sent him down for writing poetry that was too cold and brainy. Thus, in a review in the *New Statesman* significantly entitled "Have a Heart", Derek Mahon detected a "gratuitous cleverness" in the poems, stating that the poet seemed uncommitted and "merely playful", and even "a little heartless" sometimes (Stine & Marowski, 1985a: 348–49). Along the same lines, Derek Stanford in *Books and Bookmen* spoke of the "trigger-happy cleverness" of Raine's poetry (349). Alan Brownjohn in *The Encounter* complained that Raine's way of writing "preclude[d] much chance of normal human concerns breaking in" (349). And similarly, in the *Poetry Review* Lawrence Sail found that the writer's use of comparisons threatened to drown "feelings and attitudes", and advised Raine to increase "the traffic along what he [Raine] calls in one poem 'the branch-line of the heart'" (350).

Fenton's article takes its point of departure, not in Raine's poetry, but, precisely, in the negative reception of certain aspects of the poems. More particularly, as his starting point Fenton refers explicitly to John Carey's *Prudence Farmer Award Report* of the previous year and to Julian Symons's review in *The Times* of Raine's first book. In this manner Fenton directs his subversive strategies against two particular critics in order to counter Raine's negative reception in general. He has to undermine, first of all, the dominant view on Raine within the institution of the Prudence Farmer Award.

In his article John Carey described Craig Raine as "an immensely talented and unerringly rebarbative young poet" (1977, 220), i.e. he produced Raine as a creator, but not as a creator of value. Fenton feels that the second half of Carey's pronouncement needs "some qualification" (1978: 520; all subsequent quotations from Fenton's article are from this page). While he agrees with Carey that "Mr Raine's penchant for the outrageous image can create some startling repulsive effects", Fenton, in order to counter Carey's verdict, distinguishes between two Raine personae: the poet and the journalist. In his journalism Raine's scandalous imagery appears "highly unlikely, horrible if true" and merely functioning as "unloving detail". In his poetry, however, it functions in a way that makes his work highly "interesting and original". Secondly, Fenton selects Julian Symons, who was, arguably, a reviewer with a conspicuous cultural capital.[1] The distinction between Raine's journalism and poetry is also used by Fenton in his dismantling of Julian Symons's belittling view that Raine's poems are "merely clever". "Mere cleverness" is confined to Raine's journalism, Fenton assures his readers. Raine's poetry, on the other hand, is "different". While the journalistic pieces point to the author, the poetry calls attention to the thing according to Fenton.

Fenton also takes on the charges of mere cleverness against Raine by launching what he calls "a campaign against stupidity" in contemporary poetry. In contrast to the strategy of "the second-rate" poets, which involves "the deliberate mystification of the reader", Raine writes poetry that is "complex", but "reward[ing]"; its puzzles, far from confounding the reader, yield pleasure in the process of riddling them. And, Fenton maintains, "there is more to the poetry than puzzle-solving", attributing to Raine "the phenomenological style" characterised by "a free contemplation, without ulterior motive, eager if anything for the most improbable discoveries".

In this manner, then, Fenton's article not only takes its point of departure in the negative reception of certain aspects of the poems rather than in the poems themselves, but, actually, devotes the first three of its six para-

---

1   As novelist, short story writer, poet, editor, historian, critic, biographer, and scriptwriter (Stine and Marowski 1985a: 424), Julian Symons's power to consecrate and give value was formidable by 1978. And, with respect to poetry and criticism, *Contemporary Literary Criticism* adds that Symons first made his name in the 1930s as a poet, publishing two volumes of verse and editing a poetry journal. His reputation as a critic was also established before he published his first crime novel, and he has continued to write criticism, including books on Charles Dickens and Thomas Carlyle (424).

graphs to defending Raine against charges of repulsiveness and cleverness. But why is it important for Fenton to clear Raine of these charges? Arguably they stand for something else. Repulsiveness and cleverness are symptoms, I suggest, of a really serious condition for the writer of poetry: emotional sterility. In fact, the second half of Fenton's Report is a direct attempt at absolving Raine from these charges by showing that his cleverness serves a higher purpose, by presenting him as an emotional Martian, and a leader of a school of poetry with the common project of viewing our world from an alien but sympathetic perspective.

Fenton begins this section of his Report, i.e. paragraphs four and five, by justifying his choice of Raine's poem "A Martian Sends a Postcard Home":

> The poem which I finally chose is based on a string of misunderstandings. The Martian's point of view is a useful fiction, but it is not unlike the poet's own, which always insists on presenting the familiar at its most strange. The misunderstandings, appropriately enough for an Oxford poet, are like riddles in the Anglo-Saxon mode. Once solved, they do not lose their interest. Instead there is a double pathos. (Fenton, 1978)

Fenton's justification rests on two assumptions. First, the poem is regarded as a kind of programme or manifesto poem, and, secondly, its author and speaker are considered to be identical. Thus, he regards "A Martian" as a crystallization of Raine's poetic project because of a certain similarity – a "not unlike[ness]" – between the defamiliarizing points of view of its Martian persona and its author. In this way the poem is grounded in the distinctive vision of its author, who simultaneously is produced as a creator of value. Another important criterion for Fenton concerns the poem's identity as "a string of misunderstandings" which, moreover, are "like riddles in the Anglo-Saxon mode". The Anglo-Saxon affinity is crucial to Fenton since it allows him to claim that the riddles are more than riddles. In contrast to straight-forward riddles, which become uninteresting once they have been solved, these remain worthy of attention since they serve a higher purpose by producing "a double pathos". What Fenton means by this concept is clarified in the following paragraph: "The Martian expresses his enormous sympathy for us and our world. One cannot help feeling saddened by his sadness". Double pathos seems to involve the author-persona's expression of "fellow-feeling [...] feeling-along-with the mental state and emotions, of another human being, or of nonhuman beings to whom we attribute human emotions" (Abrams, 1999: 74). Secondly, the author-persona's emotions trigger similar ones in the reader. Fenton's notion of double pathos appears to involve the dimensions of author and reader, then, linking poet and audience in common emotional concerns. Fenton also offers what amounts to an example of this concept: "Without wishing to solve any riddles, I can only say that nobody in my experience has written so feelingly about the object described in couplets 10–12". Here Fenton is referring to the three couplets that outline a telephone:

> In homes, a haunted apparatus sleeps,
> that snores when you pick it up.
>
> If the ghost cries, they carry it
> to their lips and soothe it to sleep
>
> with sounds. And yet, they wake it up
> deliberately, by tickling it with a finger.
> (Craig Raine, "A Martian Sends a Postcard Home",
> ll. 19–24, quoted in Fenton 1978)

Double pathos, in this particular case, would involve the author-persona's personification of the telephone in terms of a baby or a favourite pet, and, secondly, after the reader has successfully solved the riddle, his or her realization of the aptness of this way of conceptualising and valorising a means of communication.

Whether the Martian's sympathy really is "enormous", whether he really is feeling that sad, and whether we are really "feeling saddened by his sadness" is immaterial. Similarly, even if we admit that we are dealing with the most emotionalized conceptualization of a telephone in the history of poetry, the question of whether we are really meant to regard the baby/pet – telephone analogy seriously is irrelevant for my reading of Fenton's Report. My point is not that Fenton's reading of these lines is right or wrong. Rather, what is important is the fact that he points to the element of feeling in order to account for the value of the description of the telephone, and that he points to the omnipresence of pathos involving author-persona and reader in order to justify the greatness of "A Martian".

In the sixth and last paragraph, Fenton, by awarding a second prize to Christopher Reid's poem "Baldanders", tries to create the idea that we are indeed dealing with a school with masters and disciples. He stresses that Reid deserves special mention "since there is an affinity between the two poets". In fact, the affinity is so strong that he presents Reid's poem "as a minor masterpiece of the Martian school". In this way, Fenton indirectly succeeds in presenting Raine's poem as a major masterpiece. Moreover,

Fenton's integration of Christopher Reid into the Martian school involves considerations of the presence of emotion in his poem. On the one hand, it appears to be "an extended imagist joke", on the other, he detects "a Martian sympathy for the subject".

Here I want briefly to readdress the question of Fenton's seriousness I touched upon earlier. Fenton concludes his article by emphasizing that the Martian school is "a school that ought to be noticed, since it has enrolled two of the best poets writing in England today," conferring a high degree of autonomy and agency on the phenomenon. Fenton's concluding claims concerning the status of the Martian school as an autonomous agent or body with the power of enrolling poets is, arguably, the only instance in the article that can be said to have an air of playfulness about it. The notion of schools in literary matters is a metaphorical one, of course. But it is a dead metaphor. Fenton's use of the school metaphor in the conclusion of his article amounts to a literalization of the term – it is as if we are dealing with a real school which *does* enroll pupils. Appropriately for an article that outlines the poetics of the Martians, the effect is a defamiliarizing one. By literalizing the school metaphor, he makes strange the convention of literary history whereby writers are figured in terms of schools, i.e. the very convention Fenton has used in the title of his article. In short, Fenton is himself employing something akin to the Martian point of view, which shows "the familiar at its most strange", by presenting the dead metaphor of the literary school in a strange, because literal, manner. If an element of playfulness is involved in his invention of the Martian school, it concerns the "school" component only. The Martian component, on the other hand, is regarded seriously and invested with the combined cultural capital of author, genre, and context since it is related directly to the element of emotion in Raine's poetry.

By giving Craig Raine the Prudence Farmer Award and by inventing a second prize for Christopher Reid, Fenton has actually succeeded in doing several things, then. First of all, he has established that the prize winning poem forms a crystallization or reflection of Raine's Martian poetry and poetics in general, and that there exists a relation of similarity between poet and persona, making Raine the creator of value. Secondly, he has demonstrated that "A Martian", and by extension Raine's Martian poetics, are discourses of feeling, sadness, sympathy, and pathos involving poet and audience. Taken together the focus on the poet, the audience, and matters of feeling suggests that Fenton regards Raine as exemplifying a particular idea of poetry. The notion of poetry that Fenton applauds in Raine contains an expressive element. According to Abrams (1971) an expressive notion of poetry holds that: "A work of art is essentially the internal made external, resulting from a creative process operating under the impulse of feeling, and embodying the combined product of the poet's perceptions, thoughts, and feelings" (22). Fenton's Martian, who, we remember, "expresses his enormous sympathy for us and our world," is indebted to this particular tradition of figuring poets and poetry. But Fenton seems to think that Raine's poetry manifests another dimension too. By focussing on the effect on the audience – "One cannot help feeling saddened by his sadness" – Fenton thematizes the pragmatic orientation of the poem, i.e. he regards it "chiefly as a means to an end, an instrument for getting something done, and tends to judge its value according to its success in achieving that aim" (15). Lastly, apart from identifying expressionist and pragmatic orientations in Raine, Fenton has succeeded in showing that his poetics is a noteworthy literary phenomenon since it is followed by other poets, i.e. Christopher Reid, who is also displaying "Martian sympathy".

However, if Fenton's purpose were merely to give Raine the Award for the best poem published in the *New Statesman* in 1978, the above points appear immaterial. They only become fully relevant and meaningful if we regard Fenton's article as containing other purposes as well. For instance, he appears to want to consecrate Raine's poetry and poetics in general. He employs three interrelated strategies as we have seen. First of all, Fenton produces a name, literally speaking, for Raine (and Reid) – a name which is pregnant with difference. Secondly, he tries to defend him from the accusations of emotional barrenness filed by other reviewers, i.e. those representing the orthodox or dominant point of view, by distinguishing between Raine's prose and poetry, and by demonstrating that his "cleverness" serves a higher purpose. Thirdly, Fenton desecrates the consecrated producers by accusing them of stupidity and deliberately bewildering the reader. The strategies reveal another aspect of Fenton's purpose: the defence of the notion of poetry as the discourse of feeling and a particular idea of poetry's social function. I return to these issues after I have sketched out the reception of the Martians that followed Fenton's Report. Generally speaking, after Fenton's invention of the Martian school, and his related identification of expressionist and pragmatic aspects of emotion and feeling in Raine's poetry, the attention to these elements remains central. In the following I outline this concern with particular reference to reviews and discussions of Raine's *A Martian Sends a Postcard Home* (1979) and Reid's *Arcadia* (1979) and *Pea Soup* (1982).

Blake Morrison's review of *Arcadia* presents Raine and Reid as "the first mainstream British poets since 1945 to embark on a programme which makes imagination its priority" (1979: 64), and for whom "imagination is *play*". However, having mapped out the predominance of "hedonistic structures" in Reid's poems, Morrison assures his readers that, "they are not quite the poems of a dandy or aesthete: after reading *Arcadia* you feel that the world is a stranger, richer, more various place than you'd supposed, a feeling which it takes commitment of a kind to produce". The review does not specify what Morrison means by his notion of "commitment of a kind". However, it functions in very much the same way as Fenton's concern with the expressionist aspect of feeling in his Report by identifying an element of engagement, or dedication, or even devotion which is suggestive of Reid's emotional involvement with "the world". It is also interesting to note Morrison's identification of a pragmatic angle in his description of *Arcadia*'s benign effect on its readers in terms of the verb 'feel' and the noun 'feeling'. In the first case there is near synonymity between feeling and thinking. Thus, 'you feel' can easily be read as 'you think'. In the second case they are more like antonyms; certainly, 'a feeling' doesn't necessarily translate into 'a thought'. Finally it is important that Morrison rounds off his review by thematizing the issue of emotion explicitly in relation to the Martians. Speaking of the inevitability of comparing Raine and Reid, he states that "Reid's treatment of people is cooler, even crueller, than Raine's". Morrison argues, then, that the expressionist and pragmatic elements of emotion are there in the poetry of the Martians, but differences of degree in their handling distinguish them. The same point is apparent in Alan Brownjohn's review of *Arcadia* in the *Encounter*. However, in contrast to Morrison, Brownjohn finds that Reid "could turn out [...] the more sensitive and accomplished poet of the two" (Stine & Marowski, 1985b: 349).

Andrew Motion's review of *A Martian Sends a Postcard Home* basically restates the substance of Fenton's argument, "This kind of perception is more than simply a means by which the ordinary becomes strange again," he points out with specific reference to the telephone couplets I quoted above. He continues, "It's also Raine's method of realising and releasing emotion. Once, extraordinarily, he was accused of heartlessness; in fact, poem after poem registers a deep affection for what he sees. His way of looking is also a way of bearing his heart" (1979: 947). Moreover, Motion tries to narrow down the phenomenon of authorial emotion in Raine by contrasting this combination of scrutiny and sympathy characteristic of "A Martian" and earlier poems with "a disquieting development" (948) in recent examples of Raine's poetry. According to Motion certain poems in *A Martian Sends a Postcard Home* involve a tendency "to be knowingly tender, and thereby have too palpable a design on us", i.e. they manifest a blatant concern with their audience. In this way the important element of emotion in Raine is defined as quietly expressionist and pragmatic.

Around this time (December 1979) Raine himself intervened in this discussion concerning emotion in his poetry. In *The Poetry Book Society Bulletin* he stated: "I have deliberately chosen a neutral, objective tone which allows the images to speak for themselves – under authorial supervision, of course, but without overt moralising. I hope no one will be stupid enough to mistake this tone for lack of feeling" (quoted in Hulse, 1981: 15–16). The references to "a neutral, objective tone" involving "authorial" presence "without overt moralising" bears close resemblance to the kind of authorial emotion Motion isolates in his idea of Raine's mode of seeing as "a way of bearing his heart". Michael Hulse, in his favourable article on Raine, accepts Raine's own interpretation of the matter: "No doubt Raine's somewhat arrogant tone here will not endear him to his detractors, but, on the other hand, he is entitled to establish his own aesthetic standpoint, and the point he makes is good" (16).

The same tendency to allow for a kind of hidden emotion in Raine's poetry is part of John Bayley's review of *A Martian Sends a Postcard Home*. Having wondered "who but Craig Raine would want to [...] sympathize " (1980: 1) with the highly mundane objects in his poetry, and after having noticed how particular elements in the poetry force "us to identify" (2), and how "the best poem in [the collection] creates a whole climate of feeling out of the simplest possible repetitions and connections", we are told that "Raine has far too tight a grip for things to need to display feeling: it would be the most unfortunate thing if he felt he had to go on to do so, in the same way that every novelist today is required to be 'compassionate' as well as clever" (3). Bayley, then values Raine's handling of the expressionist element of feeling without "display". Further, he senses that Raine goes against the grain of the expectations of contemporary readers, who demand emotional enhancement, and "find it irresistible that the poet should deepen and develop a heart".

In a 1981 interview with John Haffenden, Raine again tries to carve out his relation to emotion by developing a notion of poetic carefulness that contrasts with the contemporary readers' views on feeling mentioned by Bayley. Commenting on a poem from *A Martian...*, he states: "In 'The Butcher' I describe the man very carefully. For me, 'careful' also means full of care: it's a tender, teasing poem – the way you tease someone you like" (Haffenden, 1981: 181). Later in the same interview he says that "Currently we have a very crude view of what constitutes feeling; there's is a terrible dead orthodoxy about what poets are allowed to feel" (183), suggesting that his idea of poetic carefulness is the fresh and unconventional way of incorporating feeling into poetry.

From the reviews and interviews the concern with emotion eventually finds its way into Blake Morrison and Andrew Motion's *The Penguin Book of Contemporary British Poetry*, which collects what they "believe to be the most important achievements and developments in British poetry during recent years" (1982: 11). In their introduction to the Martian school they comment on the predilection of Craig Raine and Christopher Reid for establishing "connections and relationships" (18), and, reiterating Motion (1979), they point out that: "Though [they] are artfully arranged, it would be wrong to think that the Martians' ingenuity prevents them from expressing emotion: their way of looking is also a way of feeling". Moreover, they suggest that it is precisely the expressionist element of feeling that "explains why Raine and Reid have proved so influential in a comparatively short time".

Published by Penguin Books, the Morrison and Motion anthology forms the culmination in the consecration struggle concerning the Martian school. The subversive strategies have succeeded, the avant-garde is fully consecrated, heresy has become orthodoxy, and the previously dominated producers are now the dominant ones. However, the struggle in the field of production is a never ending one, and Martin Booth's review of *Pea Soup* in *British Book News*, February, 1983, although it, too, casts the Martians as constituting the dominant producers, continues the battle of consecration by taking up a different position in the field of production:

> Christopher Reid's second book of verse [*Pea Soup*] furthers his emerging reputation as darling of the new poetocracy, the movement that seems to draw its inspiration from the technique of metaphor, even at the expense of emotion, that core of verse-making, and which is rapidly succeeding in its takeover bid for contemporary British poetry. His work is characteristically shallow in its observation and depends much upon a witty modernity for its impact, seeking to study as it does the world of today [...] (Stine and Marowski, 1985b: 351).

Here Booth speaks from the point of view of the dominated producers and against the consecrated ones, "the new poetocracy", which refers unequivocally to the Martians and their partiality for metaphor. The tables, then, are turned, or almost turned since the consecration of the Martians appears not to have been fully achieved after all, judging from Booth's use of the progressive tense in his diagnosis of "the movement [...] which is rapidly succeeding in its takeover bid for contemporary British poetry". However, Booth's subversive strategies include features which were also found in the defensive ones of the early reviewers. For instance, the image of Reid as "darling of the new poetocracy" constructs him as a poet whose claim to importance rests outside himself, i.e. with the movement ruling the British poetry scene at the moment. The early allegations of coldness reappear, too. In Booth's case the charge of emotional superficiality is present on two levels. First of all, the project of the Martians is described as an almost monomaniacally reductive one tuned solely to "the technique of metaphor" with the result that the essence of poetry, i.e. emotion – "that core of verse-making"– is sacrificed. Secondly, the poetocracy's own strategy in the struggle for consecration is conceptualised in shallow economic terms as a "takeover bid", as if Booth wants to push the Martians away from the pole of genuine poetry towards the commercial one. Conversely Booth's strategy becomes a 'return to roots strategy' since he appeals to the fundamental quality of the poetry genre.

The same year, i.e. 1983, also saw Fenton's attempt at desecrating what he tried so hard to consecrate five years earlier. In his "The Manifesto Against Manifestoes", Fenton not only confesses that he invented the term "in an irresponsible fit" (13), i.e. he tries to undermine the authority of his 1978 Report, he also makes it quite clear what he thinks of Raine and Reid's proselytes: "But soon the pupils were lining up at the door, while the teachers [i.e. Raine and Reid], quite rightly, had slipped out the back way. The students broke into the classroom and pilfered everything they found. England had not witnessed such a wholesale robbery for half a century". While the references to pupils, teachers, and classrooms continue the school metaphor, which was intended playfully as a defamiliarizing device in the 1978 Report, the images of crime involving breaking and entering, pilfering, and robbery emphasise its inadequacy now. But not only are we dealing with a situation involving robbery rather than enrolment; it is a particular kind of juvenile delinquency according to Fenton: "Considered theft is a considerable tribute. One could wish, though, that the thieves were less prone to smear the walls with their excrement." Fenton's scatological imagery effectively desecrates the followers of Raine and Reid by diagnozing an embarrassingly facile expressionism, a symptom of strange fits of passion, indeed. However, Fenton's attempt at terminating the notion of the Martian school once and for all by desecrating it is the starting point of a renewed strategy intended to consecrate Craig Raine. And, interestingly, this attempt also involves the identification of the element of emotion in the poet Craig Raine, whom he regards as "much misunderstood and misread" (15). Raine is, in Fenton's book,

> [P]rimarily, an emotional, an erotic poet. It is perhaps the eroticism which is in advance of his day. When a poet looks at his wife and thinks of a tomato, one may feel that he lacks feeling. But when he further shows that his feeling for tomatoes is more deeply affectionate and more sexually alert than most poets' feelings for their first girlfriends, one is obliged to think again. Obliged to feel again. (15)

Fenton's second attempt at consecrating Raine explicitly produces him as an avant-garde poet, who differs from his contemporaries by being "in advance of his day". But the difference which characterises Raine in relation to his contemporaries according to Fenton is basically a restatement of his earlier idea of double pathos involving both the poet's strange yet deep affection and its effect on his readers.

Thus, the early reception of the Martian school, the story from its birth to its proposed death and dissolution, the struggle concerning its consecration and desecration, is very much related to the issue of emotion. Moreover, as we have seen, the topic is unflaggingly addressed with reference to (either) the poet and/or the audience, i.e. the matter of feeling in relation to the poetry as poetry is never actualized. In other words, feeling's objective orientation, its capacity of generating unity or coherence in a poetic text – is regarded as irrelevant compared to its expressionist and pragmatic orientations. The various notions that can either be extracted directly from the reviews and interviews or generated from them: "double pathos" and "Martian sympathy" (Fenton, 1978), "commitment of a kind" (Morrison, 1979), scrutinizing "deep affection" (Motion, 1979), covert "feeling" (Raine quoted in Hulse, 1981), undisplayed "feeling" (Bayley, 1980), poetic carefulness (Raine in Haffenden, 1981), sympathetic scrutiny (Morrison and Motion, 1982), emotional "shallow[ness]" (Booth in Stine and Marowski, 1985b), and Fenton's idea of a strange yet "affectionate" eroticism, are designed to conceptualize a characteristically Martian (or in the case of Fenton (1983) Rainean) concern with, or, for reviewers like Booth, indifference to emotion. But why is emotion, and, more particularly, why are its expressionist and pragmatic aspects so important for both the subversive and the defensive participants in the history of construction I have outlined so far? I think there are two related answers. One has to do with the particular notion of the nature and function of poetry which is assumed by the reviewers, the other with the specific idea of reviewing and criticism that is taken for granted.

Concerning the issue of poetry, T. S. Eliot's essay "The Social Function of Poetry," originally published 1945, makes explicit the assumptions of the contributors to the early reception of the Martians. Poetry, says Eliot, "is the vehicle of feeling" (1979: 19); it "has primarily to do with the expression of feeling and emotion". Further, "feeling and emotion are particular". But it is a special kind of particularity Eliot is talking about since it involves the poet's "race and language" (18) rather than his class, gender, age, or his own unique personality. Eliot advocates, then, a kind of national or racial expressionism where the poet expresses the emotions of his people rather than his own. However, Eliot qualifies this idea by subordinating the poet's duty to his people to his duty to his language: the poet must, first and foremost, work at preserving, extending, and improving his language:

> In expressing what other people feel he is also changing the feeling by making it more conscious; he is making people more aware of what they feel already, and therefore teaching them something about themselves. But he is not merely a more conscious person than the others; he is also individually different from other people, and from other poets too, and can make his readers share consciously in new feelings which they had not experienced before. That is the difference between the writer who is merely eccentric or mad and the genuine poet. The former may have feelings which are unique but which cannot be shared, and are therefore useless; the latter discovers new variations of sensibility which can be appropriated by others. And in expressing them he is developing and enriching the language which he speaks. (20)

Thus, the social function of poetry is no laughing matter. In fact, according to Eliot, the stakes are extremely high, indeed: "we cannot afford to *stop* writing poetry," he argues, since the absence of poets produces a kind of domino effect: "unless they go on producing great authors, and especially great poets, their language will deteriorate, their culture will deteriorate and perhaps become absorbed in a stronger one" (21).

I want to suggest, then, that the participants in the production of the Martians, both the defensive and the subversive ones, are fuelled by beliefs in the social importance of poetry akin to those formulated by Eliot. Both parties agree that real poetry ought to form "the vehicle of feeling". I also think that they pledge themselves to the notion that "the genuine poet" is a disinterested discoverer, teacher, and sharer of feelings – a kind of altruistic explorer of the continent of human emotions. Both parties would also agree that literary criticism, the art of reviewing literature, and discourse on art in general involves the discovery of the absence or presence of the thing that justifies the poetry, i.e. emotion. But if both sides in the debate ultimately appear to be employing defensive strategies designed to endorse particular ideas of poetry and the discourse on poetry, who is the subversive player they are responding to in the consecration struggle? Arguably, we are dealing with something like Eliot's worst case scenario, but the disruptive voices threatening language and culture are for a large part foreign to the cultural field in Britain, which, nevertheless, is in the process of being infiltrated by them at this time. I am thinking in particular about the impact of French structuralism and post-structuralism in Britain. Let me give just one example of this influence, David Lodge's study *The Modes of Modern Writing*, originally published in 1977, which among other things, introduces "the *nouvelle critique*" (1983: 57–71). This is, in part, how Lodge sums up the lesson of this particular intellectual tradition: "Poems are not made out of experience, they are made out of poetry – the tradition of disposing the possibilities of language to poetic ends" (70). Although Lodge tries to naturalize the idea by referring to Eliot's "Tradition and the Individual Talent" as "a classic exposition of the idea" (70), his general exposition of Roland Barthes's theories of writing undermines the notion of the genuine writer as a creator of expressive discourse that we saw advocated by Eliot. Lodge, for instance, quotes the following statement by Barthes:

> [L]anguage cannot be considered a simple instrument, whether utilitarian or decorative, of thought. Man does not exist prior to language, either as a species or as an individual. We never find a state where man is separated from language, which he then creates in order to "express" what is taking place within him: it is language which teaches the definition of man, not the reverse. (Roland Barthes, "To Write: an intransitive Verb?", quoted in Lodge, 1983: 70)

Barthes's ideas attack Eliot's notion of the poet as someone who "discovers new variations of sensibility which can be appropriated by others," and who "in expressing them [...] is developing and enriching the language which he speaks". Barthes's subversive strategy is particularly visible in his reversal of the relationship between man and language. Note also how Barthes' discourse literally subverts the idea of expressionism by placing the verb within inverted commas.

III

My discussion of "the site of the struggles for the monopoly of the powers to consecrate" (Bourdieu, 1993: 78) has shown two things. First, I have outlined how the Martians went through several stages of production. Given Bourdieu's emphasis on the power of difference to produce time, exemplified, for instance, by the epigraph to this essay, it is not unreasonable to summarize these stages in terms of a story: after the strong disagreements on the value of Raine's poetry and, in particular, after the accusations of coldness voiced by important players in the field of production, Fenton's 1978 Report formed a significant turning point. Fenton literally invented the Martian school and gave value to their writing by, among other things, attempting to identify a specific kind of emotion in Raine and Reid's poetry – a kind that made a difference. In perpetuating the theorisation of the specificity of the idea of emotion in their poetry, the subsequent discourse on the Martians comprised a kind of rising action culminating in the inclusion of the school into *The Penguin Book of Contemporary British Poetry*. But that did not bring about a neat ending to the tale of the Martians. Instead of a *denouement*, the struggle was renewed and the Martians, this time in the role of the dominant producers, became the target of subversive strategies. Secondly, I have also demonstrated how the defensive and subversive voices agreed on one thing: that the value of poetry is intimately related to the presence of emotion. And I have suggested how, on another level of struggle, the two apparently competing voices in fact constitute a single pole from where a particular notion of poetry is defended against the subversive strategies of the avant-garde, represented by, for instance, French structuralism and post-structuralism and their British middlemen. Perloff (1998) is an example of the fact that this struggle is still going strong today.

Ultimately, then, the agents' defensive strategies are directed against the principles which, through Bourdieu's influence, inform my own approach to the field of production of the Martians. In this way I have inscribed myself into the struggle between the dominant and the dominated producers concerning the power to consecrate real poetry and genuine poets – the very struggle that I have tried to examine rather than take part in. Inserting yourself into, in this case, the field of production in this manner is inevitable. If, according to Bourdieu, you cannot take a stand outside the field, what are the consequences for the status of my own "examination" of the production of the Martian School? Certainly, I cannot claim to have discovered the truth about the rise of the Martians. But I hope to have shown that Bourdieu's notion of the field of production as a site of struggle is a useful one since it allows me to suggest both explicit and implicit stakes in the particular struggle concerning the Martians. Moreover, the identification of these stakes form the first step in the creation of a map of the field of production in Bourdieu's second sense, i.e., as "a system of objective relations" (1993: 78). But that is the purpose of another essay.[2]

References

Abrams, M.H. (1971) *The Mirror and the Lamp: Theory and the Critical Tradition.* Oxford: Oxford University Press

——. (1999) *A Glossary of Literary Terms.* New York and London: Hartcourt Brace College Publishers

Bayley, John (1980) "Making it Strange". *Times Literary Supplement.* January 4. [http://galenet.galegroup.com/servlet/li...org&g=Craig+Raine&DT=Criticism+OR+Top] – last consulted July 2001

Bourdieu, Pierre (1993) *The Field of Cultural Production: Essays on Art and Literature.* (Edited and Introduced by Randal Johnson). Cambridge: Polity Press

Carey, John (1977) "The Prudence Farmer Award". *New Statesman.* 12 August 1977. p. 220

Drabble, Margaret and Stringer, Jenny (eds.) (1991) *The Concise Oxford Companion to English Literature.* Oxford and New York: Oxford University Press

Eliot, T.S. (1979) "The Social Function of Poetry". *On Poetry and Poets.* London and Boston: Faber and Faber

Fenton, James (1978) "Of the Martian School". *The New Statesman.* 20 October 1978. p. 520.

——. (1983) "The Manifesto Against Manifestoes". *Poetry Review.* Vol. 73, No. 3. 1983. pp. 12–16.

---

2 This essay is part of a project dealing with *The Production of the British Author, 1970—The Present.* Apart from Raine and Reid, this project focuses, so far, on Martin Amis, Jeanette Winterson, Will Self, and Tibor Fischer.

Haffenden, John (1981) "Craig Raine". *Viewpoints: Poets in Conversation with John Haffenden*. London & Boston: Faber and Faber

Hamilton, Ian. (ed.) (1994) *The Oxford Companion to Twentieth-century Poetry in English*. Oxford and New York: Oxford University Press

Hulse, Michael (1981) "Alms for Every Beggared Sense: Craig Raine's Aesthetic in Context". *Critical Quarterly*. Vol. 23. No. 4. 1981. pp. 13–21

Johnson, Randall (1993) "Editor's Introduction: Pierre Bourdieu on Art, Literature and Culture". Pierre Bourdieu (1993) *The Field of Cultural Production: Essays on Art and Literature*. Randal Johnson,ed. Cambridge: Polity Press

Lodge, David (1983) *The Modes of Modern Writing: Metaphor, Metonymy, and the Typology of Modern Literature*. London: Edward Arnold

Morrison, Blake (1979) "A Bookworm in the Kitchen". *New Statesman*. 13 July 1979. p. 64

Morrison, Blake and Andrew Motion (1982) "Introduction". *The Penguin Book of Contemporary British Poetry*. (Edited by Blake Morrison and Andrew Motion). Penguin Books

Motion, Andrew (1979) "Alien Eyes". *New Statesman*. 14 December 1979. p. 947

Osborne, John (1978) "The Incredulous Eye: Craig Raine and Post-Modernist Aesthetics". *Stone Ferry Review*. Vol. 2. 1978. pp. 51–65

Perloff, Marjorie (1998) "What we Don't Talk About When We Talk About Poetry: Some Aporias of Literary Journalism". *Grub Street and Ivory Tower: Literary Journalism and Literary Scholarship from Fielding to the Internet*. Jeremy Treglow and Bridget Bennett, eds. Oxford: Oxford University Press

Stine, Jean C. and Daniel G. Marowski (eds.) (1985a) *Contemporary Literary Criticism: Excerpts from Criticism of the Works of Today's Novelists, Poets, Playwrights, Short Story Writers, Scriptwriters, and Other Creative Writers*. Vol. 32. Detroit: Gale Research Company

——. (1985b) *Contemporary Literary Criticism: Excerpts from Criticism of the Works of Today's Novelists, Poets, Playwrights, Short Story Writers, Scriptwriters, and Other Creative Writers*. Vol. 33. Detroit: Gale Research Company

Thwaite, Anthony (1985) *Poetry Today: A Critical Guide to British Poetry 1960–1984*. London and New York: Longman

The ABCs, or GHQs, of Global Text Reading

BEN DORFMAN

I would like in this essay to talk about something of an invented phenomenon – a phenomenon that, at least in my experience, I have not seen named as a part of textual studies. I will call this phenomenon the 'global text'. As I will define it, a global text is both a product of as well as representation of globalization as a historical process.

Now, it should be said that though I have not in fact seen it named before, the idea of the global text is not manufactured completely out of whole cloth. Rather, it draws on existing concepts that already appear to be associated with a 'global genre'– e.g. 'world music', 'global culture', 'transnational art' and globalization's supposed 'post-nationalism'. As such, the 'global text' is an attempt to put a number of cultural artifacts, objects and events, associated with the idea of the global under one roof and give them a singular and defined analytical basis. I see this analytical basis as a matter of common sense, and including two elements. First, global texts reflect the processes of which they are a result – they are connected to those processes, and say something about them. Second, global texts further the processes they reflect in the course of their reflecting those processes. I.e., reflection is never just reflection, but an element of historical development itself.

Now, in any essay on globalization, it is important to point out that understandings of globalization as both term and process are contested. There are a number of excellent readers on the topic that can guide students through this contested terrain (e.g. Beynon and Dunkerley, 2000). To avoid controversy, however, I will employ what I see as a relatively straightforward, generally-accepted definition of the term: in this essay, globalization will be "the set of economic, environmental, political, cultural and social processes that first connect and then integrate societies" (Cameron and Stein, 2002: 1).

Clearly, this definition of globalization raises some important points. First, it indicates globalization as a process with deep historical roots. By our definition, every instance of historical interculturalism becomes an example of globalization. The Roman Empire would be a prime example. Though Rome was important (mostly from about 50 B.C. through the first century A.D) for conquering a great deal of territory, it conquered a great number of cultures and imposed on them a political structure in doing so. This structure was known as the *Pax Romana*. Now, an oft-promoted interpretation of the *Pax Romana* is that it was not cultural – its effect, goes this interpretation, was to leave cultures intact and only demand that conquered territories play by Roman economic and political rules (see e.g. Ward, et. al., 2003 for good general introductions to Roman society and culture). However, one might consider this emphasis on economics and politics a particular cultural emphasis or trait on the part of Rome. As the orator Aristedes suggested, Romans may have thought that what made Rome great was its "harmonious, all-embracing union" that "[kept] no man from being a citizen" (Aristedes, 1998: 89). Therein, Rome represents an example of how globalization might be an essential element of history generally. Any movement of people, history of conquest or multi-national empire is, like Rome, an example of cultural 'connection and integration,' as I posed in our definition of globalization.

Secondly, however, by my definition of globalization, there is a difference between global history as a whole and its specific division (e.g. Roman history, Greek history, or any modern national history). Like the globalization as a general process, what 'global history' is on a specific basis has also been a point of extended debate. Here, however, I will also try to be 'common sense'. "The 'limits'" of global history, as one recent book expresses it, are (and always have been) the globe itself (Guha, 2002). This means that global history is the unfolding of the history of the world on its full scale. It also means that global history only involves historical processes that are able to operate on such a large scale, as well as across social and cultural boundaries. Roman history, for example, may have played a role in global history. Alone, however, it was *not* global history, even within the specific period of the Roman Empire under *Pax Romana*.

Given these points, I will make several moves over the next pages to deepen our understanding of the 'global text'. First, I will look at how global texts reflect global history. The question here is simple: how is it possible to look at what I am calling global texts and see global history as embodied, or represented in them? One might think of this another way: how do global texts 'symbolize' global history and its processes? How can they be seen as 'referring to' globalization as a historical process? These questions, however, lead to another point I would like to address: how, per the definition of the global text, do global texts further and perpetuate globalization and, because of globalization's historical nature, global *history*, as such? In other words, once understanding how global history may be read in the global text, I would like to ask how global texts help make that history. In conclusion, I would like to abstract our methodology. The question here might be understood as whether it is possible to find a *logic* for the interpretation of global texts, especially in cultural and historical terms.

Graceland (With an Excursus on Deterritorialization and Time-Space Compression)

Before we begin answering the above-listed questions, we actually need to backtrack. This is because, although 'connection' and 'integration' are useful concepts for defining globalization, we might be able to be more specific in terms of understanding global *history*. In other words, are there processes that underlie social connection and integration and, form a long-term perspective, make them possible, as such? Might we identify something more fundamental to the genealogy, or 'family history', of the global present – something that extends into the past to make *it* (that past) global as well? My answer (not surprisingly) is 'yes'. Two ideas should be considered in this context: *time-space compression* and *deterritorialization*.

I will attempt to illustrate these ideas. First, we might note that one of the elements making global history unique is that it functions quite abstractly. Of course, this could be said about any history. Indeed, as I write here largely for a Danish audience, it seems appropriate to ask what Denmark is but an idea – a concept – as such? In other words, we may understand Denmark as a conglomeration of historical circumstances – the Christianization of the Danes, power struggles in the Kalmar Union, the

Reformation, etc… However, what makes that conglomeration of circumstances *Denmark*, except for an *idea* of Denmark, or at least an idea of *that history*? Still, despite the ideological nature of all histories, we can recognize the historical-conceptual processes of globalization as of a special variety: *they are processes that must at least have the potential of functioning across the boundaries of the globe at all times*. Indeed, from the standpoint of historical analysis, it is best if they actually have done so. Therein, the conceptual process of nation formation, a process we can see at work in nation-states (like Denmark) is not directly part of the globalization process. As a number of scholars have pointed out, this does not mean that it is not part of the globalization process at all; nation formation is a concept globalization relies on to successfully 'connect' and 'integrate' different nations, their societies and culture (see e.g. Held, et. al., 1999: 32–85). However, the establishment of what we might think of as 'pre-' or 'non-' global borderlines, for example, the national world as opposed to the 'global' world, is a prerequisite of globalization. As is the case with 'prerequisites', it is the 'pre-' that matters – the pre-required element has to come before the new process and is thus only part of the new process structurally, making it *not* the process itself.

How, then, does globalization 'connect' and 'integrate' the 'pre-' or 'non-' global? Let us look at this in concrete terms – how, for example, has it been possible to integrate regional societies and their cultural expressions? How has it been possible to move them beyond their boundaries, and establish socio-cultural groupings, identities and practices that we might consider 'trans-regional', e.g., Danish to Scandinavian, Danish to 'European,' or, Danish (or, for that matter, German, French, British, Canadian or American – or anything North American or European) to 'Western?' There are, of course, a great number of specific answers. However, in order to speak at the level of global history – as opposed to, for example, the level of a national history – the answer is *deterritorialization*.

Generally, deterritorialization amounts to what it sounds like – the removal of entities away from their expected territory, at least on a partial basis. In one of the formative statements on the topic, the French philosophers Gilles Deleuze and Félix Guattari define deterritorialization as a matter of "passages of flux" and "displaced limits" (Deleuze and Guattari, 1983: 232). Now, let us convert this into slightly more concrete terms. If we consider Danish society and culture as entities, for example – discrete elements existing in the world – a part of them has to be transported *out* of Denmark and placed in a wider arena (Scandinavia, for example) in order for part of Danish society and culture to flow through that larger arena (e. g. Scandinavian society and culture). The same could be said about the other European and North American societies mentioned above in terms of locating part of those societies in the framework of 'Western society'. The point is simply that trans-regional cultural groupings cannot exist without elements of the regional cultures involved being transported out of their 'home' locations. Again, I cannot underline the abstract, or conceptual dimension heavily enough as concerns global history. Concrete elements are involved in the histories of social and cultural transportations – configurations of political blocs (Scandinavia, for example, has a varied territorial history in terms of political rule), migration (Scandinavia has also had interregional migration), ideas, and certainly the linking of different regions economically. However, this is where the conceptual power of deterritorialization comes in: it brings these elements under a singular heading, or one that can be seen as having the possibility of functioning from global location to global location, and thus be said to be functioning at the level of global history. Deterritorialization, on the global scale (if we were to put it that way) could be said to be the sum of all the local deterritorializations at work in different global locales in a historical sense. It becomes, as such, a first principle in global history.

To that extent it is hard to say whether deterritorialization precedes or follows on the heels of time-space compression. In other words, deterritorialization may be *a* first principle of global history, but is it *the* first principle? I.e., if we think about social connection and integration, we can note certain phenomena at work beyond deterritorialization alone. First, societies and cultures previously existing separately have to be brought closer to one another, either geographically or conceptually. That this has happened is one of the central points of the formative statement on time-space compression, the 1989 text *The Condition of Postmodernity* by the American geographer David Harvey. In the case of Denmark and Scandinavia, for example, economies, languages, politics, if not populations themselves, had to be first introduced to one another. Here, we get a sense of shrinking social distance. Societies need to be 'mixed' with one another – and that 'mixing', if it is to amount to 'integration', has to be on a more or less permanent basis. This furthers time-space compression; in a conceptual sense, the time and space between societies connecting and integrating becomes radically smaller. It becomes so small, in fact, that, at least at strategic moments, it is possible to see the time and space between societies as infinitesimal or non-existent (e.g., when one thinks about Scandinavia, one thinks in a certain way *simultaneously* about Denmark, Norway and Sweden). Clearly, the connections to deterritorialization here are obvious: time-space compression very much assists deterritorialization. The removal of entities from their expected territories becomes much easier when the time and distance involved is small either literally or conceptually. However, the same could be said in reverse: it is noticeably easier for time and space to shrink when the connection and integration made possible by deterritorialization is at work. Therein, one might say that there are, in fact, two 'first principles' of global history – two conceptual elements one may see as working across the boundaries of the globe at all time: time-space compression *and* deterritorialization.

Therein, having comprehended time-space compression and deterritorialization as underlying social connection and integration, and elucidating the connection between globalization as something more general and global history as a specific mode of understanding globalization, let us think about a global text. To draw on one of the genres I described as inspiring the idea of the global text in the introduction, I will suggest that we think about world music. Of course, world music is a well-established genre at this point (see e.g. Bohlman, 2002). However, I am going to stretch its boundaries a bit so I can get hold of an artifact that more rather than fewer of us know. I will thus suggest Paul Simon's 1986 album *Graceland* as a global text. Indeed, I would suggest that we are actually not stretching the genre of global music too far here. What makes *Graceland* a 'global text' is that it actually does precisely what world music is intended to do, and which ties it to globalization – it represents the music of more than one culture, connects them, and integrates them (again, cf. the definition of globalization offered in the introduction).

How does *Graceland* 'connect' and 'integrate'? In the first instance, I would suggest we consider the following graphic:

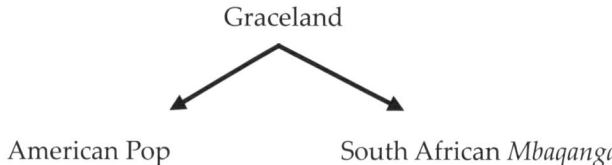

The point with this graphic is elementary: if one listens to *Graceland*, one of the things that is striking about most of the numbers on the album is that it combines Simon's recognizable American folk-rock style – which has roots in earlier American folk and rock from Pete Seeger and Woody Guthrie to Elvis – with what, to the American or European ear (or my ear, anyway) sounds like a distinctly different kind of popular music. This 'distinctly different kind of popular music' happens to be a variety of music from the South American townships called *mbaqanga*. Like Simon's folk-rock, *mbaqanga* has roots in a number of different musics: Zulu song, missionary choral singing, varieties of sub-Saharan African rhythmic musics and particular varieties of South African ragtime musics that were devised in the early years of the twentieth century (especially after the 1913 Native Land Act that effectively brought apartheid to the country – throughout the apartheid years, popular music was an important force in holding the black communities together as well as a mode of resistance). The point is that, in listening to *Graceland*, one might say that one becomes 'conceptually' transported – or at least referred to – two cultures and/or societies: 1950s to 1980s America and apartheid South Africa.[1]

Let us now consider a second graphic:

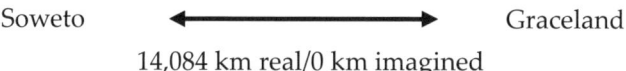

Soweto ⬌ Graceland
14,084 km real/0 km imagined

The point of this graphic, like the first, is also elementary. The idea is that beyond being 'conceptually transported' to 1950s-1980s America and apartheid South Africa, one also gets a sense of the processes that have brought these two societies into contact with one another – at least in the context of the album *Graceland* as a single text, or cultural artifact, event or object. In other words, in order to create *Graceland*, it had to be possible for cultural elements of America and South African society to exist in locations other than the United States and South Africa. Here, we might acknowledge a few facts about how *Graceland* was made. First, it was recorded in both New York and Johannesburg (as well as, it should be mentioned, London). American and South African musicians thus spent quite some time traveling back and forth between the two places. In doing so, they brought social and cultural information – their music, at the very least – to not only each other, but each other's *locations*. In short, they had to leave American and South African territory, as did a certain amount of their culture (if culture can be said to exist in amounts). This, of course, is deterritorialization,

---

[1] This understanding of *mbaqanga* is derived from Timothy White's liner notes for Simon's album.

or the removal of entities from their expected locations. However, it is also time-space compression. In deterritorializing American and South African culture, the musicians who made *Graceland* also brought about the shortening – indeed, nullifying – of the time and space between them. I have represented this in the graphic above by noting the physical distance between Soweto township, one of the well-known black townships during the apartheid period (and site of a very famous uprising in 1976 that did much to focus world attention on South Africa and apartheid) and Graceland, the gaudy home built by Elvis in Memphis, Tennessee in the U.S. – referred to by the title of Simon's album. I have then suggested the distance between Soweto and Graceland within the space of the *Graceland* album itself, designating it as the 'imagined' distance between the locations in the context of *Graceland*. Within a single artifact, these locations become deterritorialized and time-space compressed.[2]

Therein, we might create the following 'full' graphic on how *Graceland* represents global history:

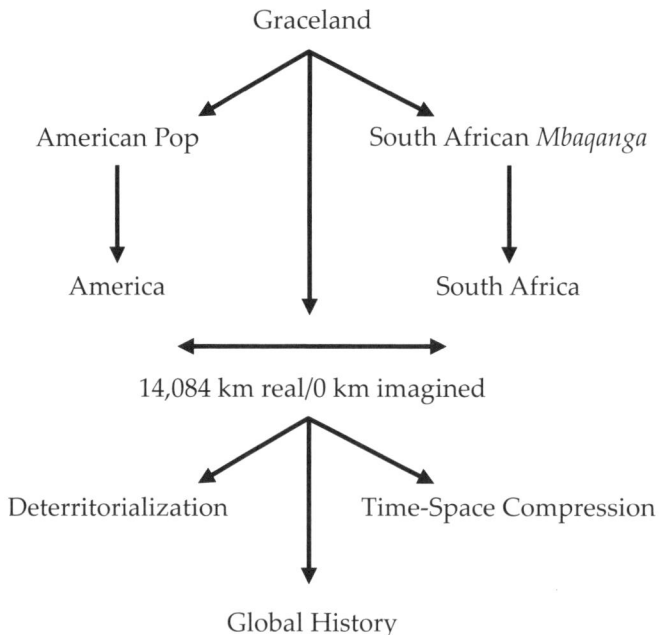

---

2 The information on the production of *Granceland* is also derived from Timothy White's liner notes.

Given that this graphic is not simply a compilation of the earlier graphics, I will explain its various dimensions. The top of it is the same as before – when we hear *Graceland*, goes the idea, we hear how the different musics in them make the 'total' music of the album. Now, as mentioned earlier, Simon's American pop and South African *mbaqanga* also have their diverse influences, so it is possible to imagine extending the portion of the graph concerned with the musics involved. For simplicity's sake, however, we will leave American pop and South African *mbaqanga* as self-contained musical/cultural entities. I would then suggest that the societies and cultures that are these musics' 'territories' are also indicated within the music – it is tough to mistake either of the musics involved in *Graceland*, for Mexican *mariachi*, for example. From there, however, I would argue that – given a bit of sophistication – we are referred to the fact that these societies and elements of their cultures have come together in a single space, which is that of the *Graceland* album itself. This is indicated by the vertical arrow extending between the line indicating the real and imagined distances between the U.S. and South Africa and the *Graceland* album itself (the top of the graph). It is then a short conceptual step to the processes that *allowed* this coming together – this 'connection' and 'integration' of America and South African culture, as it were. As mentioned, these are deterritorialization and time-space compression. And, these, of course, are the constitutive elements of global history, placing them – as well as global history – in the 'referential chain'. Now, the idea of a 'referential chain', or how and why references happen, is complex. This can especially be seen in relation to time-space compression, deterritorialization and global history; does anyone other than a cultural studies scholar think of such things when they listen to pop music, for example? However, that is precisely the point – *Graceland* is not just pop music, it is world music. It is a 'global text'. Our graph, then, might not actually be so fancy. The point of the graph is simply that, with *Graceland*, we *have* a global text – a text that is produced by the globalization process and, perhaps most importantly, a text that can be understood to represent that process. To use terms I introduced at the end of the introduction, *Graceland* is not difficult to figure out as 'symbolizing' or 'representing' the globalization process. This is especially the case if we are willing to take apart and create something of a flow chart for the cultural ingredients that went into the album's making.

Nonetheless, equally important to this essay is that we be allowed to see how global texts also *further*, or *perpetuate*, the globalization process. It is not quite the case that this is a matter of reading how *Graceland* as a global text functions from a representational perspective 'in reverse', but it is close.

To understand this reversal let us consider this section of the graph:

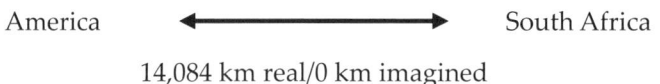

14,084 km real/0 km imagined

It is true that here, American and South African culture and society had to become deterritorialized and time-space compressed in relation to each other in order to create *Graceland* as a global text. However, one could also say that the production of *Graceland* facilitated, or was part of the deterritorialization and time-space compression processes themselves. This gets at a trait of things historical – the absolute origins of entities are hard to detect, but changes leading to them are less so. This is especially the case in relation to globalization – precisely how old are 'connection' and 'integration', or time-space compression and deterritorialization from a historical perspective? Nonetheless, we can say for sure that the processes of time-space compression and deterritorialization *have* occurred. Of course, as mentioned in relation to the examples of Danish and Scandinavian society and culture, as well as North American and European nations and Western society at-large, these causal forces can be multiple – politics, demographic-territorial movements and the transport of ideas via communication are all good examples. With *Graceland*, though, I would suggest that we have such a causal force in the form of an artifact – an artifact, incidentally, in the communicative mode, more than, say, the political or demographic (although, given that musicians had to move back and forth from the U.S. and South Africa to make the album, there is certainly some politics and demography involved). For the listener, the album *performs* time-space compression and deterritorialization. Again, we are involved with highly conceptual processes here. However, it is precisely at this conceptual level, however, that *Graceland* perpetuates and furthers the globalization process – i.e., it makes and represents global history. In representing time-space compression and deterritorialization, *Graceland* puts for the listener American and South African culture in one place. They are 'connected' and 'integrated', one might say, right before our eyes – or our ears, as the case might be. Social and cultural information and practices are blended in the text, moving across the borderlines of the territories that previously contained them and bringing them into contact with one another.

The text, however, needs to be there (exist) and conduct that blending in an active sense. The text has to *function* in a 'global genre', as such – i.e., as 'world music'. In this context, *Graceland* becomes more than a representation of deterritorialization, time-space compression and (therein) global history. It rather becomes an *agent*, or actor in those events and processes. Moreover, it should be mentioned that this process is hardly anonymous. *Graceland* brings American and South African culture to *the listener's* particular society, thereby bringing the listener (who might well be you) into the processes of cultural connection and integration as well.

There are, of course, many other global texts one could look at. Originally, for example, I considered writing this essay on Chinese Tacos – an interesting (and tasty) blend of Chinese and Mexican cuisine. I could have also looked at any number of items in interior design, fashion, landscaping or, as mentioned in the introduction, new cultural formations at larger social levels, such as new political orientations (e.g., globalization's 'post-internationalism'). The results, of such investigations, however, would be the same. Global texts represent globalization, and globalization in its specifically historical formulations, or the specific configurations of global history. As texts, these processes are embodied in their very being as texts and thus, to some extent, represent those processes, insofar as things represent what they are. In making such representations however, global texts also make global history. They bring us into globalization's conceptual sphere and perform the operations of that sphere in front of us. And, as suggested, we might thus acknowledge something extra about global texts. They bring *us* into the globalization process. However, if we think about it, this is not surprising – by the definition of global history, we were already a part of it anyway.

The ABCs of Global Text Reading

By now, we have a sense of what a global text is – a global text is a text that both is a product of and represents the globalization process. We also have a sense of *what* the globalization process is. It is the "set of economic, environmental, political, technological, social and cultural processes that first connect and then integrate societies". We further know that this is a historical process – it reflects other processes that extend across the globe's boundaries, into its past as well as into the present. We also have something to call these 'other processes': time-space compression and deterritorialization. Finally, we have seen *how* time-space compression and deterritorialization are represented in the global text – and, in the process, how global texts help make global history. The question that remains for us, then, is the last that I posed in the introduction – can we abstract a methodology for global text reading? Is there a *logic* we might suggest for interpreting global texts, or a defined way to understand them in cultural and historical contexts?

For better or worse, methodologies and logics are odd things. On one hand, the ideas 'methodology' and 'logic' sound quite strict; they are about well-established procedures and ways of thinking. However, especially with a category of text that has yet to be circulated further within discussions in textual studies (the 'global text'), one does not want to be overly strict in suggesting reading methodologies. Nonetheless, there are a few points we can make here regarding 'procedures' and 'ways of thinking' regarding global texts. I will list them numerically:

1. Global texts must be read in awareness of global history

This is a relatively elementary point in relation to textual studies in general; texts have histories, and we should be aware of those histories as we read texts. However, global history is not just any history – it is large, long and abstract, centered on the compression of space and time and the removal of entities from their expected territories. To that extent, a leading question for reading global texts should be 'Where is the space time compression?' and 'Where is the deterritorialization?' represented in the text in question.

2. Nonetheless, global texts must be read as making global history

Again, this is a relatively elementary point in textual studies – that texts make as well as reflect history. However, I have mentioned several times now, global history is a special kind of history – it always functions at the level of the global, or has the ability to do so. Therein, a 'second' leading question for global texts is 'How does the global text in question compress space and time?' and 'How does it deterritorialize?'

3. Global texts help involve us/you in the globalization process

By my definition of global history, all of the globe's inhabitants are participants, or potential participants, in globalization – globalization is, by our definition, not only *a* historical process, but *our* historical process. However, this participation has to be brought about, or caused, in some manner or another. The global text is one of those causes – not only does it compress space and time as well as deterritorialize, but it does so *for us* specifically. It is one of the ways in which we, as inhabitants of the globe, are brought into the process, in fact, of globalization.

~~~

To conclude, then, I will simply offer the following: when asked to contribute an article to this volume, I suggested that I write something on the 'ABCs' of global text reading – 'ABCs' indicating something of a primer on the subject, or basic introduction. In a way, that is what I have attempted to offer here; what we see at work when we look at global texts, how we should 'interpret' them and what we should take them to represent. In retrospect, however, I have decided that the title should be revised. As I see it upon, the question may be not so much the global text's 'ABCs', but rather understanding its 'GHQs', or that, when it comes to reading the global text, global (G) history (H) is the question (Q).

References

Aristedes, Aelius (1998) "The Roman Citizen". In *The Human Record: Sources of Global History. Vol 1.* (Edited by Alfred J. Andrea and James H. Overfield). New York: Houghton Mifflin

Beynon, John and David Dunkerley (eds.) (2002) *Globalizaiton: The Reader*. London: The Athlone Press

Bohlman, Philip Vilas (2002) *World Music: A Very Short Introduction*. New York: Oxford University Press

Cameron, David R. and Janice Stein (eds.) (2002) *Street Protests and Fantasy Parks*. Vancouver: UBC Press

Deleuze, Gilles and Félix Guattari (1983) *Anti-Oedipus: Capitalism and Schizophrenia*. (Translated by Robert Hurley, Mark Seem and Helen R. Lane). Minneapolis: University of Minnesota Press

Guha, Ranajit (2002) *History at the Limits of World History*. New York: Oxford University Press

Held, David, et. al. (1999). *Global Transformations: Politics, Economics and Culture*. Stanford: Stanford University Press

Ward, Allan, et. al. (eds.) (2003) *A History of the Roman People*. Upper Saddle River, NJ: Prentice Hall

Hollywood as Cultural Text

STEEN CHRISTIANSEN

This essay will focus on how we may consider Hollywood's products as cultural texts. Hollywood has often been critizised for its mainstream appeal, and it has repeatedly been claimed that its immense production capacity has been mainly interested in earning a profit, with considerations of art coming second, if at all.

That films are cultural products is a banal observation, yet in many ways it is also an overlooked one for it seems that most film critics have been more interested in the film-as-text aspect, ignoring many of the facets that make film a unique cultural product. The reasons for this are many, but probably the most significant one is the origin of film studies and the reception of film studies (rather than films themselves). Films were initially considered mass entertainment, popular culture made primarily to garner income to the film studios. In order for the study of films to be taken seriously, film critics had to rescue film from popular culture and instead place it as the "seventh art form" (Turner, 1993).

This move, while critical in establishing film studies as a separate branch, resulted in a field which was often dominated by discussions of the *auteur*, the genius filmmaker who fought heroically against the studios to create their own unique styles. Studio systems, especially that of Hollywood, were seen as capitalist structures interested only in creating standardised, formulaic films to as large an audience as possible, having no interest in artistic merit. While the *auteur* critics were vital for rescuing American films, and especially Hollywood films, from a lost status as mass entertainment, their one-eyed focus on the director meant ignoring any number of interesting and important films from Hollywood, simply because these films were not made by a true *auteur*.

The consequence of this biased focus was the consecration of the art-film, the film as a work of art and therefore the film-as-text. There is nothing wrong with this approach, obviously, but the emphases placed on the study of any given film were related to its artistic merits, and very often of a formal kind or alternately a psychoanalytic interest. The psychoanalytic interest in films is clearly connected to the reception of films and so will be discussed further later on. The art-film became a specific object of study and favoured the so-called artistic directors, creating a field of film study which was oriented towards individual works and directors, much like typical literary studies of what might be called 'literary fiction'. This was, to some degree, also because of the fact that literary critics began moving into film studies, bringing the concepts of literary study to film study. This only helped to solidify such assumptions as a greater respect for the individual work, as well as a high-culture patronising attitude towards commercial, popular forms of film (Turner, 1993: 2). These assumptions have of course since been challenged in film studies, as well as literary studies.

The other side of film study was the study of genre films, which usually grouped huge numbers of films together within a specific genre, studying the genre-elements rather than individual works. The individual differences of the genre films were downplayed in favour of focussing on the similarities, so that the critic was able to create coherent genres with recognisable features. Studying individual, popular films then became more an exercise in categorising the film within a specific genre, rather than studying its individual worth. Sometimes, this led to peculiar categorisations such as identifying *Star Wars* (George Lucas, 1977) as a Western because of the way certain shoot-outs were portrayed visually (Altman, 1999).

All these elements are present in film studies, but the move that is of interest here is rather that of the insertion of film studies into other critical disciplines such as linguistics, anthropology, psychoanalysis and so forth. This branching of film studies meant that suddenly film was no longer the final object of study. Rather, the process of representation became the ultimate focus of these studies. That is, typical research questions would be: what are the social and cultural processes which make images and sounds – signs in other words – mean something, often something quite specific. This change meant that film studies became part of a greater whole, namely cultural studies, and it is this specific change which means that films can be considered cultural products. Film can tell us about the processes of culture by analysing the elements that go into the film, as well as the reaction of the audience.

Having said this, let us go into the particulars of what the relations are between film and culture. It seems naive to presume that there is a one-to-one relationship between what is represented in a film and how a culture understands a given subject. This belief is grounded in a 'reflectionist' relationship between film and culture and presupposes that films reflect dominant culture unproblematically. Such readings claim that if a large number of films propose certain values (such as American 1940 musicals who were generally optimistic in tone) then this must be a reflection of society's general views (in this case, optimistic and hopeful).

Any historical consideration of films will immediately reveal that this is inaccurate, as the 1940s were also dominated by another type of film, the *film noir*. These films were far from optimistic, instead painting dark, critical views of contemporary American society. The purely reflectionist view would be unable to determine which view was the dominant. Already here we would have to take other determinants into account in order to create a proper analysis of the 1940s as reflected through films. These would include, but not be limited to, cultural, subcultural, industrial, and institutional determinants. In other words, there is a whole range of aspects to take into consideration before turning to the film(s) at hand. And here we have not even begun to take audience into account, examining the way they receive films. As many directors have learned, aberrant readings of their films are not uncommon and can often be totally counter to the intention of the director. Martin Scorsese, for instance, experienced that some moviegoers saw his *Taxi Driver* as a call for vigilante practices, while his explicit intention was quite the opposite (Prince, 2000).

Let us leave the audience for a while and instead turn our eyes back to culture. What is imperative to realize about film, is the fact that it is not reality. Godard's assertion that 'the cinema is truth 24 frames a second' ignores the fact that film like any other medium represents reality through specific codes and conventions, none of which are grounded in reality. Consider the typical shot/reverse-shot sequence of establishing for instance conversation. The effect is meant to imitate a shifting point of view, so that we see one character from the point of view of the other character. However, there are two aspects (at least) which indicate that this is a convention and not truth. First, the angle is not placed directly at the character's face so that the character looks directly into the camera. (This would break another convention of film, that of not acknowledging the presence of the camera.) Instead, the camera is placed so that the spectator can see the full face of one character, and the shoulder of the other character. However, although this emulates a point of view, it is only an approximated point of view. Second, in most mainstream films, lighting is shifted every time the camera shifts angle. Although this requires a very large change in set-up and a very costly and time-consuming rearranging, it is still done in order to create the highest-quality images. These two practices create unnatural points of view and impossible effects of light, yet we as spectators do not consider these conventions as unrealistic, but rather as indicative of realism.

If these conventions are broken (such as in *dogme* films) we react differently, considering the film in question to have a specific, unique style. This actually creates a peculiar shift in the perception of reality since the *dogme* films, for instance, used on-setting lighting and sound rather than going through the costly process of using artificial light and sound. However, although the filmic image is less standardized according to typical Hollywood conventions, it is perceived as being more distinct than the typical mainstream production and so further removed from the standard, 'realistic' approach to film.

This consideration should make us realize how films are actually carefully constructed in order to fulfil certain expectations. These expectations, while they guide the spectator's reception of the individual film, are tied up in what we may call the institutionalisation of film reception. This institutionalising effect comes from the film industry itself, yet is also part of a cultural production. In other words, it is this institutionalising effect which is the interest when discussing films as having a relationship with the surrounding culture. The result of this process also means that the individual work of representation is of less specific interest in a general sense, though of ultimate interest when analysing certain moments and genres.

The reason for such an approach is quite simple; it is unwieldy trying to include an analysis of all determinants within a given moment in history. The realisation should instead be that both production and reception are of critical importance in relation to the cultural dimension of a film text. And even here we encounter difficulties for, as we have already seen, the film industry is just that, an industry intent on making money which means that no production can be totally ignorant of the reception of a given film. As such, the industry's film production is intricately mixed with that of expected audience reception and a discussion of film production must consider the fact that the production expects a certain specific reception to take place. That is, anyone making a film will inevitably consider the target audience. Therefore, production and reception are not discrete units within the film text but ultimately mixed up in a larger process. However, it is necessary for our purposes here to separate them just so; simultaneously discussing production and reception is unwieldy, so let us instead divide the two and later return to unify the two again.

The first discussion here will be of production since this must be said to come first (even with production's expectation of reception). Hollywood, the case of interest here, is today clearly the most influential national film production system in the world. Although India's Bollywood system makes more films per year than does Hollywood, it does not export anywhere near the number of films which Hollywood does. Bollywood represents an immense national production system, whereas Hollywood in many ways is an international production system, despite the fact that it technically is a national system. Hollywood is international because it draws so many people from other countries to its system, whether they have had success in their own national cinema.

This domination which the American film industry has over other Western countries' film industries is very visible today, but it has not always been so. There are several historical factors which need to be underlined before we move on. While sound is one of the elements which helped shape this dominance, the most important reason is probably that of war, World War I. Most European countries had booming film industries, especially France and Italy, and no real need for or interest in American film. However, with the beginning of World War I, Europe's film industries began to slow production as emphasis was obviously placed on the war effort. This allowed American product, uninhibited by the costs of a war, to move in on these foreign markets. People still wanted to see films, after all, even if their own countries did not make as many. Here the lack of sound probably helped the American industry, since there was no language barrier to overcome.

This momentary control over foreign markets might very easily have dwindled after WWI, but here it is important to realize that the Hollywood system was not only very large but also made high quality films. The latter part has to do with the studio system, which we shall return to a bit later, but the size of the American industry comes from a very basic but important fact: USA is a very large country. This simple fact meant that it was possible for Hollywood to turn a profit on practically any production within their own country. As such, they were never dependent on export to save high-risk ventures. In the end, this resulted in a very competitive national cinema.

Here we have to make a brief return to reception. The major point for the rest of the essay lies in the very fact that the American feature film industry did not need to consider any other nation's reception of their films. They could simply tailor their films directly to the American audience and not care if another national audience liked it. But if another national audience wanted to see the most expensive and most technologically advanced film, they would have to see an American film. Very little has changed in that regard since the 1920s.

This total domination of their home market also made a major change in the structure of the US film industry; vertical integration. Vertical integration is a term meaning that a studio controls not just its own production, but also the distribution as well as the exhibition of its products. Vertical integration was not something specific to USA (France was the first country to achieve it in 1920), but it did have an impact as film studios began to expand their interests and their need for money. What this did was solidify the studio system, so let us now look closer at this element of film production.

In essence, what the studio system did was own, or control, a number of stars, scriptwriters, directors, designers and other people generally involved in making films. The final decision of how a film was made or what to remove from a film lay with the general manager, or overseer of the studio, typically the vice-president (Hayward, 2000). What this resulted in was a distinct feel and look for each major studio, since the same people were constantly making films together. Furthermore, each major studio was specialised even more as they usually kept to certain specific genres (Fox Film Corporation made musicals, Paramount Pictures Corporation made comedies and so on). The production practices were in many ways an assembly line process, where formulaic films were made for sure returns. While this did lead to a standardizing effect in films, it also quickly and surely created recognizable genres, even genres with a greater sophistication than might otherwise have been made, as variations were always needed. Even today, after the studio system has collapsed, Hollywood remains the greatest producer of genre films.

This standardizing effect of the studio system is what has made Hollywood most reviled by critics and sophisticated spectators, since very little true innovation ever occurred. This is what led to the creation of *auteur* theory, since a number of directors did make films that diverged from the norm, certainly from a critical point of view. However, what this attitude towards Hollywood forgets is the fact that a large number of very skilled people within their field is actually placed together, and that this inevitably results in what Thomas Schatz calls "a melding of institutional forces" (Schatz, 1998).

So the studio system cannot be said to have been all negative, but it did do one thing, and this was create an environment in which it was very difficult for minor studios to thrive. This almost-monopoly meant that smaller studios needed something which set them apart from all the rest. In 1927 Warner Brothers' new idea was sound. Actually, the idea was hardly new since the possibility of sound had existed ever since the creation of film, it had merely not been used, and perhaps with good reason. See for instance Dwight MacDonald's backlash on the introduction of sound: "The silent film had at least the *theoretical possibility*, even within the limits of Mass Culture, of being artistically significant. The sound film, within those limits, does not" (MacDonald, in Rosenberg and White (eds), 1965: 64). Here we can see how moving closer to reality is seen as detrimental to the artistic impulse of the medium. The parallels to today's reality shows are clear.

What can be said about the introduction of sound was that while it was an attempt to create attention and move audiences and while it did succeed, it was not the novelty of the technological advance which made it successful. Later attempts at increasing attendance solely through technological advancement shows how this tactic is not certain; witness such elements as the resistance to colour, the 3D-failure and the limited success of cinemascope etc. Instead, we have to realize that the notion of realism, although, as previously mentioned, it is a difficult thing to get a grip on, has followed film more than any other medium with the possible exception of TV. Sound added to the reality effect of the film and was accepted as such by the audience. This acceptance, however, must not be located solely in the interest in increasingly higher degrees of reality reproductions. If this was the case, any other technological advance would also have been immediately accepted and, as noted, this was not the case.

Instead, what made sound so successful, despite the costs connected with updating theatres all over the world, was the creation of a new genre which depended on sound; the musical. In many ways, the musical can be seen as a form of response to the fact that while sound films (talkies) drew larger audiences to the cinema, language became a barrier. All of a sudden, other nations needed to create subtitles and this did hurt the export of American film. The musical, then, created a new combination between film and vaudeville where the main attraction was stars. Stars that would not otherwise have shared the stage with each other would do so in musicals, and this became an obstacle which was difficult for non-American nations to overcome. The musical still remains a firmly American genre.

The studio system was ended by the US Supreme Court in 1948 and this meant that the major studios had to change their business strategies. What they chose to do was to keep their distribution and let go of their exhibition venues. Distribution has become the focal point of the film industry, where getting the right number of films to the right number of theatres is imperative in creating a successful film. So much so that films will never be made if they cannot ensure proper distribution. American director Terry Gilliam, for instance, has seen two projects fail in recent years (*Don Quixote* and *Good Omens*) because it was not possible to get an American studio to distribute the films in the US.

Of course, factors other than simple distribution expertise drive a studio's ability to get a film to the audience. Genre and stars are the main elements that make a film potentially profitable. The term 'bankable' covers a star which will guarantee a profit for the film, but even this system has begun to collapse. Genre has also become more commercialised as can be seen in the term 'blockbuster' which solely describes the cost of the film, rather than any particular style, mode, narrative or any other typical element included in genre discussions. Still, one can say that the blockbuster mark does indicate something, namely what might be best termed as the 'a bit of everything' mentality where the film includes elements of practically all major genres, presumably in order to make sure that there will be something for everyone. While the blockbuster film attempts to generate as large a profit as possible, this does not always succeed so the term is not dependent on actual profit, nor can *The Blair Witch Project* be termed a blockbuster despite its large returns.

On the other hand, today we see how films have branched out into other media. Whereas adaptations of novels, plays, TV series, comics, computer games and so forth move to the film, we see how major film productions now turn to these same media, along with a host of others, in order to generate even more profit, sometimes necessary profit. Certain remediations have even become almost standard. *Star Wars, Harry Potter, The Lord of the Rings, The Matrix* and many other films inevitably become computer games in addition to all the other forms of merchandising that such blockbusters generate.[1] Of all these cases, *The Matrix* seems the most interesting as it has moved into practically every form of media, be it short stories, comics, animated shorts, computer games and so forth.

It is clear that by covering all these different media, the intention is to create not just greater awareness of the film itself, but also create a larger profit. Distribution is clearly influenced by these practices, especially also such elements as the soundtrack, particularly in the case of song soundtracks rather than a score soundtrack. For instance, *Tomb Raider: The Cradle of Life* has a song by popular group *Korn*, a song which is not featured in the film itself, but is still meant to influence the audience to go see the film. However, the distribution side of the film industry lies well beyond the scope of the present essay, important as it might be. Instead, we shall turn to what happens once the film has been distributed and people go to see it.

The reception of film is an obvious element to include when discussing the cultural production of films. However, some reception theories have gone as far as to practically eliminate the side of the production, be it author, director or any other producer, claiming instead that only the reader creates meaning. For the present purposes, however, that is going too far and in addition to this, we need to realize the difference between 'the reader' and 'the readers'. The emphasis on plurality is essential to reception which is relevant here, since we are dealing with a system of production which attempts to reach as large an audience as possible.

There is, however, one element regarding audience reception which needs to be specifically addressed: psychoanalytic film theory. These theories revolve around the pleasures of cinema, identification with the film text, and most importantly the gaze of the spectator. Far be it from this essay to thoroughly investigate all the aspects of psychoanalytic film theory, but there is one conclusion which these theories make which must be countered. The audience does not react as a homogenous mass, Dudley Andrews's assertion that "Desiring to possess the film, we are confined to merely viewing it" (Andrews, 1984: 148) does not correspond to reception research. As the previous example of Scorsese's *Taxi Driver* shows, the au-

---

1 Apparently, however, only films of the fantastic mode become computer games, since it is rare to see other than fantasy, horror and sf films make this transition. Perhaps this has something to do with people's reception of computer games. So far the computer has not been accepted as an 'apparatus of reality', i.e. as something which can represent reality in an acceptable manner (Turner, 1993: 12), but with the advent of such games as *The Sims* or Sony's new PS2 camera EyeToy, this may change in time. That, however, is a different can of worms not to be opened here.

dience does not respond similarly to the same text, nor is there a specific way to control the reception of the text.

However, even if we do agree that meaning is generated by the audience, and even if we agree that it is necessary to speak of meanings rather than one meaning, there seems to be a logical gap in granting the audience total freedom over the text and then still discuss and analyse texts in a meaningful way. If readings and interpretations of texts are infinite, how can we say that a text is a reflection of the surrounding culture? The answer seems to lies in Stuart Hall's assertion that formal properties create a 'preferred' way for the text to be understood. More importantly, this preferred way to understand a text is in accord with the dominant culture (Hall, 1977).

In other words, we play cultural games when we watch films; while employing our awareness of genre-conventions, cinematic codes and so on, we inscribe ourselves into our own culture. When we as spectators correctly guess the ending of *Sleepless in Seattle*, we do so by drawing on our knowledge of genre but also by drawing upon cultural competence. This confirms our membership of our own culture[2] and in turn gives us pleasure. Note that this pleasure can still be subversive in nature, such as denying the pleasurable elements of *Pretty Woman* because we know how it will end. Also, staying with the subversive vein, disruptions of genre and conventions still remain within the mainstream of culture and not necessarily outside, as *Deep Blue Sea* is an example of. Approaching the action genre elements with an ironic twist, the black character survives (explicitly parodied by LL Cool J saying: "Ooh, I'm done! Brothers never make it out of situations like this! Not ever!") and the masculine white hero is not united with his female love interest, who is instead devoured by a shark as she heroically tries to save him. Far from challenging cultural and generic conventions, the film simply parodies them. However, note that while the film parodies certain clichés, it still draws upon other clichés without parodying them. The black character still refers to black people as 'brothers' for instance.

However, all is still not well with reception, since the above-mentioned games presuppose a specific element which is taken for granted, and that

---

2 This is the main reason for critics of race and gender to be critical of mainstream cultural texts; they do not offer possibilities for eg. blacks to inscribe themselves into the mainstream culture. As such, mainstream culture is seen as homogenous and exclusive, but this is a discussion far too large for this essay.

is competence. The audience of a film is not homogenous but often quite diverse, certainly large-scale Hollywood productions depend on a large audience, which must necessarily become diverse. When considering the audience it seems peculiar if we did not realize that even if the film proposes a 'preferred' reading, no one is required to accept this reading, as witnessed by the subversive reading mentioned above. Yet it seems logical to accept that competence varies depending on the audience. Note that this notion of competence has little to do with any correct or acceptable understanding of the text, but simply an awareness of or belonging to a particular element in society. This does not just apply to knowledge of generic conventions, such as romantic comedies always having happy endings, but also to positions of class, race, gender and so forth. For instance, how may I as a white spectator from Denmark judge the reality portrayed in John Singleton's *Boyz N the Hood*? I might form certain opinions on whether I can trust the film in any sense of the word, but in many ways I am not a competent reader and there is good reason to expect that I might not follow the film's preferred reading simply because there are elements in the film I do not recognise. Yet this does not necessarily disqualify my understanding of the film although there is reason to take my background into consideration when analysing my reception.

What we have to realize here, then, is that there are as many determinants within the audience as there are within the film's production. For Hollywood, the audience is not something to take lightly when it comes to ensuring a reasonable profit on a multimillion dollar film. One part is obviously marketing and the amount of money spent on promoting a film (often this sum is larger than the costs of the film itself), but this is beyond this essay. Instead, there are other considerations when making film, and in Hollywood this is known as the 'Peter Pan'-effect. In essence, this covers the belief that girls will watch anything boys will watch, and younger boys will watch anything older boys will watch. In effect, this results in most films targeting a 19-year-old white male audience. Clearly there are plenty of exceptions to this, but the larger and more costly a film is, the more it will turn to this segment of moviegoers. Of course, this target audience is not grabbed out of the blue, but rather reflects the fact that the largest segment of moviegoers are within the 12–24 age bracket. As such, the 'Peter Pan'-effect represents a reasonable middle-ground. Of course, this is not to claim that all films are exclusively made for this age group, but rather that films made for audiences outside this segment are produced as well as promoted differently, often explicitly excluding any assumptions of a mass audience, preferring to orient itself towards a far more specific group. There is definite potential in an analysis of film aesthetics and Bourdieu's concepts of cultural production and distinction, but this essay will not attempt this. Instead, let us return to the question of cultural positions inscribed into the film text.

The impulse to read films as expressions of culture is in many ways a structuralist impulse. As such, it follows naturally to see culture not as monolithic but instead made up of binary oppositions. In following this train of thought, it is fruitful to see films, and especially their narratives, as ways to resolve these binary oppositions. In other words, films attempt to resolve cultural oppositions in symbolic ways. For most mainstream films, the resolution and the preferred reading which the film creates would then be a mirror, in some ways, of the surrounding culture. Hollywood, then, is a most interesting production system to consider in that it does not depend on other cultures to import its films and so can finance large-budget films as completely national endeavours. Yet, because of Hollywood's domination of at least the European market, these films are still seen as representatives for American culture, and not just representations.

Considering the film as a 'battleground' for contradictory cultural positions, we may consider the 'victor' to reflect the dominant belief within the culture, the correct set of values to have within the given culture. What is important to realize about Hollywood films specifically, is that we, as spectators, are aware of watching a Hollywood film and that because of this, we, and quite possibly Americans themselves, accept this imported system of meaning in order to enjoy the film. This is relevant because it means that one does not have to adopt a specific cultural viewpoint in order to watch the film. Despite the fact that many American films portray a certain gung-ho attitude towards justice this does not mean that the spectator will automatically approve of vigilante justice or swift, violent justice. It is clearly possible to navigate specific conventions without subscribing to the values implicit in the film.

It is also relevant to keep in mind that although mainstream films often reproduce the values of the dominant culture, they can sometimes challenge them. One such example would be *Se7en*, where the ending of the film follows the pattern of so many other police thrillers, where the criminal is killed in punishment of his crimes. However, the narrative has been set up so the killing of the criminal actually fulfils the criminal's goal. So, to some degree, the film undermines the typical style of this particular genre, but also the typical viewpoint of killing the criminal. This opens an interesting discussion, as we can see how there are (at least) three ways of understanding the end of the film. One is the one mentioned above, seeing the ending as subverting the cultural dominant, while the other is seeing the ending as poorly made; the film has simply failed to live up to its generic demands of satisfying closure. The third is that the film falls prey to the typical, expected ending of such genre films, choosing the easy path instead of dealing with the difficult questions that would arise were the criminal brought to trial.

These three readings all seem quite possible and valid ways of interpreting the film's ending. It also seems difficult to agree on the film's preferred reading without concluding on the film's specific intention. If the ending is poorly made (reading 2 above) then we assume that the film has meant to be a typical genre film but that the filmmaker[3] failed to follow the conventions of the genre. Reading 3 can be said to be the subversive reading of reading 2, in the sense that it presupposes the same setup, that this is meant to be a genre film, but instead sees the film as being too typical, following too closely to genre standards and thereby succeeding only in repeating the same old formulas. The first reading is the most dynamic, seeing the film as a specific comment on American culture's 'bloodlust', refusing to create a satisfying ending that will in effect enforce the view that criminals must be punished by death. This reading, however, presupposes that most spectators will agree on the cultural dominant established in other films, rather than seeing the convention for what it is; a generic short-hand for narrative closure.

While these different readings imply a lot about the film in question, they also speak volumes about the interpreter of the film (hence I shall not venture my own opinion). However, it is undeniable that when interpreting the film, the potential cultural positions of the film are brought into play. In whatever way the film is interpreted, it is done so on a basis of cultural background on behalf of the spectator, in connection to a certain position of the film, which must often be inferred by the spectator. It is clear that the aesthetic choices made in connection with a film will influence the understanding of the film, so in this way textual analysis becomes a tool to understand the cultural position of the film. For instance, to continue with *Se7en* it is possible to analyse certain aesthetic elements of the

---

3 Here 'filmmaker' is meant to indicate the collective team of collaborators, from actors, director, scriptwriter, producer and so forth, in order to avoid the complications of choosing one specific person as the final author of the film.

film as belonging to the *film noir* genre, such as lighting, camera angles and framing. This type of analysis pushes the analyst in the direction of the first reading presented above, seeing the film as being critical of American culture. This is done by linking the visual style of the *film noir* with the thematic elements typical of a *film noir*, disillusionment, pessimism, and dissatisfaction with American culture during the 1940s. While this linking seems a logical choice, there is no specific reason to assume that it necessarily holds true; obviously *Se7en* could borrow the visual style from *film noir* without bringing the rest of the elements into the film. Certainly the pastiche-like properties of many postmodern texts perform exactly this operation. Therefore, it becomes necessary to analyse other elements in the film, in essence reading *Se7en* as partly belonging to the *film noir* genre.

Now we are entering a hermeneutic interpretative process, but rather than continuing this, it seems more logical to stop and realize that text-based analysis, close readings if you will, become vital for determining a text's preferred reading, in addition to uncovering the arguments for 'subversive', alternate readings. This brings us back to Stuart Hall, but with the added bonus of having created a dynamic web of determinants, one set of determinants located in the text itself and the other set located in the spectator. The basic advantage of this is the fact that we can now appreciate the spectator both as an individual but also as having different cultural competences based on race, gender, class, but also on genre knowledge, cultural knowledge and so on. In reading a film, the spectator will employ these competences as the film requires but also as s/he requires to appreciate the film.

So, to conclude, Hollywood functions as a cultural text because it has created specific codes and conventions that drive our understanding of its films. These codes go beyond 'mere' formal and generic devices of how conversation is represented, how satisfying closure is created etc., but also an understanding of which cultural dominants are present in these films and how we can navigate them. We recognise these cultural positions based on our competences, and accept or reject them as is necessary for our appreciation of the film. We may dislike the typical happy ending of most Hollywood films, but we can still enjoy the film if we 'read around' this convention. This suggests an important point, namely that we can obviously choose to not read a film for its cultural position (hard as it can be sometimes) and appreciate other aspects of the film, be it specific star performances, well-portrayed generic elements, unusual visual styles and so forth. Not all pleasures are located in the cultural dimension.

In arguing for such a position, I am clearly going against Colin MacCabe's claim that a realistic film cannot criticise the dominant values or beliefs, since a realistic fiction depends on the conventions of the dominant culture to assert itself as realistic. That is, the realistic fiction can only be considered realistic as long as it follows the values of the dominant cultural belief system, quite simply because reality equals the dominant culture (MacCabe, 1985). Although there might be some truth to this notion, it seems to present a quite limited view on what realism is or can be. Certainly realism is a system of signification like any other, and as such it is not necessarily tied to a specific cultural standpoint. While an understanding of realism might be culturally determined (see for instance E.H. Gombrich's *Art and Illusion* for more on this) that does not imply that one has to move outside the realistic in order to find films (or any other text) which criticise dominant culture. This is certainly also true for Hollywood, even if it has been continually critizised for aiming for the 'lowest common denominator'. The point is that realism is not a true depiction of reality, but rather a representation of what we consider to be realistic.

In order to get a better appreciation of this, we can turn to John Fiske's notion of the producerly text (Fiske, 1989: 103). Fiske places this type of text between Roland Barthes's readerly and writerly texts. Barthes's distinction, briefly, is that a readerly text is consumed passively by the reader, who also accepts its meanings inherent in the text. The writerly text, on the other hand, challenges the reader to make sense of the text, to draw upon the reader's competences to understand the text and construct the text's meaning individually. Fiske then posits the producerly text as a sort of midway between the readerly and writerly; as a popular writerly text. It achieves this by having the accessibility of the readerly text and it is also possible to read the producerly text as a readerly. However, by being open to cultural production it also reveals its own limitations and its own preferred meanings. Having these internal contradictions are vital to these texts, even if they create a specific resolution to these contradictions, because it makes the spectator active within a controlled environment, so to speak. So even if the text cannot control the variety of readings it may reproduce the struggles within culture and so engage the spectator in the text even if the cultural dominant is not accepted by the spectator. Hollywood specifically depends on the producerly aspect to ensure large attendance but at the same time opens its texts to subversive readings.

References

Altman, Rick (1999) *Film/Genre*. London: British Film Institute

Dudley, Andrew, (1984) *Concepts in Film Theory*. Oxford: Oxford University Press

Bordwell, David and Thompson, Kristin (1997) *Film Art: An Introduction 5th edition*. New York: The McGraw-Hill Companies, Inc.

Bordwell, David, Staiger, Janet and Thompson, Kristin (1985) *The Classical Hollywood Cinema: Film Style & Mode of Production to 1960.* London Routlege

Fiske, John (1989) *Understanding Popular Culture*. London and New York: Routledge

Gombrich, E.H. (1977/1996) *Art and Illusion: A Study in the Psychology of Pictorial Representation*. London: Phaidon.

Hall, Stuart (1977) "Culture, the Media and the 'Ideological Effect'". *Mass Communication and Society*. James Curran, Michael Gurevitch, Janet Wollacott, eds. London: Edward Arnold

McCabe, Colin (1985) *Theoretical Essays: Film, Linguistics, Literature*. Manchester: Manchester University Press

Neale, Steve (1989/1998) *The Genius of the System: Hollywood Film-making in the Studio Era*. London: Faber and Faber

Prince, Stephen (ed.) (2000) *Screening Violence*. London: Athlone

Rosenberg, Bernard, White, David Manning (1965) *Mass Culture: The Popular Arts in America*. Glencoe: The Free Press

Staiger, Janet (1992) *Interpreting Films*. Princeton: Princeton University Press

Thompson, Kristin and Bordwell, David (1994) *Film History: An Introduction*. New York: McGraw-Hill, Inc.

Turner, Graeme (1993) *Film as Social Practice*. London and New York, Routledge

Down With the Rebels!
David Foster Wallace and Postironical Literature

TORE RYE ANDERSEN

In the novella "Westward the Course of Empire Takes Its Way" (1989) the famous postmodern writer Professor Ambrose (a thinly disguised John Barth) collaborates with McDonalds' advertising director on the opening of a franchise of Funhouse Discotheques. The name of the franchise is of course a reference to John Barth's collection of metafiction, *Lost in the Funhouse* (1968) and the novella consequently examines how the originally anticapitalistic phenomenon of postmodernism has itself been subsumed by commercial forces.

The author of "Westward" is the young American author David Foster Wallace, born in 1962 and one of the leading figures in the current American showdown with the postmodern and ironical literature of the sixties and seventies – e.g. John Barth, Robert Coover, Thomas Pynchon. In his work Wallace argues that irony, which had an oppositional role in the literature of the sixties and functioned as an important critical weapon in the struggle against the establishment, has lost its literary value in the nineties. In the fifties and sixties, irony was first and foremost a characteristic of marginal literature, the avant-garde, where it served as an effective critique of society. In an interview, Wallace has said:

> Irony and cynicism were just what the U.S. hypocrisy of the fifties and sixties called for. That's what made the early postmodernists great artists. The great thing about irony is that it splits things apart, gets up above them so we can see the flaws and hypocrisies and duplicities. The virtuous always triumph? Ward Cleaver is the prototypical fifties father? Sure. Sarcasm,

parody, absurdism and irony are great ways to strip off stuff's mask and
show the unpleasant reality behind it. (McCaffery, 1973: 147)

At its point of departure, postmodern irony was thus a healthy, critical reaction against the System and a way of unmasking the conservative establishment, of shaking the monolithical power in Washington. However, during the eighties and nineties, the System – as Fredric Jameson has argued[1] – has transformed itself: it is no longer a monolith that can be toppled over, but has increasingly turned into a flexible, adaptive network, which has the ability to contain contradictions within itself. An important result of the increased adaptability of the System is its elastic assimilation of the ironical counter-language of the sixties. The mainstream culture of television has simply taken over the previously effective catalogue of countercultural strategies, causing the rebellious and norm-breaking irony to lose its critical potential and become a norm in itself.

Consequently, the rebellious and ironical attitudes of early postmodernism can today be traced in a wide spectrum of popular culture. Advertising slogans such as Hugo Boss' "Don't imitate, innovate!" and Macintosh's "Think different" cultivate the rebellious and the marginal and constitute a marked contrast to advertising slogans of the fifties, or even the seventies, which celebrated community and played on the fear of being different. Today you have to stand on the outside to be a part of the community.[2]

A cynical, snarling irony pervades sitcoms like *Frasier* and constitutes the dominant rhetorical mode in e.g. Jay Leno's and David Letterman's popular talk shows.[3] And in Hollywood, traditional and linear narrative patterns are broken up and replaced by the a-chronological, fragmented patterns that characterized the literature of the sixties. This broken chronology is for instance a feature of one of the most influential movies of the nineties, *Pulp Fiction*, which at the same time serves as an illustration of irony's

---

1 For instance in the seminal essay "Postmodernism, or The Cultural Logic of Late Capitalism" (Jameson, 1984).

2 For a further discussion of the cooptation of irony, see Naomi Klein's *No Logo*, especially chapter 3.

3 Wallace's short story "My Appearance" from the collection *Girl With Curious Hair* is precisely about David Letterman's hyperironical talkshow. An actress who is scheduled to appear in the show is afraid of being ridiculed by Letterman. In consequence, she devises a complex strategy where she will make a fool of herself before Letterman gets to her. In other words, she hopes to pre-empt Letterman's ironical barbs through self-irony. The results of this strategy are, as it turns out, disastrous.

subtle transformation, when transferred from genuinely critical art to mainstream culture. In the best postmodern literature irony serves a clear purpose. It is directed toward a well-defined goal and is a means of communicating a political message. In Tarantino's movie, however, irony has become its own end. According to Wallace, "[i]rony's useful for debunking illusions, but most of the illusion-debunking in the U.S. has now been done and redone [...] Postmodern irony and cynicism's become an end in itself, a measure of hip sophistication and literary savvy" (McCaffery, 1993: 147)

The irony in a movie like *Pulp Fiction* does not serve a visible purpose besides maintaining and polishing the shiny facades of the characters. It is an example of what Jameson calls "blank irony" (Jameson, 1984: 65), a directionless irony which is not committed to anything but a sly grin, and which has lost all oppositional force. As a consequence of its assimilation into mainstream culture, irony has become a ubiquitous cool attitude, which has misplaced its critical potential and instead – in an implicit confirmation of the *status quo* – exempts its practitioners from taking a responsibility.

From Counter-Language to Principal Language

The main problem for American writers today is that commercial culture increasingly encroaches upon their territory, thereby rendering their art toothless, not to say harmless. One of the best examples of this apparently unavoidable tendency is the author Don DeLillo, who during the past 30 years has been engaged in an ever more desperate race with The Market. Ever since his debut, DeLillo has attempted to stay out of the commercial loop and maintain a marginal position in the society he criticizes in his novels. By staying on the edge of the System, at odds with the law so to speak, it is possible to undertake a number of critical attacks against the System like a literary outlaw, without becoming part of it. The role of the outsider endows the writer with a tinge of *charismatic authority*, which makes his statements dangerous for the *bureaucratic authority* he attacks.[4] To maintain his charisma and avoid the routinization that an excessive exposure to the media would cause, DeLillo kept out of the twin spotlights of the press and the academic circuit. At one point he even moved to Greece where he handed a single persistent interviewer a card with the pre-printed message: "I don't want to talk about it" (Nevertheless, the pilgrim got his interview). In 1981 the journal *Horizon* brought an article on "Missing Writers", discussing DeLillo's absence alongside other charismatic and invisible writers such as Salinger, Pynchon, and Gaddis. With the publication of the bestseller *White Noise* in 1985 it became increasingly difficult for DeLillo to keep the attention at bay, and when he published *Underworld* in 1997, he was transformed into a veritable literary superstar. One of the sharpest critics of American consumer culture suddenly appeared in car commercials on the Internet and sold the movie rights to his novel for more than a million dollars. The previously silent and invisible DeLillo set out on a number of promotion tours (even to tiny Denmark) and gave a series of interviews. Curiously, most interviews are still prefaced with a description of a shy DeLillo who rarely gives interviews. It's hard not to be a bit sceptical about this assertion when, for the umpteenth time, it is accompanied by a large colour photo of a smiling DeLillo, but at the same time it is interesting to notice how the media and the critics are still attempting to construct DeLillo as a marginal, rebellious figure; how they are still trying to sustain his charisma. And DeLillo himself is still handing out his pre-printed rejection slips – e.g. at the National Book Award ceremony in 1997 – while probably realizing that he has lost this part of the race with The Market, and that he *does* have to talk about it, after all. This realization, however, is not tantamount to a renunciation of his charismatic authority. Now he only attempts to counter routinization and assimilation into the System in a dif-

---

4 I have borrowed the italicized concepts from the sociologist Max Weber. In *The Theory of Social and Economic Organization* Weber distinguishes between three types of authority: the traditional/dynastic form which is hereditary; the rational/bureaucratic authority which we know from most modern societies; and finally the *charismatic* authority which is temporary and unstable, and which due to its instability will quickly be rationalized/routinized: "In its pure form charismatic authority may be said to exist only in the process of originating. It cannot remain stable, but becomes either traditionalized or rationalized, or a combination of both." (Weber, 1947: 364). Of course Weber's concepts are not originally meant to describe literature, but nevertheless they seem to provide an apt description of the continuous growth and decline of various avant-garde movements that is an essential feature of literature.

ferent manner: from within. In an interview with the Danish author Bo Green Jensen, DeLillo has said:

> It's hard to keep up your opposition. I hope that my own books demonstrate an opposition to the state and the corporations, to the whole runaway consumerism. Nobody is more free than the American author, and for the same reason he is one step from ending up as elevator music. Popular culture absorbs everything, so how do you remain a subversive force? William Burroughs did it for 40 years, but today everything turns into a t-shirt, a coffee mug, a shopping bag. There is something about the large, complex novel, which resists and hints at the fact that not all are willing to be caught up in the food chain of consumerism. In this kind of culture, the writer should always stand alone. If he succeeds, he has at least achieved *something*[5] (Jensen, 1998: 9, my translation).

In spite of his recent position in the spotlight and his newly minted membership medal for the Club of Millionaires, DeLillo evidently still insists on the importance of at least making an attempt at marginality.[6] At the same time, it seems obvious that the possibilities for an up-to-date and critical avant-garde literature are significantly reduced. As a result of mainstream culture's absorption and watering down of the previously effective counter-language of postmodernism, the genuinely critical project has been driven into a corner while the market is flooded with works unreflectively reproducing the now inoffensive counter-language of the sixties in the hope of still being able to shock readers and gaining the coveted avant-garde status. As previously discussed, David Foster Wallace is of the opinion that the rebellious postmodernism *has* played its part, and he scorns the writers who without second thought replicate the rule-breaking methods of e.g. Thomas Pynchon:

> The modernists and early postmodernists – all the way from Mallarmé to Coover, I guess – broke most of the rules for us, but we tend to forget what they were forced to remember: the rule-breaking has got to be for the *sake* of something. When rule-breaking, the mere *form* of renegade avant-gardism,

---

5 Despite its length, however, *Underworld* does not seem overly subversive. It is simply too well-behaved. In his solemn and self-conscious attempt at writing a Great American Novel that contains multitudes and masters the complex American reality, DeLillo employs a pompous style, which strokes the decade's self-complacency with the fur. To a certain extent, DeLillo's much shorter *The Body Artist* (2001), even though unsuccessful in many respects, is more subversive in its destabilization of different planes of reality. For another *Underworld*-detractor see Tony Tanner's last book, *The American Mystery* (2000).

6 For an excellent discussion of white American writers' deeply felt wish of staying marginal, at the critical edge, see Michael Berubé's *Marginal Forces/Cultural Centers* (1992).

becomes an end in itself, you end up with bad language poetry and *American Psycho*'s nipple-shocks and Alice Cooper eating shit on stage. Shock stops being a by-product of progress and becomes an end in itself. (McCaffery, 1993: 132)

These uncritical rule-breakers and old-fashioned innovators are nevertheless still received as genuine avant-garde by media hungry for the latest literary sensations.[7] However, mainstream culture has overtaken the avant-garde of the sixties long ago, and the affected avant-garde in these works at most represents a tired and unoriginal *avant-gardism*[8] whose artistic effects are no match for the historical and cultural context in which it is written.

The great challenge for Wallace and others of his generation is the creation of an updated, effective counter-language that doesn't fall into the trap of avant-gardism; the writing of a charismatic literature that resists the smooth assimilation into popular culture. According to Wallace such a project necessarily has to begin with a showdown with the ironical literature of the rebellious sixties:

> If I have a real enemy, a patriarch for my patricide, it's probably Barth and Coover and Burroughs, even Nabokov and Pynchon. Because, even though their self-consciousness and irony and anarchism served valuable purposes, were indispensable for their times, their aesthetics' absorption by U.S. commercial culture has had appalling consequences for writers and everyone else". (McCaffery, 1993: 146)

But how is it possible for these young writers to negate the ironical negativity aesthetics of the literature of the sixties, without employing its own artistic effects and thus be caught up in the very tradition they are trying to escape? How can they criticize society and their literary predecessors without automatically being accepted by a mainstream culture whose principal language is the postmodern counter-language? Wallace hints at some possible answers in several of his interviews and essays, but the an-

---

7   A case in point is the rising star of the new millenium Mark Z. Danielewski, whose much lauded *House of Leaves* (2000) utilizes 'innovative' typographical gambols already patented by William Gass in the sixties, in *Willie Masters' Lonesome Wife* (1969).

8   The distinction between avant-garde and avant-gardism is drawn from the art critic Thierry de Duve and his book *Kant After Duchamp*. De Duve defines avant-gardism as an ineffectual reproduction of a previous avant-garde; a reproduction that has no relevance for and no effect upon its own immediate context. David Foster Wallace's debut novel *The Broom of the System* (1987) can with its Wittgenstein-inspired repetition of familiar postmodern arguments itself be charged with avant-gardism, and Wallace himself has subsequently more or less disowned the novel.

swers seem at best vague and somewhat programmatical. Wallace's strength in these texts is first and foremost etiological: he argues convincingly what is wrong and why it is a problem, but fails to pose a clear, constructive alternative. However, this is not the case in his most important work, the novel *Infinite Jest* (1996), one of the key texts of the nineties, in which Wallace follows up on his acute observations and forges them into something concrete and new. The novel constitutes a foundational monument in what I propose to describe as a *postironical* movement in modern American literature. But before I elaborate upon the contours and characteristics of this movement, I will turn to its central text.

Never-Ending Fun

Infinite Jest from 1996 is in all respects a great novel. It weighs roughly the same as half a gallon of gasoline and sports 1100 densely printed pages. The last 100 pages are notes to the rest of the text, and of the 388 notes – a judicious mixture of bad jokes, scientific information and misplaced chapters – many are provided with sub-notes, printed in a vanishingly small font-size. The scene of the novel is USA somewhere in the near future. It's difficult to establish precisely which year of the Gregorian calendar is the backdrop of the action: Each year is sold to the highest bidder and instead of numbers the years now have sponsored names such as Year of the Whopper or Year of the Perdue Wonderchicken.[9] The country is lead unfirmly by the President, ex-crooner Johnny Gentle, whose main claim to fame is that he was the first president *ever* to swing his microphone by the cord during his inauguration. The North American continent – Canada, USA, and Mexico – has, with USA as undisputed leader, entered into the alliance O.N.A.N. (Organization of North American Nations). To celebrate the excellent co-operation USA has given (read: forced upon) Canada the states Vermont and Maine, while reserving the right to dump all their toxic waste there. This so-called Convexity/Concavity (depending on your perspective) is consequently an ecological disaster area, ruled by hordes of feral hamsters and mutated babies the size of houses. At the same time, a group of Canadian wheelchair terrorists from Quebec is trying to force the province's secession from the rest of Canada by disseminating copies of a lethal movie, "Infinite Jest", which is so enjoyable that you lose the desire

---

9 The novel mainly takes place in the Year of the Depend Adult Undergarment, and internal information seems to place Y.D.A.U. sometime around 2009.

to do anything but watch it repeatedly, with saliva dribbling down your increasingly comatose self. Everything is narrated in a flickering, a-chronological style, with a confusion of ever proliferating characters and shifting perspectives.

This motley and satirical universe – some would say fortunately – only plays a subordinate part in relation to the main action of the novel, which takes place in a fictitious part of Boston, Enfield, at the two nexuses Enfield Tennis Academy (E.T.A.) and Ennett House Drug and Alcohol Recovery House [sic]. At a first glance, the two institutions seem to have absolutely nothing in common. The tennis academy is a hatchery of up and coming tennis stars, a playground for privileged kids, which is symbolically situated at the top of a large hill. At the bottom of the hill, in the literal shadow of E.T.A., is Ennett House, a halfway house that for its occupants is a way station between drug and alcohol abuse, and a hopefully new beginning.

At E.T.A. the main character is the lexical genius and tennis talent Hal Incandenza whose eccentric family has quite a few things in common with J. D. Salinger's Glass family. Hal's father, James Incandenza, was the founder of E.T.A. in addition to nurturing a career as an avant-garde filmmaker. After founding different aesthetic movements and dead ends such as anti-confluentalism and radical realism, he created the lethally pleasurable movie "Infinite Jest", whereupon he committed suicide by sticking his head in a cleverly altered microwave oven. The mother Avril is the daily leader of the tennis academy, and in her spare time she struggles with various neuroses and phobias. Finally Hal has two brothers, one of whom is a deformed dwarf with a heart of gold. The novel follows Hal's daily round at the academy and describes how he, parallel to his promising tennis career, embarks on a dangerous course of marijuana abuse. Tied up between the high expectations and the iron discipline of the tennis academy on the one hand, and an increasing dependency upon marijuana on the other hand, Hal slowly disintegrates and in the midst of a bustle of tennis students he becomes deeply lonely.

At the bottom of the hill, in Ennett House, we find the second principal character of the novel, the former drug addict and burglar Don Gately. After having been an inmate of Ennett House on his way out of addiction, Don is now employed in the house, keeping an eye on the other residents. At the same time he himself has to stay clean and he subsequently frequents a great number of AA-meetings in and around Boston; meetings where he takes the stand and tells his own story or sits in the nicotine haze in the room, listening to other people's stories from the dark side of society.

The way out of substance abuse is a slow, hard, and frustrating one, but nevertheless Don Gately moves in the right direction, while Hal at the top of the hill continues his deroute.

As is hopefully evident, addiction is a central theme in *Infinite Jest*. The characters of the novel are addicted to everything from alcohol and hard drugs, to pet abuse and the TV-show M*A*S*H. As such, *Infinite Jest* is an urgent corrective to the sixties' mythologization and glorification of drugs, and rather than – like for instance Pynchon – focusing on the colourful and unauthorized states of mind caused by drugs, Wallace concentrates on the humiliating debasement involved in the desperate struggle for one more fix.

Wallace's investigation of the many facets of addiction is not just a corrective to the sixties, but also to the American "pursuit of Happiness," which is written into the very Declaration of Independence as a self-evident truth. The freedom to choose and the fear of letting your life and your choices be dictated from above have always been important themes in American literature.[10] Personal freedom has always been something of a sacred cow, which not even the most critical voices have dared disturb. Of course Wallace is not of the opinion that there is something inherently wrong with the personal freedom to choose, but he *does* argue that this freedom doesn't necessarily lead to our common good. According to Wallace, this is nevertheless a common American assumption, and at one point in the novel he lets an American government agent state that "The American genius, our good fortune is that someplace along the line back there in American history them realizing that each American seeking to pursue his maximum good results together in maximizing *everyone's* good," and that USA is "a community of sacred individuals which reveres the sacredness of the individual choice" (Wallace, 1996: 424). The novel argues, however, that Americans manage their free choice at best dubiously; that rather than preserve a genuine freedom they choose to submit to some higher purpose, be it religion or the uncontrollable dictate of addiction. The valued independence thus often leads to a form of dependence, and the American citizen turns into "the slave who believes he is free" (108).

The novel's central metaphor of this thematic cluster is James Incandenza's movie "Infinite Jest", which truly maximizes the pleasure of the viewer; in fact, it provides so much pleasure that you lose the urge to do anything but watching it repeatedly, in an infinite loop guaranteeing infinite

---

10 As has been demonstrated by e.g. Tony Tanner in his *City of Words* (1971).

pleasure, infinite jest.[11] Therefore it is the perfect weapon for the Canadian wheelchair terrorists,[12] whose plan merely consists of making the movie available to the American citizens, trusting that the free choice of the Americans will do the rest of the work.

The common title invites a comparison between Wallace's novel and Incandenza's movie, and Wallace's novel is certainly also a pleasurable affair. But where the movie "Infinite Jest" encourages passive consumption and surrender, the novel *Infinite Jest* demands that the reader take active part in integrating the fragments of the novel into a more or less coherent vision. In interviews Wallace has stated that *Infinite Jest* is an attempt at striking a balance between the pleasurable and the difficult, thus providing the reader with an incitement to undertake the comprehensive and sometimes difficult interpretational work demanded by the novel in order to surrender meaning. This aesthetic strategy is, like so many of the strategies of the novel, encapsulated in a discussion about James Incandenza's moviemaking, in this case the so-called "anticonfluentalism." The filmography of Incandenza, exhaustively described in the novel's note 24 (8 dense pages long), constitutes a veritable catalogue of the techniques of *Infinite Jest*, and the descriptions of the various aesthetic movements of the director therefore often function as a mise-en-abyme of the novel itself. Of anticonfluentalism we are told: "An après-garde digital movement, a.k.a. 'Digital Parallelism' and 'Cinema of Chaotic Stasis,' characterized by a stubborn and possibly intentionally irritating refusal of different narrative lines to merge into any kind of meaningful confluence" (996). This possibly intentionally irritating lack of narrative convergence is an essential trait in *Infinite Jest*. Plotlines peter out, never meet, are dropped not to be picked up again, and after finishing the novel you are left with a number of unanswered questions. The lack of narrative convergence is, however, far from synonymous with a lack of connections between the elements of the novel. *Infinite Jest* contains a large number of latent connections between its characters and events; connections which are never made explicit, but which are nevertheless discernable through readings and re-readings of the novel. An example of such hidden dendrites in the novel is the young Marlon Bain whose parents were killed on the freeway by a crashing press helicopter.

---

11 The title of the novel and the movie hails from the churchyard scene in *Hamlet*, and besides commenting on the American "pursuit of Happiness", it introduces a father/son-theme which is acted out in Hal's relationship with his father.

12 The novel was written in an innocent decade long ago when it was still possible to joke about terrorism.

Elsewhere in the novel we learn that the secretary of E.T.A., Lateral Alice Moore, has received her moniker because she can only move sideways after having survived the crash of a press helicopter. The connection between Marlon and Alice is never made explicit, but it is nevertheless present as a latent circuit waiting to be completed by the attentive reader. What on a superficial reading seems to be a mess of unconnected events and persons, on closer inspection reveals itself to be a complex network, a densely woven expanse of more or less hidden patterns, of "the connectedness of all events" (96).[13] The apparently different worlds of E.T.A. and Ennett House thus have several points of contact, and during the novel a considerable exchange takes place – both literally and metaphorically – between the overworld of the tennis academy and the underworld of the halfway house.

This essential feature of *Infinite Jest* has much in common with Umberto Eco's well-known theories of *the open work*.[14] Eco developed his reception aesthetics through readings of e.g. Joyce's *Ulysses* and *Finnegans Wake*, and he defined the open work as a new, ambiguous depiction of the world, where the emphasis in the interpretational work was shifted from a sender-oriented to a receiver-oriented understanding. The open work creates a kind of *organized disorder* in order to increase the number of potential meanings and undermine the dominant cultural codes. In this context it is important to stress the fact that the apparently chaotic form of the open work is meticulously constructed, and that rather than being genuinely formless it creates the perfect *illusion* of formlessness.

The carefully constructed chaos of art is an important part of the attempt to avoid a mere reproduction of the system against which art is in opposition; a system which often administers its power through causal chains of command. The apparently absent causality in the open work means that it is the reader/receiver who actualizes the latent structures of the work – a fact that has been pushed to the extremes by the critic (and not the crooner) Tony Bennett. He argues that we should not talk about the "interpretation" of a text, but rather the reader's "productive activation" of the many potential discursive formations of the text (Bennett, 1983: 14). The result of all this is that each reading of an open work – each productive activation of its latent patterns – differs according to the perspective of the

---

13 This statement would seem to echo Pynchon's famous dictum in *Gravity's Rainbow*: "Everything is connected" (Pynchon, 1973: 703).
14 Originally proposed in *Opera Aperta* from 1962.

reader. The reader of *Infinite Jest* has the freedom to choose (there it was again: the freedom of choice) which patterns to construct, and as a result of the many possible combinations, the novel theoretically has an infinite potential of meanings, a charisma that is renewed through each reading.

Even the interpretations of radically open works like *Infinite Jest* have a tendency to converge towards some kind of common denominator, to coagulate in a broad consensus. The interpretations of *Finnegans Wake* thus resemble each other more closely today than they did 50 years ago. Such an interpretational consensus is in reality synonymous with a reduction of the potential meanings of the work and thus a routinization of its charisma. Wallace is fully aware that the originally wildly divergent interpretations of his novel will gradually be caught up in a bell curve – the curve of a normal distribution – but in order to counter this as effectively as possible he has sprinkled his novel with a number of unbridgeable inconsistencies and narrative canyons which are so deep that they will hopefully ensure continued disagreements among the literary critics and sustain the manifold potential of the work.

The greatest gap in *Infinite Jest* is the one between the first chapter of the novel and the rest of the book. As the only chapter in the novel, the first chapter takes place in the Year of Glad, one year after the main action in the Year of the Depend Adult Undergarment. The bookish Hal, who knows most of the Oxford English Dictionary by heart, is at an admission interview at a university. When he finally opens his mouth in order to impress the academic panel with his oral talents (which are amply displayed in the rest of the novel) he is met with terrified looks. The panel simply cannot understand a word of what he is saying, and they experience his attempts at communication as a series of frightening, inarticulate noises, reminding one of them of a "goat, drowning in something viscous" (Wallace, 1996: 14). They subsequently wrestle the uncomprehending (and unintelligible) Hal to the floor and send for a psychiatric ambulance. Thereafter the chapter ends, and that is the last – chronologically, that is – we see of Hal. And then the rest of the novel begins.

It is never explained how this significant communication breakdown can possibly have arisen during the gap between November Y.D.A.U. – where the main action of the novel ends – and November Year of Glad. We are provided with a few hints during the novel that Hal, as a result of his marijuana abuse, experiences an increasing isolation, a solipsistic introspection,[15] but at the same time it is made clear to us that Hal has been lonely since infancy. It is also suggested that James Incandenza made the dangerous movie "Infinite Jest" in a failed attempt at communicating with Hal (838), and that Hal has possibly seen the movie and lived.... or that he has experimented with the potent psychedelic drug DMZ, which at one point – in typically involuted fashion – is described as "acid that has itself dropped acid" (214). Several possible explanations are offered for Hal's severe communication breakdown, but the vectors refuse to converge in a satisfactory and consistent interpretation. The space of *Infinite Jest* cannot be completely closed as a result of the "stubborn and possibly intentionally irritating refusal of different narrative lines to merge," and Wallace's anticonfluential novel thus offers an effective resistance to the literary critics' attempts at routinizing its charisma.

David Foster Wallace's reader-activating aesthetics are not exactly a new invention and can also be found in postmodern works by for instance William Gaddis and Thomas Pynchon. In reality, *Infinite Jest* sometimes seems to be a rewriting – though a competent one – of postmodern monstrosities like *The Recognitions*, *Gravity's Rainbow*, *Giles Goatboy*, and *The Public Burning*. These novels are likewise characterized by complex structures completed by the reader, high information density, non-linear chronology, and metafictive sequences. When Wallace nevertheless succeeds in distancing himself from the predecessors he seeks to escape – the postmodern patriarchs – is has to do with his unflinching focus on the problems under his scrutiny. Here there is no skating over the events, no ironical distance, but rather a strong insistence upon telling us of the pain of the characters, of the hard work and the "raw, unalloyed, agendaless kindness" (203) that are prerequisites for finding your way back to at least some kind of dignity after your substance abuse.

As part of this intrepid confrontational strategy, *Infinite Jest* escorts Don Gately to numerous long AA-meetings where the air is thick with cigarette smoke and clichés. The AA meetings are an "[i]rony-free zone" where the stories you tell about your previous substance abuse have to be "the truth unslanted, unfortified" (369), and where clichés like "Easy Does It" and "One Day At a Time" are surprisingly frequent. Initially, Don finds it difficult to cope with this "unromantic, unhip, clichéd AA thing" (350), but to

---

15 Solipsism is an important theme in the novel, and it is given concentrated expression in the character Nell Gunther who has a glass eye and who likes wearing it with the pupil and iris facing into her head (Wallace, 1996: 362–63).

his surprise he gradually comes to realize that the clichés and the almost insufferable sincerity actually work; that "the vapider the AA cliché, the sharper the canines of the real truth it covers" (446).

In these long AA sequences Wallace himself is not afraid of seeming banal or practising an "unhip earnestness" (689). *Infinite Jest* often moves dangerously close to the border of the Land of Clichés, but in the end it does not cross the border, as a result of Wallace's self-awareness of the banality of the subject matter and the lack of irony. He actually insists upon telling us the truth, yet he is fully aware that a 'true' and 'real' art is a fragile project in our times. This awareness is expressed through Mario, Hal's gentle and deformed brother:

> It is increasingly hard to find valid art that is about stuff that is real in this way. The older Mario gets, the more confused he gets about the fact that everyone at E.T.A. over the age of about Kent Blott finds stuff that's really real uncomfortable and they get embarrassed. It's like there's some rule that real stuff can only get mentioned if everybody rolls their eyes or laughs in a way that isn't happy. (592)

With *Infinite Jest* Wallace attempts to create an updated, complex realism, a "radical realism" (836), which consists of "density plus realism" (491). In a way the novel combines Raymond Carver's realist fiction with the formal complexity of postmodernism, and it is an ambitious attempt at creating a constructive alternative to the ironical postmodernism. The sword with which Wallace tries to cut down irony and self-consciousness is two-edged: On the one hand Wallace employs the already mentioned irony-free, 'banal' sequences, which in their insistence upon telling the truth are vulnerable and easy to ridicule. On the other hand the novel contains passages where Wallace confronts the ironical self-consciousness of postmodernism directly and turns its own arsenal against it. In these passages Wallace is not only self-conscious, but conscious of this self-consciousness and furthermore conscious of this self-conscious self-consciousness etc., in self-consuming spirals of what Wallace calls "Marijuana Thinking": "labyrinths of reflexive abstraction that seem to cast doubt on the very possibility of practical functioning" (1048). By applying irony on irony, and self-consciousness on self-consciousness, Wallace lays bare the aporia lurking at the bottom of all postmodern literature, at the same time showing how the concepts are finally in danger of imploding under their own burden. The meta-ironical and meta-metafictive labyrinths into which he casts the reader seem destined to give you a headache, but they nevertheless express a genuine wish to clean the slate. The method reappears in condensed form in the short story "Octet" from 1999, where a reflective Wallace tries to write himself through layer upon layer of self-consciousness in order to reach a core of heartfelt honesty. You actually believe Wallace when, in "Octet" as well as *Infinite Jest*, he insists that he really *means* it, that he truly wishes to overcome the looming solipsism and solitude and reach a new common ground, a new basis of communication. Wallace's ambition is to blow a hole in the self-conscious and ironical fortifications of the reader, to establish a direct channel between the lonely author and the lonely reader, and to bring about what Thomas Pynchon in a previous novel about communication and solipsism has called "the secular miracle of communication."[16]

The Postironical

As suggested in the first part of the essay, David Foster Wallace is not alone in his insurrection against those iconoclastic writers of the sixties who themselves have turned into icons. The revolt against postmodernism is one of the most visible tendencies in recent American literature, and even though it cannot be said to constitute an organized movement with a clear agenda, its practitioners nevertheless have so many traits in common that it makes sense to provide the tendency with a name: the postironical.

The most outstanding postironical figures in USA – besides of course David Foster Wallace – are the writers Jonathan Franzen (*The Corrections*), Rick Moody (*The Ice Storm, Purple America*), and Dave Eggers (*A Heartbreaking Work of Staggering Genius*). In addition to this central quartet one could mention authors such as Jeffrey Eugenides, Donald Antrim, George Saunders, and – perhaps surprisingly – Thomas Pynchon and Don DeLillo. Pynchon and DeLillo occupy a somewhat special position within postironical literature, since they are among the very authors rebelled against, while they themselves in their later novels, e.g. *Mason & Dixon* and *Underworld*, have moved beyond postmodernism to seek new grounds.[17] A beginning revolt against postmodern irony can also be traced without the American borders, even though the need of an insurrection is not as urgent here as in David Letterman's native country. In Scandinavia, an artist as for

---

16   *The Crying of Lot 49* (Pynchon, 1966: 180).

17   Pynchon's self-criticism was already initiated in his foreword to the collection *Slow Learner* (1984), where he dissociates himself from some of his earlier works. I have borrowed the term 'postironical' from Pynchon who in a recent blurb has called a novel by Emily Barton "blessedly postironic".

example Lars von Trier exhibits strong postironical traits (I will return to von Trier later).

As shown in the analysis of *Infinite Jest*, the postironical does not represent a clean break with postmodernism, but rather a revised continuation, which is simultaneously a break and an extension. As such, postironical literature is by and large related to postmodernism as postmodernism is related to modernism. Each employs formal traits from its predecessor, while at the same time exposing its aporia. Both come into existence when the predecessor becomes seriously aware of itself as a literary system: a self-awareness that enables one to move beyond the system – to regard it at a distance and decide where it is solid and where it is unstable.

Among the most important postironical characteristics is an increased focus on family, at the expense of the postmodern focus on society and the System. The changed focus is perhaps caused by the endless sitcoms that Wallace's generation has been brought up on, but the influence of Raymond Carver should probably also be taken into account.[18] In postironical literature the instrumental ties of society are to a large extent replaced by the ties of blood, and the intimate system of the family is set forth as a human counter-system to the System. It should be emphasized, however, that the families of postironical literature are far from idyllic and in fact tend towards the outright dysfunctional. The family in Rick Moody's *The Ice Storm* (1994) is falling apart due to infidelity and hypocrisy, and in *Purple America* (1997) by the same author a man leaves his sclerotic wife because he simply does not have the energy to nurse her anymore. Enid Lambert in Jonathan Franzen's *The Corrections* (2001) desperately wishes to gather her splintered family for one last Christmas before her husband is finally lost in the confusing labyrinths of Parkinson's. In Jeffrey Eugenides' *The Virgin Suicides* (1993) the five Lisbon sisters commit suicide one after the other, without any obvious reasons, and in *Infinite Jest* James Incandenza likewise kills himself, leaving a family in ruins.

Another characteristic of postironical literature can be summed up by Hal Foster's slogan "The Return of the Real." This inclusion of reality into the world of fiction manifests itself either through a simple insistence that you are telling the truth (as in *Infinite Jest* and "Octet"), or through the inclusion of the author's own life as an explicit subject matter. Moody's short story "Demonology" from the collection of the same name is about the

---

18 As should Don DeLillo's *White Noise* and Pynchon's *Vineland*, both family-centred narratives.

tragical death of his sister, and it ends with Moody apologizing for the fact that he has been unable to fictionalize the account more than is the case (and this almost confessional mode is continued by Moody in his memoir *The Black Veil*). Dave Eggers' genre-busting memoir/novel *A Heartbreaking Work of Staggering Genius* (2000 – by the way: how should one react to a title like that?!) describes how Eggers within one horrible month lost both his parents to unrelated cancers, whereupon this immature 20-year-old was left with the scary responsibility of raising his 8-year-old brother. Woven into this shocking and exceptional account are a number of silly fictitious sequences, blatant lies, exaggerations etc., and the reader is not sure whether to laugh or to cry. The inclusion in the novel of reality and the personal constitutes a clear contrast to the postmodern insistence that everything – even human identity – is a fiction, and at the same time it makes the postironical self-consciousness seem honestly self-revealing and painful rather than a cool, aesthetic calculation.

The postironical focus on near things, on family and the personal, is not synonymous with a desertion of political awareness in favour of self-centred navel contemplation. There has only been a slight adjustment of postmodernism, so that the political is now presented through the personal rather than vice versa. In postmodernism we were often represented as products and slaves of the System, whereas postironical literature seems increasingly aware that we in fact *constitute* the System and that our role as helpless victims of this System tends to be caused by our own free choices, or at least by our habit of running away from responsibility. As previously discussed, Wallace argues that the free choices of Americans often lead to voluntary enslavement, and Dave Eggers makes the following comment on the multinational corporations that were so feared back in the sixties: "no matter how big such companies are, and how many things they own, or how much money they have or make or control, their influence over the daily lives and hearts of individuals [...] is very very small, and so hardly worth worrying about" (Eggers, 2000: colophon). The postironists root their political awareness deeply in the human sphere.

The most important characteristic of the postironical – the characteristic that justifies the name of the burgeoning movement – is of course the reckoning with the irony that mainstream culture has taken over from the postmodern rebels and made its own. This reckoning constitutes the central axis around which the postironical project revolves, but at the same time it is paradoxically its weakest and most fragile part. To support this claim you only have to turn to Danish movie director Lars von Trier's Golden

Heart-trilogy,[19] which distances itself from his previous ironical phase. The main problem for this trilogy is that its creator, after ironical and metafictive works such as *The Element of Crime* and *The Kingdom I–II*, has a hard time being taken seriously in his attempts to employ a larger degree of pathos in his work. I do not believe that the church bells at the end of *Breaking the Waves* are ironical, but still they tend to be perceived in that way; or if not ironical, then at least forcedly pathetic. Irony is a stronger and less fragile rhetorical mode than pathos, since it is always already attacking itself, making a show of undermining itself and thus pre-empting attacks from without. The change from irony to pathos is therefore much more difficult than the opposite movement – the ironical aura that Lars von Trier himself has constructed and sustained through his earlier productions cannot be dismantled without further ado, and subsequently also extends itself to the trilogy.

At its point of departure the revolt against irony is therefore on somewhat shaky ground, and a further destabilizing factor is to be found in the fact that the revolt to some extent springs from a reductive – not to say outright faulty – understanding of the postmodernism that is under attack. It is as if the postironists tend to forget that their original enemy is not postmodernism itself, but rather the assimilated and watered-down version of it that is found in mainstream culture. As a result of this, their blazing guns are often aimed at postmodern literature itself,[20] or more precisely at a (mis-) constructed version of it, made expressly for this very purpose. In order to make the attack more forceful, a small zone of postmodernism – the metafictive and introverted self-reflection found in some of John Barth's, Robert Coover's, and William Gass' books – is made to represent the entire field of postmodernism. This somewhat facile strategical move naturally results in a strong distinction between a postmodern, self-reflexive and ironical literature on the one hand, and a non-ironical, extroverted realism on the other hand; a distinction that is unfortunately

---

19 This controversial trilogy of movies consists of *Breaking the Waves* (1996), *Idioterne* (1998), and the Palme d'Or-winning *Dancer in the Dark* (2000). The trilogy is loosely based on a sentimental little children's book, *Guldhjerte* (Golden Heart), about a self-sacrificing girl who hands over all her belongings to people in need. As a reward, she is finally turned into a princess – a merciful fate compared to the hardships endured by von Trier's heroines: Bess in *Breaking the Waves* and Selma in *Dancer in the Dark* are both killed (whereas Karen in *Idioterne* is let off with countless humiliations and a beating).

20 As becomes clear in the already quoted passage where Wallace lists the literary patriarchs for his patricide. Note that the 'murder motive' is not the work of the fathers themselves, but rather the assimilation of this work by popular culture.

not a monopoly of the postironists, as to a large extent it structures the reception of American post-war literature.[21] This reductive division is an extension of the deconstructive concept of irony found in e.g. Paul de Man, who describes irony as a "permanent parabasis" (de Man, 1996: 179), a fundamentally uncontrollable, form-dissolving figure which destabilizes literature's internal structures of signification and reduces the meaning of widely different literary works to the same sceptical relativization of the chances of communication. In this perspective, a text is either ironical or earnest, and a division into a playful postmodernism and a serious realism is a natural consequence hereof. The problem is that the actual American post-war literature only rarely fits into either category, and as a consequence of this, the reception often has to force the authors into these categories: the pervasive irony of a 'realist' author such as Saul Bellow is for instance often ignored, whereas the discreet irony of 'postmodern' Don DeLillo tends to be magnified.

The postironical focus on, precisely, irony is valuable in that it emphasizes how important a part of modern American literature and culture irony is. At the same time, however, it underscores the need of re-evaluating the deconstructive concept of irony and the resultant division of literature. Even if the church bells of *Breaking the Waves* were ironical, they would not automatically cancel the pathos of the rest of the movie. Irony can easily – in a rhetorical and pragmatic perspective as can be found in e.g. Wayne C. Booth's *A Rhetoric of Irony* (1974) – be perceived as a local, temporary effect that communicates a specific message and does not necessarily destabilize the whole work. Booth's pragmatic distinctions between for example stable/unstable, local/infinite, overt/covert irony, and his focus on the communicative aspects of irony, provide a number of interpretational tools that can register the many nuances of the concept of irony, consequently improving its analytical value. It is not within the scope of this essay to conduct a thorough mapping of the modern American novel, but I will argue that a slight updating and revision of Booth's typologies of irony would enable one to re-evaluate the entrenchments of

---

21 It can be found for instance in the work of the critics Frederick Karl, Malcolm Bradbury, Linda Hutcheon, Susan Strehle, Frank Lentricchia, Tom LeClair, and Brian McHale. For a non-ironical approach that provides a radically different perspective of the period, see Tony Tanner's pattern-oriented *City of Words* (1971). Another critique of the reductive understanding of postmodernism is found in Paul Maltby's *Dissident Postmodernists* (1991) where he divides postmodernism into a self-reflexive, "introverted" branch, and a politically conscious "dissident" branch. Maltby's division is a step in the right direction, but in my opinion it still represents a simplification.

the reception and demonstrate that American post-war literature, from Bellow to Barth, in reality forms a wide spectrum of ironical practices.

With a more varied concept of irony it would also be possible to conceive irony and avant-garde as two separate entities. In recent years there has been a tendency to unite these concepts in a purely formal conception of the avant-garde, where avant-garde and irony are in reality made synonymous.[22] As argued in the first part of this essay, however, the current reproduction of the ironical avant-garde of the sixties merely represents an ineffective avant-gardism. A genuine avant-garde necessarily has to move concurrently with the context against which it defines itself, in a continuous series of slight adjustments. Like Weber's charismatic authority it cannot exist as a stable entity, only in the process of originating, making it more difficult to maintain a stable concept of the avant-garde than to nail a blob of quicksilver to the table. In order to provide the concept with any critical relevance, it first has to be re-historicized. (With re-historicization I do not mean a rehabilitation of the historical avant-garde – whose charisma has long since been routinized – but that the concept should be understood as historically determined, as a specific reaction to a specific context).

With its questioning and critique of the ironical consensus of mainstream culture, and its attempt at plotting new courses for art in the 21st century, postironical literature fulfils some of the most essential criteria for a genuine avant-garde. In their self-perception – the feeling of a revolt, of carrying on the critical torch – authors like David Foster Wallace and Jonathan Franzen are avant-garde, and as such, they, and the other postironists, are marked by a complex double awareness: the wish of being marginal *and* accepted at the same time. Wallace is fully aware that the avant-garde traditionally has been more or less invisible from the mainstream, and that its very naming as an avant-garde at the same time represents an assimilation into a mainstream hungry for revolt, and thus a loss of critical potential, of charisma. Nevertheless, he and the rest of the postironical authors have an ambition of being something as apparently self-contradicting as a popular avant-garde, an avant-garde which in the midst of admiration and

---

22 This is for instance the case with the influential critic David Lehmann, who contends that "irony is the very essence of the avantgarde" (See Lehman, 1998).

accept succeeds in maintaining its charisma.²³ This seems to be one of the only options for a contemporary avant-garde, since an avant-garde like the one of the sixties, an avant-garde outside the System, on the margins, no longer seems to be a real option. Today, where establishing a critical position beyond the System does not seem feasible,²⁴ the resistance has to take place within the System, in full visibility.

It is still too early to decide whether the postironical literature can be described as a genuine avant-garde, as it constitutes but one of many potential paths on our way ahead. Seen from here, its complex critique of the literature of the sixties and its assimilation by the Market seems both necessary and productive, but only time will tell whether the postironical is a cul-de-sac, or whether it – like the truly original avant-garde: the exposed vanguard of the military – is capable of leading us to a new and still unknown territory.

References

Bennett, Tony (1983) "Texts, Readers, Reading Formations". *Journal of the Midwest Modern Language Association*. Vol. 16. No. 1. pp. 3–17

Berubé, Michael (1992) *Marginal Forces/Cultural Centers: Tolson, Pynchon, and the Politics of the Canon*. Ithaca: Cornell University Press

Booth, Wayne C. (1974) *A Rhetoric of Irony*. Chicago: The University of Chicago Press

De Duve, Thierry (1996) *Kant After Duchamp*. Cambridge Ma.: The MIT Press

De Man, Paul (1996/1977) "The Concept of Irony". *Aesthetic Ideology*. Minnesota: University of Minnesota Press

---

23 An excellent case in point here is Jonathan Franzen, who in his *Harper's* essay from 1996, "Perchance to Dream", outlined his ambition of writing a genuinely critical novel that reached a mainstream audience. And in 2001 he *did* deliver on his promise, with the publication of *The Corrections*, a brilliant and truly critical send-up of USA on the brink of a new millennium. While being critical in the best sense of the word, the novel also reached a wide audience, culminating in the selection of the novel for Oprah's book club. This was apparently an even wider audience than Franzen had intended, and in several interviews he expressed his reservations about being identified with the other mainstream products in Oprah's book club – the rest is history.... The Oprah affair illustrates that even though the postironical authors know that they have to resign themselves to an existence within the System, they are still far more comfortable at the margins.

24 As Fredric Jameson has underlined with his idea of "the abolition of critical distance" (Jameson, 1984: 85–86).

Eco, Umberto (1979) *The Role of the Reader: Explorations in the Semiotics of Texts*. Bloomington: Indiana University Press

Eggers, Dave (2000) *A Heartbreaking Work of Staggering Genius*. New York: Simon & Schuster

Franzen, Jonathan (1996) "Perchance to Dream". *Harper's Magazine*. April 1996. pp. 35–54

——. (2001) *The Corrections*. New York: Farrar, Strauss, Giroux

Hutcheon, Linda (1996) *A Poetics of Postmodernism*. London: Routledge

Jameson, Fredric (1984) "Postmodernism, or the Cultural Logic of Late Capitalism". *New Left Review*. No.146. pp. 53–92

Jensen, Bo Green (1998) "Dødens triumf" (interview w. Don DeLillo). *Weekendavisen Bøger*. November 13, 1998. pp. 8–9

Klein, Naomi: (2001) *No Logo*. London: Flamingo

Lehman, David (1998) *The Last Avant-Garde*. New York: Doubleday

McCaffery, Larry (1993) "An Interview With David Foster Wallace". *Review of Contemporary Fiction*. Vol. 13. No. 2. pp. 127–50

McHale, Brian (1992) *Constructing Postmodernism*. London: Routledge

Maltby, Paul (1991) *Dissident Postmodernists: Barthelme, Coover, Pynchon*. Philadelphia: University of Pennsylvania Press

Moody, Rick (1994) *The Ice Storm*. Boston: Little Brown

——. (1997) *Purple America*. Boston: Little Brown

Pynchon, Thomas (1966) *The Crying of Lot 49*. Philadelphia: Lippincott

——. (1973) *Gravity's Rainbow*. New York: Viking

Tanner, Tony (1971) *City of Words: American Fiction 1950–70*. London: Jonathan Cape

Wallace, David Foster (1989) *Girl With Curious Hair*. New York: W.W. Norton

——. (1993) "E Unibus Pluram: Television and U.S. Fiction". *Review of Contemporary Fiction*. Vol. 13. Summer 1993. pp. 151–94

——. (1996) *Infinite Jest*. Boston: Little Brown

——. (1999) *Brief Interviews With Hideous Men*. Boston: Little Brown

Weber, Max (1947) *The Theory of Social and Economic Organization*. Trans. by Parsons & Henderson. New York: Oxford University Press

A Mile in Her Shoes:
Culture Metamorphoses in Rebecca Miller's
Personal Velocity

CAMELIA ELIAS

> *At once cultural texts and commodities,*
> *shoes represent the human condition in all its complexity.*
> – Susan Keiser on *Footnotes: On Shoes*

Having found the perfect pair of shoes on a trip to Sweden but not yet being convinced that I should pay the exorbitant price, I went across to a nearby bookstore and found the following words on the jacket of Rebecca Miller's debut short story collection, *Personal Velocity* (2001):

> Greta Herskovitz looked down at her husband's shoes one morning and saw with shocking clarity that she was going to leave him. The shoes were earnest, inexpensive brown wingtips. Greta was wearing a pair of pointy alligator flats… Lee was a kind, quiet man. If he ever fell out of love with Greta, she knew he would go into therapy and fix it. But she hadn't bargained on her own success. (back cover)

I bought the book and forgot about the shoes, temporarily. The fictive ones put me on a wandering path, with thoughts wondering about what it might be like to be in Rebecca Miller's shoes, metaphorically speaking. A prominent cultural figure, Rebecca Miller is the 43-year-old daughter of the most famous contemporary American playwright, Arthur Miller, and Inge Morath, the Austrian born famous photographer who worked for the prestigious Magnum Photos. (Arthur Miller married Inge Morath a year after he divorced Marilyn Monroe, which is also the year of Monroe's death.

Some of Inge Morath's most famous photos are the portraits she did of Marilyn Monroe). Rebecca Miller is also the wife of famous actor Daniel Day-Lewis (who is the son of famous actress Jill Balcon and famous father, the poet laureate Cecil Day-Lewis).

It means something to have cultural capital, I said to myself, thinking of both Miller and the French cultural theorist Pierre Bourdieu. But first, Miller: before expressing herself as a writer, Miller, who studied sculpture and painting at Yale University, tried out her talent as an actress in a couple of movies. Then she moved on to directing the feature films *Angela* (1996), which won the Filmmakers' Trophy and the Cinematography Award at the Sundance Film Festival and IFT Gotham Prize, and *Personal Velocity: Three Portraits* (2002). The latter film is based on her collection of short stories, and also won the award for Best Film and Excellence in Cinematography at Sundance.

When Miller's collection of short stories came out in 2001, the critics almost unanimously agreed that a new voice had emerged in American fiction. The reviews of Miller's work make for interesting reading from several points of view. For instance, one notices immediately that critics emphasize the "new", not against the background of a larger American literary scene, but against the well established and recognized literary and visual voices of Miller's parents. On the other hand, while critics do not engage in comparing Miller's work to that of her father or mother – that would be an indication of malpractice – they all define Miller's "newness" in relational terms. Which is to say that critics make recourse to Miller's own statement regarding her choice to opt for the film genre which combines drama (the father's legacy) and visual arts (the mother's legacy). Says Miller in an interview: "I always had this compulsion to tell stories and I was so visual at the same time. Making films just seemed the right way to unify those things" (Dougan, 2003: http). Statements such as these tap into the critics' already made up mind that Rebecca Miller is genetically endowed and thus able to mark herself as an artist in her own right. For Miller, drama and the visual have a combinatory function which is both synchronic and diachronic. "Combining those things" is a phrase which reflects both Miller's own inclination (synchronically contingent) and the disposition of her parents. The latter, although individually expressed at different poles, was passed down to her as a unified family tradition (diachronically contingent).

A look at the titles of the multifarious review essays, both on the book and on the film, makes one join the consensus, and declare: indeed, Rebecca

Miller could not have become a truck driver. "Out of the Shadows", "Miller's Crossing", "Personal Tenacity", "Escape Velocity", are titles with both a declarative and an imperative ring to them: they all seem to indicate the necessity to create for oneself an individual identity which would be recognizable against the background of parental (or otherwise) heritage and influence. Paradoxically enough, while the public's expectations from figures such as Miller go in the direction of demanding that Miller establish herself as radically different, they also circumscribe this difference not in radical terms, but in a limited way. In this context radical difference does not transcend the dominant group which successfully produces and exchanges culture for economic benefits.

As far as Miller herself is concerned, growing up in a culturally and economically rich environment constitutes a head start in the development of her identity, insofar as the 'rich and famous' epithet does not allow for a stage of 'beginning from scratch', as it were. Here I would say that Miller's own "personal velocity" is not so much driven by concerns with classical issues of identity anxieties (as critics would have it when they make pronouncements on the significance of stepping out of the parental shadow). Miller aims more sophisticatedly at inventing for herself an 'interesting' identity that would distinguish between what is already there and what else is available. If one accepts the default situation of being an artist simply because everybody else in the family is one, one would have to come up with new ideas that would define the same field, yet in a different way. Miller suggests this much herself when she says: "Probably given the fact that everybody in my family's an artist, I became one. But I think that happens with doctors too" (Stuart, 2002: http). Thus while she acknowledges the benefits of a culturally rich environment, Miller also wants more. For her, the question that poses itself here is what to do with inherited influences and how to make them work towards defining an identity in terms of capabilities that are equally good or better than those shared by other agents in similar positions.

Miller grounds her own success in a matter-of-factness situation in which the parental influence is not only welcome but embraced. Her strategy in dealing with this influence is to place herself within the same artistic field, yet in a relation of difference which is marked not by radicalness but by degrees of interestingness. Trying out several ramifications of the profession of artists – which according to her own statement has the potential to perpetuate itself from generation to generation – may be the element which bestows interestingness on the already established identity. Miller's own contribution to the artistic scene has been marked, not by a single debut but by at least five: as a painter, sculptor, actress, director, and writer, in each field obtaining various degrees of success. Furthermore, the metaphorical implication of words such as "velocity" – a concept which saturates all of Miller's works – substantiates her suggestion that the move from artist to artist, or doctor to doctor, is not dictated by some wind blowing in all directions, but by the speed and force of the personalities involved. But before I go into expanding the idea of 'interesting identity' and how it finds expression in Miller's short stories, I would like to return to the question of what it means to have cultural capital in light of Bourdieu's theory.

Culture Exchanges

Bourdieu's notion of cultural capital is an investigation into what constitutes non-economic and immaterial forms of capital, namely cultural and symbolic capital which can be exchanged and converted into other forms, including economic capital. One of the main claims in Bourdieu's work *Distinction: A Social Critique of the Judgement of Taste* (1984) is that cultural practices increase when economic capital decreases in a society. Cultural capital for Bourdieu, while convertible, is irreducible to economic capital insofar as it consists of non-economic forces such as family, background, social class, prestige. Bourdieu distinguishes between two types of classes each claiming a right to access culture, here in the form of art, music, literature. The dominating class appropriates culture via economic investment for the sake of acquiring status symbols, or the preservation of conservative values. This class is identified as holding bourgeois values. The dominated class appropriates culture symbolically, for example, through the knowledge of art, or the creation of artefacts which distinguish themselves as works of arts and reflect the manifestations of a certain group or community. This class is identified as being intellectual, progressive, and capable of creating avant-garde movements. Furthermore, what differentiates the two classes is also their approach to the acquisition of art. Insofar as the dominated class has fewer economic means, it engages in producing works of culture, while the dominating class, possessing economic capital, engages in investing in the preservation of works of art. In other words, while art for the bourgeoisie is stripped of culture, for the intellectuals, culture is heralded as a form of art.[1]

Between classes and within each class, however, there are gatekeepers who ensure that the production and exchange of culture occurs according to the rules and conventions which designate their respective canons. In other words, even with the right shoes on, it is not easy to walk in. Here, Bourdieu's concept of symbolic capital becomes relevant. For Bourdieu, the symbolic capital is part of the embodied cultural capital, or *habitus* which designates an individual's dispositions, cultural values and personal acquisitions held in esteem in the individual's, or agent's given context. An agent's *habitus* relates to societal issues, class, ethnicity, family, and ultimately constitutes identity. Symbolic capital is defined by "prestige, celebrity, consecration of honour awarded an agent by other agents acknowledging his work or competence" (Bourdieu, 1993: 77–78).

Bourdieu's other two forms of cultural capital besides the embodied state, are the objectified and the institutionalized states. The objectified state of cultural capital consists of ownership of cultural goods such as books, paintings, monuments, instruments, machines (Bourdieu, 1986: 246). These materials can be appropriated either by economic investment or symbolic investment, the latter by exercising what Bourdieu calls "a form of knowledge, an internalized code or a cognitive acquisition which equips the social agent with empathy towards appreciation for, or competence in deciphering cultural relations and cultural artefacts" (Bourdieu, 1993: 7). The institutionalized state of cultural capital consists of academic credentials. Academic qualifications create "a certificate of cultural competence" (Bourdieu, 1986: 248), they are proof of an agent's versatility in respect of culture. Whereas the objectified state of cultural capital is the exercising of the embodied state, the institutionalized state can be used as a conversion rate into economic capital, depending on the demand for the specific academic qualifications. Cultural capital, then, consists of *habitus*, cultural competence, and institutional recognition.

The acquisition of cultural capital varies from context to context, and an agent's access to it and means to increase it are largely determined by the previous investment in her skills or talents by the family. In the case of

---

[1] This statement is obviously a generalization which yet is not always valid. As long as the dominating class can also buy knowledge for itself, and the dominated class also includes incompetent intellectuals, the approach to art will thus be context-situated before it is institutionalized as such.

Rebecca Miller, the already invested cultural capital is ready to be converted more quickly into economic capital. When a predetermined path is available and accepted, one does not waste time figuring out what kind of an individual one is, what skills one has, and how to create strategies for institutional recognition. As Bourdieu says: "the initial accumulation of cultural capital, the precondition for the fast, easy accumulation of every kind of useful cultural capital, starts at the outset, without delay, without wasted time only for the offspring of families endowed with strong cultural capital" (246).

Cultural heritage here delineates the space of positions or movements within a field and it leads to what Bourdieu calls "position-takings". For instance, art for Bourdieu, exists only for those who have acquired enough cultural capital to enable them to understand, or perceive, and decode the art at stake. Understanding art is however also situation-based, insofar as it is institutionalized, or grounded in a relation to the "ensemble of the works forming the class to which it belongs, and to these works only" (Bourdieu, 1993: 222). When the agent is fully capable of decoding art, he is also capable of rejecting the conventions that make it art. On this point, Bourdieu makes many references to Manet's example of refusal to follow the injunctions on art enforced by institutions such as *École des Beaux-Arts,* which had it at the time that a work of art is defined by a narrative content, a message, and a theme usually dealing with 'high' or 'noble' issues. Manet's famous painting *The Absinthe Drinker* is thus first a representation of manifestations within a specific culture, that of the lower class, and then a work of art in pictorial terms.

The positions that an agent takes vis-à-vis communicating his competence in relation to decoding is similar to the strategies of interpretation which the agent uses as a matter-of-course in the sense that interpretation, or criticism, is based on a legitimacy claim. The formation of a literary canon is, for instance, a question of who holds the necessary authority to enforce the validity of definitions of literary works. These definitions are thus grounded in a pre-determined position of legitimization. Determining what works form a literary canon is, however, an ethnocentric enterprise, which is to say that the agents forming the literary field judge and determine the works of the literary canon according to their norms and regulations. An ethnocentric approach to literature, or society for that matter, means the incorporation in the canon of those works which correspond to the views of agents in the field of literature. The agents mean to establish that since they have been educated to appreciate a certain type of literature, this literature works for them. In the ethnocentric approaches, then, there is no space for the recognition of "otherness" or "difference". Consequently, the agents take it for granted that everybody else must accept their views. However, this is not always the case, and thus we have, in response to traditional literary canons, formations of other literary canons dealing, for example, with feminist, queer, or postcolonial issues. In other words, the literary or artistic field becomes both a "field of forces" where competing discourses take place, and a "field of struggles", where legitimacy is sought. Says Bourdieu in *The Field of Cultural Production* (1993):

> The *space of literary or artistic position-takings*, i.e the structured set of the manifestations of the social agents involved in the field – literary or artistic works, of course, but also political acts or pronouncements, manifestos or polemics, etc. – is inseparable from the *space of literary or artistic positions* defined by the possession of a determinate quantity of specific capital (recognition) and, at the same time, by occupation of a determinate position in the structure of the distribution of this specific capital. The literary or artistic field is a *field of forces*, but it is also a *field of struggles* tending to transform or conserve this field of forces. (30)

In tandem with Bourdieu's statement here, and his general critique of theories which fail to question their own position in the field, I refer to a concrete example where the artist takes issue with what position and space her art assumes, both in relation to society and in relation to a conventional canon. Rebecca Miller's film *Personal Velocity – Three Portraits* is an interesting example of how an artist who comes from the field of literary fiction and painting approaches the field of movie production and direction: in her case, sideways and backwards. In several interviews Miller explains that originally she wanted to make movies but had gotten tired of waiting for her projects to be endorsed and consequently financed by producers. Thus, not having been able to access the field of movie making, she turned to writing fiction because, as she claims, the desire to tell stories was very strong. However, once the short stories came out, Gary Winick, a producer and friend of Miller, saw the opportunity to turn some of the stories into portraits that could be shot on digital video. The result is not a mainstream film and both technically and thematically the film is different from most American productions. As Miller herself evokes, not only does the film emphasize character rather than plot, thus aligning itself with the French tradition, but it is also digitally shot (Dawson, 2003: http). This technique requires an experienced photographer, and it is interesting to note the reason why the award winning cinematographer Ellen Kuras wanted to be involved in the making of the movie, and how she viewed the collaborative process between a fiction writer and a photographer. Kuras's response indicates that a reputable gatekeeper, such as herself, has the power not only to endorse Miller's project but also to find a way to accommodate Miller's poetic idiosyncrasy. Says Kuras:

> I was very interested in working on the film because it was a whole different format; almost like three short stories […] Rebecca and I talked about visual metaphors and "macro-epiphanies" where a series of close-ups are visuals to a state of mind, particularly with Greta and Paula. I was wrestling with the fact that I was going to have to shoot on mini-DV so one thing I decided was to try and make the film a visual poem. In poems, you can do anything, you can leave out your punctuation, but when you put in your punctuation it means something. So I decided that I would leave all the doors open and try to make it an expressive piece in service of the narrative. I usually shoot a lot of bits and pieces and sometimes they don't make it into the film and sometimes they do. The great thing about Rebecca as an editor/director, thank God, is that she recognized those moments in the footage and then put them in the film. The movie is really about the movement toward these realizations, toward these poetic moments. (Torneo, 2002: http)

Miller's own statements about her movie emphasize a scholarly aspect: she analyzes not only themes but also the form, the use of language and rhetoric in her film, which betrays her knowledge of literary criticism and her awareness of a kind of eclecticism which she brings to the field. The combination of still photography in the movie with the choice of colour palettes to enhance a certain mood provides not merely an 'explanation' of the artistic value of the work from an aesthetic point of view, but also a 'statement' on Miller's engagement with situating the work in a political discourse which has the situation of women (as underachievers, battered wives, or confused subjects) at its forefront. Insofar as the movie layers different material (painting, photography, narrative), the viewer is confronted with Miller's underlying aim: the movie must have the viewer in mind and the kind of emotional responses she engages with, but it must also address its own status as a work of art and what it intends to legitimize. There are several kinds of metamorphosis that the film proposes to engage with, and these constitute a reflection of the multiple messages and intentions of the work. One can contend that as a work of art Rebecca Miller's film is not entirely self-referential, yet as a work of culture, it represents an element of self-referentiality insofar as it questions and verifies its own presuppositions in relation to its intended multiple messages. Miller's statements, which are both didactic and anchored in scholarly culture, parallel Bourdieu's thesis (with a note on Heidegger) which claims the following:

> Educated people are at home with scholarly culture. They are consequently carried towards that kind of ethnocentrism which may be called class-centrism and which consists in considering as natural (in other words, both as a matter of course and based on nature) a way of perceiving which is but one among other possible ways and which is acquired through education that may be diffuse or specific, conscious or unconscious, institutionalized or non-institutionalized. "When, for instance, a man wears a pair of spectacles which are so close to him physically that they are 'sitting on his nose,' they are environmentally more remote from him than the picture on the opposite wall. Their proximity is normally so weakly perceived as to go unnoticed." Taking Heidegger's analysis metaphorically, it can be said that the illusion of the 'fresh eye' as a 'naked eye' is an attribute of those who wear the spectacles of culture and who do not see that which enables them to see, any more than they see what they would not see if they were deprived of what enables them to see. (217)

For Rebecca Miller, the sense of seeing is not far removed from institutionalized taste. When she recounts that her mother took her to museums from the time she was four, she acknowledges that, for her, the value of art is inscribed in her scholarly and cultural awareness as a social condition. Bourdieu's "class-centrism" which manifests itself as a natural way of perceiving finds resonance in Miller's emphasis on the social aspect of museum-going, a habit which was religiously enforced by the mother. As she puts it: "she was always talking to me about painting, composition. She taught me a lot about seeing in a disciplined way" (Guthmann, 2002: http). Possessing 'scholarly culture' is thus a disciplined act of perceiving.

Knowledge about the social world in which one acts as an agent is based upon the construction of divisions which organize the image of the social world. When Miller refers to "seeing in a disciplined way", she does not refer only to the influence of that kind of seeing on her art, but also to the context which, on the one hand, situates her work in a process of distinction, and, on the other hand, functions as a marker of social orientation. Here, Miller's ambition to be other than her parents can be understood in terms of a socially constructed reality. This reality confers on her identity the degree of difference needed to be interesting, insofar as the dominating class (to which Miller belongs) sets 'interestingness' as one of its most exchangeable forms of cultural capital. When asked about her relationship to success, Miller, however, rejects the idea that her success is based on ambition. "Ambition can be a disease", she says, "and it feeds on itself. I have a real resistance to giving myself over to it, partly because there's something a little bit anti-human about it" (Wood, 2003: http). Her stance on the question of ambition – which is a very strong theme in her book – is further related to her ability to position herself in a different stance than her parents by being suspicious of her background. Here she says:

> I don't have the kind of dream that I might have about the idea of being successful which I think I would if I was completely innocent of it. Though I have to admit, my parents lived in a very simple way. I grew up in a farmhouse in Connecticut. There were no limos, no first-class flights. It was not a particularly extravagant way of life. But I did know what fame is, obviously, so… I guess you have to just keep your eye on what you're doing, and not think about the smoke it gives off. (http)

Thus, while Miller acknowledges the influence of her parents, she is not interested in questioning their way of doing things. Her own dispositions are set in a contradictory relation to her background in the sense that her suspicions revolve not around influences as such, but around the positions she assumes in relation to those influences. When one walks the same path, it is less interesting to know things about the route. What counts are the shoes one wears. As a person, she belongs to the dominating class. As an artist, she belongs to the same dominating class but at the same time is dominated by the gatekeepers in the field. Ultimately, the relationship between dominated and dominating forces is what forges dynamism and creation in the field in which one chooses to operate.

Shoe Anxiety

The shoe metaphors are useful here insofar as they illustrate the point that there is a difference between filling someone's shoes and following in someone's footsteps. In the first case, it is harder to fulfil someone's expectations and carry on a task that has been previously designed and made to fit certain requirements. An artist who makes claims to originality indirectly points out that the inherited shoes do not fit. Consequently, the work of influencing 'fathers' is rejected in order to create space for individual artistic production. In the second case, following in the footsteps of an established artist implies accepting a degree of that artist's influence on one's own work, and acknowledging that even if one does not fit the shoes, the path one walks deserves the effort. Followers are not interested in grounding their own work in some original manifestation. A work is deemed worthy when it opens itself up to encounters with other ideas which foreground dialogue. Both cases are, however, marked by an anxiety of inadequacy. One is reminded here of Harold Bloom's theory of the anxiety of influence which also operates with similar distinctions. In Bloomian theory, developed in several works, there are two types of poets: strong and weak. The strong poets – whose 'drives' are put into action by what Bloom says is the tendency "to think of themselves as stars because their deepest desire is to be an influence, rather than to be influenced" (Bloom, 1975: 12) – have to define the originality of their work against the achievement of their predecessors, or father-figures. Further he claims that even in the strongest, "whose desire is accomplished, the anxiety of having been formed by influence still persists" (12). Bloom's theory of poetry is a theory of influence, claiming that poetry is not about anxiety but *is* an anxiety about a poet's relation to a previous poet (Bloom, 1973: 94). For Bloom, a powerful anxiety of influence renders literature the scene of an Oedipal struggle; the beginning poet, or in Bloom's words, the "ephebe", engages in a struggle in which he uses any means to repress – through creative acts of misreading, or "misprision" – the influence of powerful "forefathers". He writes:

> Every poem is a misinterpretation of a parent poem. A poem is not an overcoming of anxiety, but is that anxiety. Poets' misinterpretations or poems are more drastic than critics' misinterpretations or criticism, but this is only a difference in degree and not at all in kind. There are no interpretations but only misinterpretations, and so all criticism is prose poetry. (94–95)

For Rebecca Miller, being close to so many artistic expressions, originality becomes a strategic battle for position-takings. Avoiding using her father's fame to enter his literary field, her husband's fame to enter his motion pictures field, or her mother's fame to enter her field of still photography, Rebecca Miller tries to shift fields by using nevertheless the same prerequisites which define each of them. Knowing that there is no guarantee for success across any of these fields, Miller approaches drama through visual arts (by making films), visual arts through fiction (by basing her films on her writing), and fiction through character portrayal (her stories are extended portraits of individuals). Her strategy of dealing with these fields and the famous people who delimit them through their work is to make her approach interesting in a relational way. For each field has its gatekeeper. If we take the example of Daniel Day-Lewis, we remark that his highly profiled statement on his talent as an actor has some bearing on his wife's position vis-à-vis his field. When he says: "I suppose I have a highly developed capacity for self-delusion, so it's no problem for me to believe I'm somebody else" (Day-Lewis, 1993: http), we sense that Miller's preference for writing for the movies goes in the direction of establishing herself as herself and not as somebody else who is somebody through somebody else. What goes for Day-Lewis, whose formidable talent sets the standard for outstanding acting, goes only partially for Miller. Her performances have been praised but none were unforgettable.

Another aspect of gate-keeping is seen in the reception of Miller's work. Gaby Wood, the critic who entitles her interview/review of Miller's film "Miller's Own Tale" (2003), establishes her academic credentials by alluding to Chaucer's *A Miller's Tale* and perhaps Schubert's song cycle, *Die Schöne Müllerin*, two works which pose the question of the artist who is engaged in shifting fields and positions. Chaucer's pilgrim miller tells a narrative which is meant to stand alongside the narratives of other 29 pilgrims of both high and low standing, all on their way to Canterbury. Schubert's wandering miller tells a narrative about wooing and desiring a better position for himself. While Schubert's music in the first lied "Das Wandern" is downright an homage to trekking-boots, Chaucer's miller praises the silk shoes of Alison. The reader endowed with the necessary cultural competence will identify the contrast between Schubert's romantic idealism – paralleled in the interview by references to Ireland, a perfect wandering place for millers, and Rebecca Miller's adopted country where she now lives with her husband – and Chaucer's world of emblematic images, which in the interview is symbolised by a reference to Miller's wearing and commenting on her new silk shoes.

Miller's strategy of securing for herself a space in the field of cultural production can be said to combine an awareness of who the gatekeepers are with an originality which is meant to fit her and their shoes simultaneously, both in a 'proper' and an 'improper' way, according to each field and situation. Literally wearing silk shoes in rural Ireland can hardly be deemed proper. Yet, it is always proper to make oneself interesting, insofar as interestingness sparks dynamism and creates a tension which is beneficial for every act of creation. Miller's anxiety of influence, then, finds resolution, not in the usurpation of the influencing factors, but in distinguishing between filling the wrong shoes and following in the right footsteps, yet wearing unfitting footwear. Positioning herself 'out of the shadows' is in Miller's case, not an instance of *being* a 'wanderer', but *becoming* one, thus metamorphosing each field according to the shoes she wears. This much is suggested also in the review essay, "Miller's Crossing", which, with a wink to the title of the Coen brothers movie, makes a reference to Miller's versatility in shifting fields of creative production.

Culture Fitting

In Miller's book, *Personal Velocity*, which comprises seven stories about seven women, shoes can be said to function as a master metaphor for the characters' desire to make their lives something different from what they are. What Miller is interested in is not how to make her characters, women with different social backgrounds, escape their situations, but how to engage them in becoming more interesting in the same context. While the women in Miller's book nevertheless all walk away from the lot that life has dealt them, they do not walk very far. And this is what makes the work interesting. While Miller employs thematically the reaching of a crossroad, her characters are not allowed to develop as they would in a traditional *Bildungsroman*, in which we may have a feminist, or realist approach. Metaphorically speaking – and in places, literally problematized – the characters, while at the crossroad, do not make the realization that they have to make a decision about which way to go – the answer to that question comes to them naturally and unambiguously. Rather, they make the realization that they wear the wrong shoes. They are not interesting enough. Thus, at the crossroad the characters try to compensate for the lack of that attribute by putting on a new pair of shoes to go with their ambitions even when these are not yet realized, or are in a state of latent manifestation.

Interestingness for Miller is directly linked to individual struggle, emotional survival, and personal responsibility. Each story is structured as a portrayal, and shows Miller's mastery at depicting images of forceful character. Her writing technique borrows elements from her father's dramatic portrayals of the simple and common, yet dignified people, and her mother's photographic portraits which always focus on the subject's personality. The short and well cadenced sentences together with the right metaphors make her style almost aphoristic, which adds a layer of incontestability to the content of the stories. In the first story, "Greta", the protagonist, a Harvard educated woman coming from a family with high economic and cultural capital, is yet an obscure cookbook editor and the wife of a shallow man. She wears cheap pumps. One day her boss calls her into his office and asks her to meet with the best selling author in America who is with a competing publishing house. They are both very surprised, Greta, because she has never edited fiction, and her boss, because the author, who specifically asked for her, had called her an excellent editor. Each anticipates in their own way the opportunity to have the best selling author change publishing houses. As Miller writes, Greta's anticipation revolves around projecting an image of the professional who knows what it takes to make it. She thus "went straight out to the most expensive shoe store she had ever heard of and put the alligator flats on her credit card. She couldn't even begin to afford them, but she needed to feel worthy, she needed to feel like a pro" (Miller, 2001: 3).

Style in writing as an important element in the field of cultural production, here literature, is paralleled with style in fashion, style in witty conversation, and style in negotiation. At the meeting, the best selling author, who is a refugee from Laos writing a new book based on his experiences of his escape from his country, enlightens Greta as to his choice of her editorial help: Greta was good at "trimming fat", a competence which grew out of her years at Harvard. At the restaurant where they first meet, the exchange between Greta and her author is mediated by a third person narrator who registers the style shifters that take place not only in the dialogue between the two characters, but also throughout the entire story. As the next passage illustrates:

> On the day of the meeting she wore a red suit with a fairly short skirt – just above the knees. It was a cool, clear spring day. She was twenty minutes early, so she walked over to the Museum of Modern Art and wandered around the cluttered gift shop with the fixed stare of a sleepwalker, little charges of anxiety going off in her belly […] Then she rushed over to the restaurant, sat down at the corner table that had been reserved by Mr. Gelb's secretary, and took out her notebook so she'd look busy. Inside was a shopping list: bananas, clementines, toilet paper, rice, batteries, tampons. She looked up and Thavi Matola was standing there.
>
> "Greta Herskovitz?" he said.
>
> "Yes – oh, hi!" Greta stood up, adjusting her hair band. She felt off-kilter. She should have been watching for him. Thavi sat down. He was slender and androgynous-looking, with smooth brown skin and short curly hair. His mother was Laotian, Greta remembered. Father, Italian-American soldier, dead. Refugees. Hard life. Three sisters, two left behind in Laos because of that government.
>
> "I really loved your first book", she said.

> "It's a piece of shit," said Thavi in a slight accent, lighting a cigarette.
>
> "I think that's pretty common," said Greta.
>
> "Second thoughts?"
>
> "Self-hatred." A minor convulsion of amusement forced the smoke out of Matola's nose; he fixed his gaze on Greta like a child surprised to hear a stranger call him by his nick-name. (3–4)

Here, the reader begins to get a sense of Miller's direction in terms of style. The scarce use of redundant sentences, the choice of just the right word, or metaphor, is Miller's way of carving out the personality of her characters. Attention to culture-marking details enriches her portraits and one finds oneself spending time thinking about them. While there is a contrast between Greta and Matola, it is clear in the quoted passage that their differences meet on common ground. Greta's presuppositions regarding the tough life of refugees do not go any further than her deciding, later in the following passage, that the author must be gay, as he is slender and "androgynous-looking". Being a foreigner in a foreign country does not call for further speculation as Greta herself comes from a family with a history of migration. She is Jewish, and her mother was even a survivor of a concentration camp. Thus, Matola's success as a writer in exile does not strike her as eminent, as her own personal field of reference includes a family that managed to succeed in spite of obvious hardship. The father, a top lawyer, who set up office and home in a top Manhattan location, sent her to top schools, and expected from her the 'top'. When Matola wants some information about her in return she responds:

> "Manhattan, I was born in Manhattan, went to the Flemming School uptown – a small private, you know – and then to boarding school, then to college, then to law school, but I quit – my father's a lawyer, we're not speaking, my mother is – well, dead. They're divorced. I mean they were. I'm twenty-eight. My father has a three-year-old". *God almighty please let me shut up*, she thought. Her steak arrived. She cut into it vigorously.
>
> "My friend Felicia Wong said you were good at trimming fat," he said, watching her do so. Felicia Wong had written short stories at Harvard. Greta had been one of the editors of *The Advocate*. She had an eye for the inessential and would sift through the undergraduate fiction, culling every superfluous word. The writers had called her the Grim Reaper. Yet they all wanted Greta Herskovitz to comb through their work. She had been a bit of a star at Harvard.
>
> "I have a tendency to overwrite," he said. I need someone to kick my ass."
>
> "I can kick your ass," said Greta accommodatingly, wondering if he was gay. (5–6)

The fact that Greta does not do any research into Matola's ethnicity, which is also the background for his book, enforces the point that, for her, one's identity is not about questions of ethnic affiliation alone. Prior to their meeting she goes to the Museum and is more interested in her shopping lists. On the other hand, her own cultural experiences have taught her not to pry and be free of prejudices. The meeting with Matola on untainted ground, as it were, acquires for Greta a different significance. Whereas her desire to distinguish herself from her father and be other than him is legitimized, her ambitions take her on exactly the same path which characterizes her father's success. Getting hired to edit for Matola gains her a strong reputation and prestige and constitutes also the moment of reconciliation with her father who throws her a big party, where he invites, not Greta's friends, but his own.

To the Herskovitzes, Greta's sudden success – when people had stopped expecting anything of major importance from her – means, on the one hand, gaining access to a class of people with economic capital – and on the other hand, enforcing one's belonging to the same class who also appreciates culture and personal achievement. Greta's assets are suddenly converted into money and prestige. At the party she reflects that her newly gained reputation as a competent editor enables her to open her own publishing house, if she wanted, with investments she would receive right then and there from her father's network of rich people. This realization makes her acknowledge two things: first, that she does not wish to dissociate herself from a family whom she previously saw as being "uncivilized", in the sense that they were "always yelling out ideas over dinner like they were selling fish in a souk" (15–16) – here in contrast with her husband's family of Germanic origin who always behaved in a disciplined manner, who "said grace and 'please pass the bread'" (15) at the table. Secondly, as it becomes apparent to Greta that selling ideas is a much more interesting enterprise than repetitive discipline, she is willing to endorse the thought that her best attributes are due to the fact that she is "rotten with ambition". Consequently, when her father proudly makes the public pronouncement that "everyone has their own personal velocity" (27) – implying that with his investment in Greta, she could not be anything but successful, even when she has been slow in becoming so – Greta realizes that her husband and herself do not walk at the same pace. However, she does not decide to leave him either for that or for his "lack of ambition", but simply because he wears cheap shoes.

From a cultural point of view this is an interesting denouement in the story. Miller's choice to make such decisions as getting a divorce a matter of distinction – expensive vs. cheap shoes – finds justification in the fact that materiality and triviality are factors of social orientation which anticipate and negotiate the values of cultural capital in relation to economic capital. Greta's expensive shoes are emblematic of the conditions under which she is able to produce autonomously something of cultural and social value. Applying Bourdieu's theory to Greta gives us an example of an agent who finds herself in the middle of the struggle between dominating forces in the cultural field. Bourdieu's examples of consecrated artists vs. striving artists, novel vs. poetry, art for art's sake vs. social art, are manifested as metamorphoses of cultural capital in Miller's story. Greta's move within the positions available to her, from striving for recognition to becoming a consecrated editor, not of cookbooks (socially determined), but of novels (aesthetically determined) expresses the dynamics of the field of cultural production. Greta's challenging of the established traditions, both of her family as well as her husband's family constitutes the driving force in the negotiation for a space and a position within the cultural field. As Bourdieu claims:

> Every position-taking is defined in relation to the *space of possibles* which is objectively realized as a problematic in the form of the actual or potential position-takings corresponding to the different positions; and it receives its distinctive value from its negative relationship with the co-existent position-takings to which it is objectively related and which determine it by delimiting it. (Bourdieu, 1993: 30)

Greta's negative relationship to the world of her father does not find resolution in a repudiation or denouncement of that world, but in repeating it and reproducing it. Bourdieu identifies this movement as a form of "heretical break" characterized by the use of pastiche or parody "as the indispensable means of objectifying, and thereby appropriating, the form of thought and expression by which they were formerly possessed" (31). Greta's example, in which she appropriates her father's dictum on "personal velocity" only so that she can dismiss her husband on account of cheap shoes, is a reflection of Miller's parodying the ways of portrayal in which the character must be in the possession of 'noble' or 'true' thoughts. Greta is shown to exhibit 'nobility' the moment she realizes that there is nothing nobler than using shoes as a reason for "personal velocity". As Miller writes in the lines which conclude the story:

> In the morning, she showered and dressed for the new job. When she came out of the bedroom Lee was already reading the paper. The coffee had been made and there was a brown paper bag full of fresh muffins on the table. Greta kissed Lee on his head, took a muffin, and poured milk into her coffee, observing the light that spilled sparkling through the window onto the blond wood table, the white china, Lee's white shirt, his golden hair. And then she looked down at his shoes. Suddenly a terrifying thought came into Greta's mind, clear and cruel. Tears of shame filled her eyes. She was going to dump her beautiful husband like a redundant paragraph. She reached out impulsively, as if she'd stumbled, and grabbed his arm.
>
> "What is it?" he asked. But it was too late. Greta felt herself falling away at tremendous speed, her hair whipped back, the skin vibrating against her face. There was nothing she could do. (29)

Interesting identity as a form of cultural capital can thus be acquired by engaging in a process of metamorphosing the system of differential positions in relation to the space of position-takings available. Going for the interesting is, however, no new thing, especially when one thinks of another literary giant, Virginia Woolf, who said that every position a woman takes is interesting, and that shoes are as interesting as a war or an earthquake. Thus, one of the overall messages in Miller's work – and in addition to Bourdieu's discussion of the field of cultural production – is that women make themselves available by putting interestingness at the top of their agenda. Women metamorphosize culture, and culture buys them interesting shoes.

References

Adams, Sam (2002) "Miller's Crossing". *Philadelphia City Paper*. Dec. 5–11. [http://www.citypaper.net/articles/2002-12-05/movies2.shtml] – last consulted Jan. 2006

Benstock, Shari and Ferries, Susanne (eds.) (2001) *Footnotes: On Shoes*. New Brunswick: Rutgers University Press

Bloom, Harold (1973) *The Anxiety of Influence: A Theory of Poetry*. Oxford: Oxford University Press

——. (1975) *A Map of Misreading*. New York: Oxford University Press

Bourdieu, Pierre (1984) *Distinction: A Social Critique of the Judgement of Taste*. Cornwall: Routledge

——. (1986) "Three Forms of Capital". *Handbook of Theory and Research for the sociology of Education*. John Richardson, ed. New York: Greenwood Press

——. (1993) *The Field of Cultural Production*. Cambridge: Polity

Dawson, Thomas (2003) Interview: "Rebecca Miller – Personal Velocity". *BBC – Movies*. 2003/02/27 [http://www.bbc.co.uk/films/2003/02/27/rebecca_miller_personal_velocity_interview.shtml] – last consulted Jan. 2006

Day-Lewis, Daniel (1993) *Entertainment Weekly*. December 28/93

Dougan, Andy (2003) "Out of the Shadows". *Evening Times On Line*. - [http://www.eveningtimes.co.uk/lo/extra/7006505.html] – last consulted Jan. 2006

Guthmann, Edward (2002) "Director Miller Attains Escape 'Velocity'". *San Francisco Chronicle*, Sunday, December 1. [http://www.sfgate.com/cgi-bin/article.cgi?f=/chronicle/archive/2002/12/01/PK70349.DTL] – last consulted Jan. 2006

Miller, Rebecca (2001) *Personal Velocity*. London: Black Swan

——. (2002) *Personal Velocity: Three Portraits*. DVD Producer: InDigEnt, et al.

Stuart, Jamie (2002) "Rebecca Miller: Personal Tenacity". *Movie Navigator*. [http://www.movienavigator.org/perosonalvelocity.htm] – last consulted Jan. 2006

Torneo, Erin (2002) Interview: "Cinematography As Poetry: Ellen Kuras Talks About The DV Challenges of 'Personal Velocity'". Indiwire – People 11/25/02 [http://www.indiewire.com/people/int_Kuras_Ellen_021125.html] – last consulted Jan. 2006

Wood, Gaby (2003) "Miller's Own Tale". *The Observer*. Sunday March 9. [http://www.film.guardian.co.uk/Print/0,3858,4621199,00.html] – last consulted Jan. 2006

Transtextuality, Paranoia, and Apophenia in *Pattern Recognition*

STEEN CHRISTIANSEN

> *"Call me Ishmael," she says, walking on.*
> *"A girl's name?" Eager and doglike beside her.*
> *Some species of weird nerd innocence that somehow she accepts.*
> *"No. It's Cayce."*
> *"Case?"*
> *"Actually," she finds herself explaining,*
> *"it should be pronounced 'Casey,'*
> *like the last name of the man*
> *my mother named me after.*
> *But I don't."*
> – William Gibson

This discussion of the protagonist's name in William Gibson's *Pattern Recognition* inevitably opens the caskets of several textual ghosts; textual ghosts that will haunt the reader who recognizes them and be invisible to those who do not see them. This function is hardly rare or unusual; perhaps even one of the basic elements of literature. However, it is a function which is explicitly commented on by the text in question, and the text itself is certainly also filled with such possible ghosts. What is interesting is how we react to these ghosts as readers. Most assumptions of reader competence would have us look for these ghosts, to invest them with meaning, to examine their referential value and their interpretative potential. Yet there is another way to react to these ghosts and that is the "weird nerd innocence" mentioned above, by the reader who does not recognize the name Ishmael as anything significant, even to the extent of not knowing whether it is a girl's or boy's name. This is a different reading strategy, in a sense a lack of specific competence, which will create a different understanding of the text in question.

This difference in reading strategy – of investing fragments with meaning and the potentially dangerous aspects of this reading – is discussed in Gibson's text usually with a favouring of not drawing connections, of being wary of seeing ghosts and even more wary of what these ghosts might mean. Voices beyond the grave should not be taken lightly, especially not if they are revealed to be ourselves speaking, saying things to comfort us. This will be the focus of the present essay: how do we as readers react to such voices and should we always trust what we hear from them? How does literary competence work in such cases of explicit and implicit references?

I use the word 'ghosts' because there is a ghost in the text; Cayce is haunted by the ghost of her father (!), lost on September 11, presumed dead – but Cayce refuses to believe this. She constantly sees traces of him around her, but can never be sure that it is him. Does she find traces of him or does she read random objects to be traces of him? This is one of the elements of the story, but perhaps it would be better for our purposes here to find a different word than 'ghost'. Fortunately, Gerard Genette has created plenty of words for us to draw on, so let us instead begin with examining how his basic term transtextuality may help us in understanding the way that texts draw upon each other and create webs of references. Transtextuality is of course a heading for a number of other, more specific, textualities, each with its own distinct function.

Genette proposes, in his book *Palimpsests* (1982, translated into English 1997), five types of transtextual relationships: intertextuality, paratextuality, metatextuality, hypertextuality, and architextuality. These different relationships often flow together and separating them is not always a simple matter. Intertextuality is, in Genette's term, a reasonably limited form of textual reference, as it presupposes a direct relationship to another text in question, such as a quote or plagiarism. Some allusions are also considered intertextual if the allusion requires the knowledge of the other text to make sense. Paratextuality refers to the text which surrounds the text in question, such as cover, title, recommendations and so on. As such, the paratext often changes from edition to edition, or between publishers. The paratext is the one element connected to a text which is more or less in constant flux, as it is not (always) under the direct control of the author. Metatextuality consists of comments about a given text, such as criticism and reviews. Conceivably, any comment made on the text constitutes a metatext, but Genette realizes the impossible task to gather all such metatexts as many of them are verbal rather than written. Some parts of metatexts on the given text often become part of the paratext in the form of 'blurbs', at least if the metatext is positive in nature. Hypertextuality is the relation of one text (the hypertext) with another text before it (the hypotext). In this manner, *The Odyssey* is the hypotext of the hypertext we know as *Ulysses*, to use one of the best-known examples. Of course, today, hypertext also refers to another textual function, but we shall not broach this subject as it falls outside our current discussion. Architextuality is Genette's term for texts that use the same genre or mode, in whatever form we may choose to use the term. In this way, all novels share specific elements which make them novels, and that can be termed the architext of novels, and the same goes for poems, epics, and so forth. The term also deals with more professional genres, such as detective stories, romances and similar (or not so similar) genres. The main point is that we understand such texts in relation to all other texts of the same architextual type (at least those we have read, but also more).

All these categories are mainly useful for understanding how we read texts in relationship with each other (the topic of poetics, Genette calls it), and as such they begin to explain why some texts are understood in particular ways by some readers, and in other ways by other readers. This discussion is part of the issue of reader competence, something which Genette does not deal with explicitly only implicitly in the sense that he presupposes that we recognize the relations, while realising that not all readers will do so. The point is that if we as readers do not realize the transtextual relations that a given text has, we can easily misunderstand it, or at least elements of the text. While this relationship with other texts differs greatly from text to text, we must always be aware that there is at least the potential of a relationship with one or more texts. The more we read, the more we recognize these relations, and the more aware of their existence we become. Some texts will require us to become historians or even archaeologists, digging to find the original text used in the text we have just read. Sometimes, this relationship is of course reasonably open and straightforward, as is for instance the case with Kathy Acker's novel *Great Expectations*, where the relationship with Dickens' text is openly acknowledged and necessary for the full appreciation of Acker's text. In this way, serious students of literature will always be on the lookout for interesting relationships between texts. The point of this essay is to illustrate to what extent these relationships provide significance for us as readers and how we can be sure that the relationships signify what we think they do.

After this discussion of literary archaeology, let us return to the names mentioned at the beginning of this essay. The invocation of Ishmael in this specific form is most definitely what Genette would call an intertextual reference, since it is lifted verbatim from Melville's text. Note that I immediately presume that anyone will recognize this quote as being from Herman Melville's *Moby Dick*, yet Voytek (the poor nerd in question) does not. At the same time, however, his reaction immediately prompts us to ask "what is the meaning of the reference?" Clearly Cayce is striving for humour but when that fails, the issue of recognition and competence comes into question. We, as competent readers, recognize the reference, understand the joke but might very well ask if there is more to this reference

There might be: Cayce is certainly on many searches in this text, for her father, for the deeper meaning and maker of certain film fragments, as well as a more concrete search for a rare and unusual calculator. Yet understanding the reference as directed at Cayce's searches seems so banal that we are almost embarrassed to accept this as the meaning of the quote. Certainly there have been many texts that include a search for something without having to specifically invoke Melville. Gibson's first novel *Neuromancer* also had this search as the structuring element of its narrative, although the search was not for a computer. So, we may ourselves search for other meanings to this quote, but a specific connection to the quote seems difficult to find Perhaps it would be better to look elsewhere to find clues to unravel the text.

Here, it would be more interesting to look at *Neuromancer*, as there is also something about Cayce which might be a direct reference to that text. Although Cayce's name does not look like a one-syllable word, we learn that it is pronounced Case rather than Casey. This seemingly innocent difference in pronunciation is actually quite significant in relation to *Neuromancer* as the main protagonist there is called Case. Again we are confronted with a reference which seems quite clear; a reference Genette might call a hypertextual relationship, with *Neuromancer* being the hypotext of *Pattern Recognition*'s hypertext. In fact, whether we see the name as a case of intertextuality or hypertextuality depends on how much significance we subscribe to the reference. If it is nothing more than a simple evocation of the earlier text, we would probably regard it as intertext, while if we deem the reference more significant, we would regard it as hypertext. The significance of this relationship is obscure, yet persistent. Clearly we cannot argue that Gibson coincidentally names the protagonist the same, since the name is not normally pronounced the same way, so by having the character insist on pronouncing it Case, Gibson seems to create a deliberate effort to connect the two texts.¹ But how, and why? Again, we are left with a peculiar embarrassment because of the simplicity of the reference. If Cayce is like Case in a metonymic relationship, what deeper understanding do we get from this? The only real similarity between them is the fact that they are both searching for a rare, elusive object – much like the connection with *Moby Dick*. One other connection can also be made, and that is the fact that both characters excel at navigating webs of information all around them; in *Neuromancer* Case is an expert on cyberspace, while Cayce is a 'cool hunter', able to locate the best brand icons. In a more abstract way, one can say that they are both expert semioticians, having an almost mystical understanding of signs and their meaning. While this connection might seem more relevant than the quest-structure from *Moby Dick*, the fact is that both characters are simply representatives of a very small architext, namely Gibson's texts. All of Gibson's texts have protagonists who are 'semiotic navigators', capable of understanding and manipulating cultural codes – particularly the deeper codes beneath the immediate surface – Case, the structure of all computer networks; Cayce, the structure of all branding.

Our initial analysis of both of these two transtextual relationships has yielded disappointing results, in that we see the relationships but our hopes of locating significance in them are not met. This does not mean that the text does not hold any direct relationships where are our expectations of them can be met. At one point, Cayce is trying to determine if someone has broken into her apartment:

> She remembers an eerily young Sean Connery, in that first James Bond film, using fine clear Scottish spit to paste one of his gorgeous black hairs across the gap between the jamb and the door of his hotel room. Off to the casino, he will know, upon returning, whether or not his space has been violated. (Gibson, 2003: 42)

She later uses this trick, but the reference here makes perfect sense. This reference is not so much a hypertextual one (although to some degree it is), but rather it is also an architextual marker. We are meant to read *Pattern Recognition* in the same way we read James Bond movies. The use of this

---

1 Gibson himself has said that there is no connection, that he "is just being apophenic" (Leonard, 2003). Whether we choose to believe him, is another matter. Certainly, his comment constitutes a paratextual metatext, and hence not something which is part of the text itself. As such, we may discard it at will, but also at our own risk.

marker means that we realize that this text falls into the genre of the spy-thriller, so that we can expect double-crosses, fancy hotels, chases, technological gadgets and so on. All of these expectations, if we have them, are fulfilled and our understanding of the text increases. Again, the reference only works if we can understand it; that is if we know of James Bond movies. Here, however, the relationship is established directly, so even people who have not heard of the James Bond movies will know that there is a relationship, even if they cannot see its significance. In this way, this overt reference makes it possible for those so interested to locate the specific text and retroactively understand the significance of the reference.

Here we can see how an intertextual dependence on another text may actually prove useful for the understanding of the current one, so let us not stop here, but let us immediately locate another example. One literary connection which the text establishes, implicitly rather than explicitly like the Bond reference, is one which can in many ways be seen to be as close to literary fact as is at all possible. The relationship between William Gibson and Thomas Pynchon, in a literary sense, has been made quite clear several times. Gibson himself has often invoked Pynchon as a major influence (McCaffery 1991: 272), while Pynchon's *Vineland* is often seen as indebted to Gibson and cyberpunk in general. In *Pattern Recognition* we find a number of parallels to Pynchon's *The Crying of Lot 49*, perhaps clearest in Cayce Pollard's reminiscence of Oedipa Maas.

Compare Cayce's reaction to the Tommy Hilfiger logo with Oedipa Maas's reaction to the TV screen. Gibson's first:

> When it starts, it's pure reaction, like biting down hard on a piece of foil. A glance to the right and the avalanche lets go. A mountainside of Tommy coming down in her head. (Gibson 2003: 17)

and then Pynchon's:

> Oedipa stood in the living-room, stared at by the greenish dead eye of the TV tube, spoke the name of God, tried to feel as drunk as possible. But this did not work. (Pynchon 1966: 1)

The similarity here is not so much in the reactions themselves, but rather in the cause of the characters' reactions: modern life and the empty signs that follow. Both characters seem to be deadened by the proximity of the modern, mediated world. These media signs carry no signification, only emptiness and entropy. Both protagonists are in essence allergic to modern life. Of course, the similarities do not end here, as both women are also on their own private detective-quests. There is also a stylistic parallel which is interesting, and this is the fact that both novels are restricted to one perspective, that of the main protagonist, and there are no real timelapses. While Pynchon has since moved away from that style, it is a new style for Gibson whose previous novels have all been characterised by multiple perspectives and multiple ellipses. Because of this unusual feature from Gibson, it is something to note and the similarity between the authors becomes even greater. This is of course without even mentioning the fact that this is the first non-science fiction novel Gibson has written, which in itself represents a break. Already here we can see how even Gibson's own architext becomes unstable in this novel.

The interest here is less on the narrative parallels, since they are no greater than those to *Moby Dick* or James Bond, but rather the thematic connections. *Pattern Recognition* takes place in a maze of paranoia, completely similar to Pynchon's text, though the level of satire is different. The paranoia in Gibson's text is very real, far more oriented towards the spy genre than Pynchon's entropic evasions. Pynchon's paranoia remains a far more playful and slippery trope, in opposition to Gibson's more structuring narrative device.

Interestingly, however, the concern seems to be the same in the two texts: to what extent is the world connected, and to what extent should we see sinister plot formations behind events? This concern is often made quite explicit in *Pattern Recognition*, such as when Bigend remarks: "Everything, today, is to some extent the reflection of something else" (Gibson, 2003: 68), or when Parkaboy states that "Homo sapiens is about pattern recognition" (Gibson, 2003: 22). This is the basic truth which lies at the heart of Gibson's text and is, as Parkaboy says, both a gift and a trap. One cannot escape making connections between things, just as we cannot help but think that *Pattern Recognition* is an intermodal transmodalization as well as a transmotivation[2] of Pynchon's text. But Pynchon's text is never invoked specifically in the same way that James Bond is, so the question remains to what degree is the connection 'true'?

---

2   Genette defines intermodal transmodalization as any kind of alteration involving a shift from one mode to another (Genette, 1997a: 277), in this case from Pynchon's mode to Gibson's. Transmotivation is defined as when the original motivation is displaced by a new one (Genette, 1997a: 330), and in this case we see how Pynchon's original paranoid parody becomes more serious in Gibson's work.

This insecurity creates a level of paranoia on the level of the reader which is parallel to the paranoia of Cayce. Much as she becomes paranoid because the Asian Sluts website moves to the top of her browser's history without her knowing how, we become paranoid when Pynchon's text moves to the front of our reading, instead of Gibson's own. This seems a true example of a palimpsest, where we continually glimpse the text beneath the current we are reading. Here, it is not so much a matter of architextual genre markers, but a clear example of a hypertext. The recognition of the hypotext is of course limited to those who have read Pynchon's text or are otherwise reasonably familiar with it. As such, certain aspects of the text are only accessible to some, and closed to others. Since we may never really know what we are not identifying in the way of references in a text, we all become paranoid readers, wondering what is not accessible to us, and attempting to find relevance in the connections we can find.

Paranoia has been a favourite reading strategy for postmodernist texts: to constantly locate other forces at work behind the present one. Paranoia has been a master trope for Pynchon in all his works, but this current can be located in many other authors, such as Don DeLillo, Joseph Heller, William Burroughs and Gibson himself. The notion of connecting elements in a text runs even deeper, from Donald Barthelme to Paul Auster. The point being that Gibson enters into a deep-seated interest and suspicion inherent in American postmodern literature, and he does so very explicitly with one major element in his text: Fetish Footage Forum. The assemblage of meaning from the fragments of film by an unknown creator parallels the search which Cayce is otherwise engaged in, although it does not appear connected. The revelation is that these two disparate elements of Cayce's life are connected, just as they are connected with her father's disappearance.

As the basic premise for the novel, it is not so surprising that things are connected, what is perhaps more interesting and more unsettling is the way they are connected and why. Cayce is part of an elaborate plot to acquire a very rare calculator, but it turns out that her own search for the creator of the Feetish Footage film fragments and her hope to learn what happened to her father are also part of this plot. The interesting thing to note here is the way that discovering the connections between the calculator, her father and the film fragments follows the same path as the understanding of the film fragments. As Cayce becomes more caught up in the plot and the paranoia of being followed and under surveillance, the more she also discovers about the meaning of the fragments. In this way, the internal search for meaning to the text of the film fragments also becomes the search for the meaning behind the plot. It is crucial that Gibson's novel takes up the discussion of the production of meaning of the fragments, as this also begins to reveal ways to understand the plot Cayce is caught in.

While paranoia will make the reader search for clues anywhere, and the parallel between the meaning of the film and the meaning of the novel's narrative is one such clue, there is another related response which is brought forth in the text with connection to the footage: Apophenia.

> Apophenia... the spontaneous perception of connections and meaningfulness in unrelated things [...] What if the nascent meaning they all perceive in the footage is simply that: an illusion of meaningfulness, faulty pattern recognition? (Gibson, 2003: 115)

Here the connections that we make as readers of this text are brought into serious doubt. We may see a meaningfulness in the parallels between the footage and the plot, and we may see meaningfulness in comparing *Pattern Recognition* to *The Crying of Lot 49*, but to what extent are these connections completely our own? Of course, we may say that there is no difference between the text and our understanding of the text, and that is also something which the novel itself brings up, when Bigend says:

> One day we'll need archaeologists to help us guess the original storylines of even classic films [...] It's as though the creative process is no longer contained within an individual skull, if indeed it ever was. Everything, today, is to some extent the reflection of something else. (68)

The question of paranoia, apophenia and transtextuality is implicit in this quote, which seems to indicate that a work of art cannot be controlled, that the text will always differ from any intentional meaning and that intentional meaning is therefore relatively unimportant.[3] The issue of transtextuality is inherent as everything is always connected. What seems to be the real issue here is whether or not we may conclude that there lies a meaningfulness behind these connections. Julia Kristeva would of course say that there are always connections to other texts, while Michael Riffaterre would even include texts later than the origin of the text itself. Harold Bloom would most likely see the issue at hand as a form of kenosis within

---

3   This implicit discussion of aesthetics and reading practices is not a new thing in Gibson's work, but rather a continuous occupation with him. See Christiansen 2001 for more on this.

Pynchon's text, unless his speedy reading made him conclude that Gibson's text was wholly original.

The fact is that the text is open to any number of connections, but that it explicitly makes us aware that these connections are not there in the text itself, but are made by us as readers. This does not make the connections totally irrelevant, but it means that we should consider what the connections bring us. While we may feel confident that Gibson's text 'wants' us to read Pynchon's text into it, we can never be certain. There are most definitely enough peculiar leads and references that seem without meaning for us to unproblematically posit Pynchon's text as more meaningful than the others. There is of course also always the paranoid reaction of fearing the existence of transtextual relations to texts we cannot recognize, of there being connections we cannot make that are meaningful and should be made. As such, paranoia is the fear that we have missed something vital, while apophenia is the compulsion to make connections without knowing whether they are there. In this way they can be seen as two sides of the same coin, but with different results.

What we have to focus on here is not so much what people may categorize Gibson's text as, but rather the way in which the text itself is aware of this process of categorization. It seems most definite that this text (if not Gibson himself) wishes to escape categorization; the first clue to this being the fact that this is not a science fiction novel, despite the fact that this genre made Gibson popular. The constant invocation of other texts also means that we can never gain full control of the text, or if we do then we make certain connections that we can never be sure are correct. The text itself works with this suspenseful notion and the conclusion is two-fold. While Cayce discovers who made the film footage, there is no real success inherent in this discovery – rather the revelation becomes anti-climactic because it means that the interest in the footage is lost ("So mystery Internet movie is out, yoghurt drink is in" (Gibson, 2003: 352)). The message seems clear: when a reading becomes solidified it ceases to be interesting. A text is only interesting as long as it is open for further reading and re-reading. Gibson's novel seems to place itself within both an open and a closed framework. This draws on Umberto Eco's distinction between open and closed work.[4]

---

4 One could also draw on Roland Barthes's notion of readerly and writerly texts as Eco's and Barthes's concept pairs are similar enough to be practically interchangeable.

Gibson's text seems to be positioned between both an open text and a closed text, simply because we as readers may approach it in two different ways. One is seeing the text as a spy-thriller, and so reading for the plot and the resolution of the story and protagonist. Another reader may come to the text with the same expectations, but soon realize that far more is going on, and that the interest of the text is perhaps less in what happens as how it happens and what the reader's reactions may be. This second reader is the one who recognizes the different texts which Gibson's novel invokes, whether intertextually or hypertextually, and realizes that the novel is interested in questions of the paranoia of reading, as much as the paranoia of the narrative. The closure of the novel seems to indicate this interest, because it ends anticlimactically as the calculator is revealed as a MacGuffin[5], the footage loses interest when the creators are discovered and the final question of whether Cayce's father is alive or not is not resolved at all, only given an unsatisfactory 'maybe' as answer.

Readers for the plot are justified in feeling cheated, but the other readers, the 'informed' readers are left with an equal sense of letdown, since the text does not fulfil the elements one might expect from an open text either. An open text cannot afford any interpretation, argues Eco, only the interpretations that the text itself wants. But this is problematic in this case because the text does not want you to make any interpretations or any connections, it simply points out that pattern recognition is a basic human state. This is why it is both a gift and a trap: simply because we cannot help but have expectations of a text, nor can we help to revert to specific codes when we read a text. Eco himself would agree on this, and in this case one code can be that of transtextuality, but we have to approach this transtextuality both as paranoids who manically search for connections, and as selfconscious apophenics who are aware that any connection is our own connection. Gibson may seem to be searching for his literary father Thomas Pynchon in a web of kenosis, but only if we recognize the reference. As an open text creates a closed project for its reader, this text seems to demand an open reader who is aware of his or her faults, but accepts them anyway, as they are a necessary predisposition to read. We cannot help make these connections, but we can be aware of us making them.

This is relevant not only for the specific interest of this text, using paranoia and apophenia to question the validity of interpretation and under-

---

5   MacGuffin being Hitchcock's term for a plot device that advances the story but is minimally explained (OED).

standing, but also because the text itself inevitably falls victim to this plurality of codes being brought to bear on it. Any reader who approaches this text will almost without a doubt be aware of the fact that Gibson was, at least previously, a science fiction (sf) writer. Whether sf is appreciated by the reader or not, one cannot help but be on the look-out for sf elements, either to throw the book down in disgust or to enjoy the recognition of Gibson's earlier works. Critical readers, especially academics, will probably also be aware of the connections between Gibson and Pynchon and cannot help but notice the similarities. We are victims of our own codes, but we cannot escape them, as we are apophenic by nature. The reading strategies in this essay are also elements of certain codes which are then found in the text, but they are only there because we place them there. A work, or text, no matter how complete is always a work in progress. Cayce's allergic reaction to the deeper structures in advertising may seem the only sensible choice when reading: if we encounter codes let us run away from them, for fear that they overwhelm us and blind us to the text. But Cayce's reaction is also impossible, for we must read, and reading is finding codes or as Barthes expresses it: "And no doubt that is what reading is: rewriting the text of the work within the text of our lives" (quoted in Scholes, 1989: 10).

Eco's argument engages the reader, but there is the problem of who determines whether a text is open or closed. It seems that Eco would argue that this is done by the text itself, or potentially the implied author. However, it might be more fruitful to engage the reader into this determination process, since one reader might regard the text as closed, whereas another would regard it as open. This notion of open or closed is far more dependent on the reader than Eco seems inclined to accept. While he does argue that an open text may be closed by an ignorant reader, it would seem that *Pattern Recognition* problematizes this notion, as it questions the need for locating connections. Eco's smart reader is always paranoid, caught in what Brian McHale calls paranoid reading where everything is connected (McHale, 1992: 82). This is what defines his reader, as the one who is able to make connections at different levels and engage the text critically and appreciate the depth and range of the text. Gibson's text, however, seems to belong to among those novels where this connectivity is not necessarily appropriate.

Rather than create elaborate networks of interconnections, the text questions these interconnections. It freely admits to making them, but it does not admit to their significance. Instead the text emphasizes the fact that the connections are made by the reader. However, as it suspends its own connections it makes all reading valid. There is no longer a question of the text being either open or closed: that depends on the reader. The text accepts being read as a spy-thriller, and it also accepts being read as Pynchon's hypertext. It does not privilege either reading, as it seems to propose that no reading can be privileged. The only mistake a reader can make is to care about the intentions or identity of the author, as this will stagnate the reading in the same as the footage becomes uninteresting after the creators are discovered.

This acceptance of insecurity is also part of the text, in the way that Cayce never learns what actually happened to her father. Although she learns more she will never know the final truth, which is hidden behind layers of secrets and connections. She follows a trail leading to her father, but in the end she must interpret the clues presented in order to decide whether he is alive or dead. This final decision is presented thus:

> She lies there, staring up into the dark, hearing the distant drone of a plane.
>
> "They never got you, did they? I know you're gone, though."
>
> Her mother had once said that when the second plane hit, Win's chagrin, his personal and professional mortification at this having happened, at the perimeter having been so easily, so terribly breached, would have been such that he might simply have ceased, in protest, to exist. She doesn't believe it, but now she finds it makes her smile. (Gibson 2003: 351)

As we can see belief is inherent in deciding what has happened to her father and we may see beliefs as parallel to reading protocols. The death of Cayce's father can be proven by lawyers (Gibson, 2003: 352–353), but only by using the codes of law. Cayce may well believe that her father is gone but there is no evidence to directly support this belief. This is why September 11 runs as a thread throughout Gibson's entire text, not a major element of the narrative but one which lies central to the question of reading and relating to texts. The paranoia inherent in the time after September 11 becomes a trope for the way that we make sense of the world, using specific codes to relate to this unfathomable event. It is an event which defies meaning and sense, and the only way we can gain any level of understanding of the event is to inscribe it into a framework of codes, but the danger lies in seeing things that are not there. This is what the event is used for in this text, a questioning of how we make sense of the senseless. The response seems clear; we draw on a number of other texts and say that they are part of this text. Gibson's September 11 becomes a meaningless void which we can never bridge, only arbitrarily. It becomes a closed text which we can do anything with, but it is also an open text which plays along with what we do, until we realize that it is simply unstable, an event neither Cayce nor we can ever make sense of.

Transtextuality is one code which we may use to understand texts, as seeing them in relation to other text, whether in a specific or general sense. Paranoia and apophenia are different reactions to what we discover in a text. We may be paranoid about what we are missing, or we may be paranoid about overinterpreting the codes we find. Gibson's text creates an unstable environment, establishing perhaps the ultimate paranoia where we cannot even trust our own reading of the text, as we come to realize that it is in itself a fiction.

References

Christiansen, Steen (2001) *Tunnel Infinity: Mirror Into Mirror: William Gibson's Cyberspace Trilogy as an Allegory of Postmodernism.* [www.hum.aau.dk/~steen/] – last consulted Jan. 2006

Eco, Umberto (1984) *The Role of the Reader: Eplorations in the Semiotics of Texts*. Bloomington: Indiana University Press.

Genette, Gerard (1979) *The Architext: An Introduction*. Berkeley: University of California Press

——. (1997a) *Palimpsests: Literature in the Second Degree*. Lincoln and London: University of Nebraska Press.

——. (1997b) *Paratexts: Thresholds of Interpretation*. Cambridge: Cambridge University Press

Gibson, William (2003) *Pattern Recognition*. New York: G.P. Putnam's Sons

Leonard, Andrew (2003) "Nodal Point". [archive.salon.com/tech/books/-2003/02/13/gibson/] – last consulted Jan. 2006

McCaffery, Larry (1991) *Storming the Reality Studio: A Casebook of Cyberpunk and Postmodern Fiction*. Durham and London: Duke University Press

McHale, Brian (1992) *Constructing Postmodernism*. London and New York: Routledge

Pynchon, Thomas (1966/2000) *The Crying of Lot 49*. London: Vintage.

Scholes, Robert (1989) *Protocols of Reading*. New Haven and London: Yale University Press

Contributors

All contributors to this volume are currently, or have been, associated with the English programme at Aalborg University.

Jørgen Riber Christensen is associate professor; Jens Kirk is associate professor; Jesper Trier Gissel is a former teaching assistant; Lene Yding Pedersen is associate professor; Bent Sørensen is associate professor; Ben Dorfman is assistant professor; Steen Christiansen is a PhD candidate; Tore Rye Andersen is a PhD candidate; Camelia Elias is associate professor.